CATULLUS' CARMEN 61

LONDON STUDIES IN CLASSICAL PHILOLOGY

Volume Nine

CATULLUS' CARMEN 61

by

PAOLO FEDELI

J.C. GIEBEN, PUBLISHER

AMSTERDAM 1983

© 1983, by J.C. Gieben
ISBN 90 70265 62 1
Printed in The Netherlands

To Giuseppe Giangrande

CONTENTS

Preface 1

1. Poem 61 and the Literary Tradition of the Wedding-song 3

2. The Cletic Hymn. 17

3. The Encomium of the God 47

4. The Song before the Bride's House 61

5. The *deductio* and the *fescennina iocatio* 85

6. The epithalamium. 133

Conclusion 147

Bibliography 159

Indexes

– Index locorum. 163

– General index 172

– Index verborum. 175

– Index of names 178

PREFACE

My interest in Catullus was caused by a seminar organized by Eduard Fraenkel in Bari in the spring of 1966.

To the analysis of c. 61 I devoted a Latin seminar at Fribourg University in the winter term of 1969/70; I have good cause to be thankful to the students for their helpful observations. I am further indebted to the colleagues of the Faculty of Classics at Fribourg University, who enabled me to include this work in the series "Seges" and in particular to the secretary of this series, Professor Ramón Sugranyes de Franch. I have to thank also the Hochschulrat for accepting and financing the publication of the book.

Fribourg, 8 February 1972

The present English translation of my research into c. 61, published in the series "Seges" of the Éditions Universitaires (Fribourg 1972), is also a second edition; additions and alterations have been made in the light of the numerous comments on my first edition and of the most recent and valuable contributions to the criticism on Catullus. The book has been translated by Dr. Marianna Nardella.

My thanks are due to Professor Giuseppe Giangrande, Dr. Heather White and Professor Frederick Williams for their learned and friendly help.

Torre a Mare – Bari, October 1980

CHAPTER 1

POEM 61 AND THE LITERARY TRADITION
OF THE WEDDING-SONG

Poem 61 has been defined by Norden an interesting attempt to cross the hymenaeus with fescennine verses: but, it has been added, despite all the admirable details in which this poem is particularly rich, the poet has not succeeded in reconciling elements which are basically incompatible. In sharp contrast with this essentially negative appraisal by Eduard Norden[1] can be set the often enthusiastic verdicts of other critics, such as Augusto Rostagni, for whom epithalamium is among the purest and most beautiful ever written.[2] The disparity between these assessments, and the over-cautious approach of commentators on Catullus, who especially when dealing with c. 61 leave large gaps in their commentaries, prompt a re-examination of the poem in its various aspects, in an attempt to comprehend an important moment of Catullus' poetic activity.

What Norden reproaches Catullus with is not in fact one of his faults but one of his essential qualities. It is well known that elsewhere too he seeks to fuse together elements that are Greek and motifs that are purely Roman: we need only think of the famous c. 51, where the imagery is that of Sappho until the final strophe, where Catullus introduces the typically Roman theme of *otium*.[3] But with c. 61 we must consider whether the poem does in fact consist, as Norden thinks, of a straightforward attempt to combine a familiar Greek literary genre, the epithalamium, with a popular

---

1. E. NORDEN, *Die römische Literatur*, in *Einleitung in der Altertumswissenschaft*, I[3] 4, Leipzig-Berlin 1927, 30.

2. A. ROSTAGNI, *Storia della letteratura latina*, I[3], Torino 1964, 478.

3. On the meaning of the last strophe of c. 51 cf. G. WILLS in "Gr. Rom. Byz. St." 8 (1967) 193-197.

form of expression from Roman and Italian life, the *fescennina iocatio*, or whether the origins of the poem, and Catullus' intentions, are not altogether more complex.

If a contrast does exist between the various parts of the poem, this is surely to be detected in the style of the poem, and it is precisely in this area that I feel commentaries on Catullus leave most to be desired. With c. 61 people have on the whole gone too far in seeing colloquial constructions and expressions everywhere, even in the 'hymn to Hymen' (lines 1-75) where in fact the elevated language of prayer prevails. Alternatively, summary and contentious verdicts have been handed down: even in Gordon Williams' *Tradition and Originality in Roman Poetry*, much the most important work on the poetry of the first century B.C. to appear in recent years, we read that "the style is of extreme simplicity"[4] − too vague a definition, which fails to do justice to the stylistic complexity of c. 61. In fact Latin poets do not employ one single style uniformly throughout a genre: their choice of a style within the limits of the genre is profoundly affected by their subject-matter and the situations they are describing. In c. 61 we must draw a sharp distinction, above all from the point of view of style, between the cletic hymn and the rest of the poem: it is impossible to believe that the language of the hymn and that of the *fescennina iocatio* are one and the same, or even that they overlap. Most scholars strive to discover in the hymn the same popular elements which are to be found in the *fescennina iocatio*; they forget that the technique and the composition of the hymn are determined by a literary genre, that of the prayer, which is governed by rules laid down centuries before by the Greeks and observed by Catullus, whereas the *fescennina iocatio* reproduces colloquial forms and patterns from contemporary Italian life.

The use of elevated style and of colloquial language is therefore intimately related to content, as was realized by Riese when he asserted that "der Stil (ist) meist der einer eleganten Sprache, in einzelnen Stellen aber höher oder niederer je nach ihrem Inhalt",[5]

---

4. G. WILLIAMS, *Tradition and Originality in Roman Poetry*, Oxford 1968, 201.

5. A. RIESE, *Die Gedichte des Catullus*, Leipzig 1884, 112.

but his observations have not been taken up by subsequent scholars. It is certainly true that even in the hymn Catullus uses imagery which, as we shall see, does not belong to the language of the prayer; even so this imagery is never actually drawn from "Umgangssprache" and it occurs only in certain very special sections of the hymn. It is in the rest of the poem that Catullus' stylistic *poikilia*, so effectively emphasized by La Penna,[6] can be strikingly demonstrated.

In c. 61, as well as in others, we are faced with one form of a problem which has provoked much debate, and not only in connection with Catullus: is this a poem which was not merely written for an historical occasion (I do not think there can be any further doubt on this question), but intended as an accompaniment for the various stages of the actual ceremony, or did the incidental circumstances merely constitute the point of departure for a poetic creation which was not so closely shackled to actuality? Among the most distinguished supporters of the former view can be cited Lafaye,[7] for whom this poem sticks to realities so exactly and reproduces Roman customs in such a perfect way that it has been possible to draw from it the most precise and complete picture of wedding ceremonies in those days; or Pighi,[8] who proposes a rigorous distribution of the various strophes between a solo singer and a chorus.

The optimism of Lafaye and Pighi contrasts with the scepticism of Wilamowitz, according to whom "die eigentümliche Form des Gedichtes ist vielfach so arg missverstanden, dass man Teile von ihm an Chore von Jungfrauen und Jünglichen gab, also wohl gar an Aufführung wie an einem modernen Polterabend dachte ... Diese Feier aber ist selbst eine Fiktion".[9] I personally share the view of those who consider it impossible to think of c. 61 as a song accompanying the ceremony and see it as a purely literary creation. To demonstrate this requires of course a full investigation of the sources of c. 61 and of Catullus' technique. Here too

6. A. LA PENNA in "Maia" 8 (1956) 155 ff.
7. G. LAFAYE, *Catulle et ses modèles*, Paris 1894, 71.
8. G.B. PIGHI in "Humanitas" 2 (1948/49) 41-53.
9. U. v. WILAMOWITZ-MOELLENDORFF, *Hellenistische Dichtung in der Zeit des Kallimachos*, II, Berlin 1924, 281 f.

the critics are deeply divided. Lafaye[10] and Rostagni[11] harboured no doubts: for them the poem was inspired by the famous examples of Sappho's epithalamia. Wheeler, in his well-known book on Catullus, aligns himself with this view[12]; and it is true that in c. 61, despite the almost complete loss of Sappho's epigrams, some echoes of her poetry can be heard, especially in the comparisons of the bridal pair with trees and flowers, and in the delicate descriptions of the bride.

For others, Catullus' source, especially so far as the techniques of the wedding-song are concerned, must have been Callimachus: in the words of Wilamowitz, "Catull von diesem (sc. Kallimachos) die Form entlehnt hat, uns durch die Einführung eines real nicht vorstellbaren Ordners die Feier miterleben zu lassen".[13] Obviously, this would not be the Callimachus of the *Aetia*, but of the Hymns, some of which (2, 5, 6) display a mimetic-dramatic technique comparable with that employed by Catullus in c. 61. Catullus does indeed assume the functions of master of ceremonies (as Tibullus does at the feast of the Ambarvalia) and of *coryphaeus*: he invokes the god (lines 1 ff.), exhorts the maidens to sing (lines 36 ff.), turns to the bride and urges her to come out (lines 82 ff.), commands the *pueri* to wave the torches (line 114) and the *concubinus* to throw the nuts to the *pueri* (lines 124 ff.), advises Iunia on how she should enter her husband's house (lines 159 ff.), and indicates to the *praetextatus* the moment when he should let go of the bride's arm (lines 174 ff.), gives the *pronuba* the order for the *collocatio* (lines 179 ff.), and tells Manlius when he should join his bride in the bedchamber (lines 184 ff.), and, finally, orders the maidens to close the door of the bedchamber (line 224).

Among the Hymns of Callimachus it is above all the fifth (*The Bath of Pallas*) which is instructive in this respect: the situation is of course completely different, but there too the poet is speaking in the first person and addressing a group of girls, and exhorting the goddess to approach. The influence of Callimachus is evident especially in the first part of c. 61, the cletic hymn. There are, to

10. G. LAFAYE, *Catulle et ses modèles*, cit., 71.
11. A. ROSTAGNI, *St. d. lett. lat.*, cit., I³, 478.
12. A.L. WHEELER, *Catullus and the Tradition of Ancient Poetry*, Berkeley 1934, 205.
13. U. v. WILAMOWITZ-MOELLENDORFF, *Hell. Dicht.*, cit., II, 282.

be sure, important differences: for instance, in Callimachus the mythological element, on the origins and attributes of the divinity, is developed at a length which, while justifiable in the hymn, would have been out of place in the wedding-song; nevertheless, his techniques do seem comparable with those of Catullus. On the other hand, it is very far from being demonstrable, despite Wheeler's attempt,[14] that Sappho employed these same techniques in her epithalamia. In Theocritus too (*Idylls* 2, 3 and 15) we see a similar technique.[15] But, beyond individual images already present in Sappho, and techniques related to those of the hymns of Callimachus or some of Theocritus' *Idylls*, Catullus' innovations are such as to cut the ground from under the feet of those who see in him no more than a mere imitator of Sappho, Callimachus, or Theocritus; equally hazardous is the attempt of Wheeler and others to reconstruct Sappho from Catullus' wedding-songs and the theoretical analyses of the genre found in the Greek rhetoricians.

*

It is impossible to discuss c. 61 without first locating it within the development of the genre of the wedding-song; otherwise we should run the risk of misinterpreting *topoi* of the literary tradition as features of a real event. A brief survey will suffice to show how Catullus, while he reflects conventional imagery and observes the rules of the genre, succeeds, by drawing on the rich resources of the native Roman and Italian tradition, and by the originality of his treatment of Greek motifs, in giving new vitality to a genre which had long been regulated by a system of rules, and in creating a work of high poetic worth.[16]

14. A.L. WHEELER, *Catullus and the Tradition*, cit., 201 ff.; for Callimachus' techniques see also G. PASQUALI, *Quaestiones Callimacheae*, Göttingen 1913, 148 ff.; L. DEUBNER in "N. Jahrb." 47 (1921) 361-378.

15. Cf. L. DEUBNER in "N. Jahrb." 47 (1921) 376-378.

16. For a detailed analysis of the genre see V. KÖRBER, *De Graecorum hymenaeis et epithalamiis*, Breslau 1877; R. REITZENSTEIN in "Herm." 35 (1900) 73-105; E.A. MANGELSDORFF, *Das lyrische Hochzeitsgedicht bei den Griechen und Römern*, Hamburg 1913; A.L. WHEELER in "Amer. Journ. Phil." 51 (1930) 205 ff.; ID., *Catullus and the Tradition*, cit., 184 ff.; on the epithalamium in the late Latin poetry cf. C. MORELLI in "St. Ital. Fil. Class." 18 (1910) 319-432.

At the outset, a brief preliminary note on terminology may be helpful. One frequently encounters, in literary histories and even in the works of distinguished scholars,[17] some confusion between 'hymenaion' and 'epithalamium'; often the two words are used indiscriminately. Their precise meaning was made clear by Robert Muth,[18] who showed that the hymenaion is the song of the chorus accompanying the bride to the groom's house: it belongs therefore to the *deductio* stage. The epithalamium on the other hand, exactly as its name indicates, is the song sung outside the *thalamos* or bedchamber of the bridal couple. Catullus' c. 61 exemplifies this distinction perfectly: the ritual cry invoking Hymen is repeated both in the cletic hymn and during the *deductio* stage; but in the part preceding the *deductio* the refrain takes the form *prodeas nova nupta*, and after the *deductio*, in the song before the bedchamber, there is no further invocation of the god Hymen. The confusion already existed in antiquity, with the term 'hymenaeus' tending to encroach upon the area of 'epithalamium' in the strict sense: as early as Aeschylus, *Prometheus* 555 ff., the verb ὑμεναιοῦν is applied to the song before the bedchamber[19]; the use of 'epithalamium' to designate the wedding-song as a whole does not however begin before the late hellenistic period.[20]

In this investigation I have kept the term 'epithalamium' for quotations from the fragments of Sappho's collection, since this was the title given to the book by the Alexandrians,[21] for references to Theocritus, *Idyll* 18, which is an epithalamium in the true sense, and to later wedding-songs (Statius, and the anonymous *epithalamium Laurentii*) by which time the term had lost its original meaning, and, finally, for discussing the late rhetoricians, whose precepts for the λόγος ἐπιθαλάμιος cover both the hymenaeus and the epithalamium proper.

If we had only the remains of archaic Greek literary output to go by, we would be forced to conclude that the wedding-song did

17. Compare, for example, R. REITZENSTEIN in "Herm." 35 (1900) 78 n. 4; P. MAAS in "R.E.P.W." IX 1 (1914) 130 ff.; the passages by Norden and Rostagni quoted at the beginning of this study show that even these two remarkable scholars use the term "epithalamium" inaccurately.
18. R. MUTH in "Wien. Stud." 67 (1954) 5-45.
19. Cf. R. MUTH in "Wien. Stud." 67 (1954) 20 ff.
20. Cf. R. MUTH in "Wien. Stud." 67 (1954) 34.
21. On this subject see R. MUTH in "Wien. Stud." 67 (1954) 38-40.

8

not become a literary form before Sappho but it is probable that long before her time the folk-songs which accompanied the wedding ceremony had been given literary expression. Indeed as early as Homer, among the scenes depicted on the shield of Achilles there is the brief description[22] of a torchlit wedding procession to the music of flutes and *citharae*, while πολὺς δ' ὑμέναιος ὀρώρει. Moreover when Hera refers in passing (*Iliad* 24, 62-3) to the wedding of Peleus and Thetis, it is highly significant that she mentions Apollo with his lyre among the wedding guests because this detail might suggest the singing during the banquet of a song in honour of the newly-wed couple; indeed on the basis of the Homeric passage Wilamowitz[23] went so far as to posit the existence in the archaic period of a narrative version of the wedding ceremony.

Reitzenstein[24] regarded Hesiod as the author of the first wedding song, the main evidence to support this view being the citation by Tzetzes (*Schol. ad Lycophron.* 4.13 Scheer) of a fragment of Hesiod on the wedding of Peleus and Thetis (*fr.* 221, 7 ff. M.-W.: τρὶς μάκαρ Αἰακίδη καὶ τετράκις, ὄλβιε Πηλεῦ κτλ.). It seems certain however that what we have in Hesiod is a narrative of the mythical wedding ceremony and not a real song actually intended to represent the progress of the ceremony.

In the *Shield of Heracles* attributed to Hesiod (lines 273-80) we have another instance, with a greater wealth of detail, of a motif we have already encountered in *Iliad* 18, namely the representation on a shield of a wedding procession. On Heracles' shield it is the *deductio* which is depicted: while the hymenaeus is being sung (line 274 πολὺς δ' ὑμέναιος ὀρώρει as in *Il.* 18,493), and slave-women are waving torches, followed by χοροὶ παίζοντες of youths and maidens amidst the music of flutes and *citharae*, the bride is being conducted in a coach to the groom's house.[25]

The earliest fragments of *epithalamia* are those of Sappho: but, as has already been said, it is highly likely that the genre was not her creation, and that the epithalamium had already become a litereary form in other poets. It was in part Sappho's fame which

22. *Il.* 18,491-496.
23. U. v. WILAMOWITZ-MOELLENDORFF in "Herm." 14 (1879) 201.
24. R. REITZENSTEIN in "Herm." 35 (1900) 73 ff.
25. Cf. C.F. RUSSO, *Hesiodi Scutum*, Firenze 1965², 146 f.

subsequently caused the wedding-songs of earlier or contemporary poets to fall into oblivion. There is no reason to doubt the evidence of Leonidas of Taras, when he says that Alcman wrote *hymenaei* at Sparta in the seventh century.[26] It is likely that the content and tone of these *hymenaei* were not very different from those of Sappho, but we possess only fragments of them and no sound conclusions can be drawn *ex silentio*.

As far as we can judge from the scanty fragments, Sappho's wedding songs were in all probability not mere poetic exercises, but were intended to accompany the marriage ceremony.[27] It was the Alexandrians who collected these songs in a single book, with the title of ἐπιθαλάμια.[28] But there is no basis for the theory that the book contained a large number of *epithalamia*, as Mangelsdorff supposes[29]; all the evidence suggests rather that the *epithalamia* formed only a minor appendage of the poems of Sappho known to the Alexandrians, even though it must be borne in mind that not all the wedding songs were included in the book of ἐπιθαλάμια.[30]

The *communis opinio* is that Sappho became the invariable model for writers of wedding songs: a view based essentially on the trust which has been placed in the rhetoricians, for whom it is *de rigeur* to cite the name and example of Sappho in the precepts on the λόγος ἐπιθαλάμιος: cf. Himerius, *Or.* 9,4 Col. τὰ δὲ Ἀφροδίτης ὄργια παρῆκαν τῇ Λεσβίᾳ Σαπφοῖ ᾄδειν πρὸς λύραν καὶ ποιεῖν τὸν θάλαμον, 9,19 Col. πρέπει γάρ σοι τὰ τῆς Λεσβίας ἐγκώμια, Ps. Dion. Hal. 6,1, p. 270 U.-R. τινὰ μὲν οὖν καὶ παρὰ Σαπφοῖ τῆς ἰδέας ταύτης παραδείγματα, ἐπιθαλάμιοι οὕτως ἐπιγραφόμεναι ᾠδαί, Choric. *Or.* 1,15 F. ἐγὼ δὲ τὴν νύμφην Σαπφικῇ μελῳδίᾳ κοσμήσω.[31]

26. Cf. *Anth. Pal.* 7,19,1 f. τὸν χαρίεντ' Ἀλκμᾶνα, τὸν ὑμνητῆρ' ὑμεναίων / κύκνον, τὸν Μουσῶν ἄξια μελψάμενον κτλ.

27. Cf. D. PAGE, *Sappho and Alcaeus*, Oxford 1955, 120; C.M. BOWRA, *Greek Lyric Poetry*, Oxford 1961², 214 ff.

28. Cf. Seru. *ad* Verg. *Georg.* 3,31 *generum uero pro marito positum multi accipiunt iuxta Sappho, quae in libro, qui inscribitur* ἐπιθαλάμια, *ait* "χαῖρε νύμφα, χαῖρε τίμιε γαμβρὲ πολλά" *ἀντὶ τοῦ* "νύμφιε" and U. v. WILAMOWITZ-MOELLENDORFF, *Die Textgeschichte der griechischen Lyriker*, Abh. Ges. Wiss. Göttingen, IV 3 (1900) 71 ff.

29. E.A. MANGELSDORFF, *Lyr. Hochzeitsged.*, cit., 1.

30. Cf. *e.g.* 27 L.-P. and 30 L.-P.; on this subject see D. PAGE, *Sappho a. Alc.*, cit., 125.

31. Cf. E.A. MANGELSDORFF, *Lyr. Hochzeitsged.*, cit., 14.

In the few fragments of Sappho's epithalamia we do indeed find some motifs which reappear in later wedding songs: the μακαρισμός of the bridegroom (112 L.-P.), the praising of the beauty of the bridal pair by comparing them with trees and flowers (105 L.-P.; 115 L.-P.), the formula for wishing the couple well (116 L.-P.; 117 L.-P.), but there has been a tendency to rush from this starting point hastily to an assertion that later representatives of the genre are derivative from Sappho and merely repeat her themes. Wheeler[32] would even have us believe that in her epithalamia Sappho pioneered the mimetic-dramatic technique of representing and describing the ceremony. Maas[33] sensibly alerts us to the danger of such extreme views, emphasizing that there is no solid basis for asserting that the epithalamium had a fixed literary form in Sappho, that it is an exaggeration to see her influence as dominant and ever-present in Hellenistic and Latin *epithalamia*. Besides, after a careful consideration of the list of parallels between Sappho and her alleged imitators we come to realize that a most cautious approach is advisable. It is to be expected that a wedding song will include such features as praises of the beauty of the bride and groom, and expression of good wishes to the couple for a happy life, and it is hazardous to infer from the presence of these motifs in Sappho that she exercised a decisive influence on all subsequent works of the kind. These are motifs which belong to the τόποι of the wedding song, and only the unlikely hypothesis that Sappho created the genre (a hypothesis fostered by the late writers on rhetoric for whom Sappho was the most famous example and representative of the genre), could leave one to think of such τόποι as having their origin in Sappho. The single motif which in my view is specifically Sapphic is the comparison of the bride and groom with trees and flowers: but this occurs within the framework of the conventions of the εἰκάζειν.[34] As far as the alleged presence of the mimetic-dramatic method in Sappho is concerned, Wheeler's examples simply fail to convince[35]; we have already observed that this innovation, which

---

32. A.L. WHEELER, *Catullus and the Tradition*, cit., 201 ff.

33. P. MAAS in "R.E.P.W." IX 1 (1914) 132 ff. s.v. "Hymenaios".

34. On the εἰκάζειν see the discussion about ll. 16-25 and l. 102.

35. A.L. WHEELER, *Catullus and the Tradition*, cit., 201 ff. I do not understand (and, obviously, I am not interested in knowing) why Wheeler's

Catullus was to take up in c. 61, probably had its origin in Callimachus or Theocritus. Finally, Page points out a further difference in tone between later wedding songs, such as Theocritus, *Id.* 18 or Catullus, c. 61, and Sappho's epithalamia, when he does not recognize or regard as likely the presence of the element of ribaldry, which in later times was to be considerably developed[36]; however, strong doubts can be entertained on Page's assertion on the basis of the meaning of fr. 111 L.-P. ἴψοι δὴ τὸ μέλαθρον / ὑμήναον· / ἀέρρετε τέκτονες ἄνδρες· / ὑμήναον. / γάμβρος † εἰσέρχεται ἴσος † Ἄρευι / ἄνδρος μεγάλω πόλυ μέζων. It would seem in all probability that the sense of the last verse is obscene: as Kirk puts it the groom is so described "because he is fantastically ithyphallic".[37]

By the 5th and 4th centuries B.C. the wedding song has achieved the dignity of an autonomous *genre*; as such, with its own characteristic features and its own rules, it works its way into other literary *genres*; indeed the most significant examples from this period are found in tragedy and comedy. In the *Trojan Women* of Euripides (lines 308-40) Cassandra celebrates her own *hymenaeus* before the temple of Apollo; in her words we find, over and above the invocation of the god, the μακαρισμός of the

examples and arguments persuaded G. LIEBERG in "Latinitas" 22 (1974) 216; in fact, I am more concerned with stating that, in my opinion, Catullus' mimetic technique does not derive from Theocritus' epithalamium, but from Callimachus' hymns, as it is frequently asserted in this study. It is also obvious that, despite the limits I set to Sappho's influence on Catullus' poetry (exerted either directly or through the Alexandrians) I have no intention of diminishing or minimizing it. Mine is possibly a polemical stand, caused by the emphasis laid for years on the connection between Sappho and Catullus, as well as, side by side − to give only an example − the connection between Alcaeus and the Horace of the *Odes* or Archilochus and the Horace of the *Epodes*. The influence exerted by the Alexandrians (a far more determinant one, in my opinion) has never been held in due account. Anyhow, this bad habit does not affect criticism on Catullus only; indeed, it reflects some prejudices − which die hard even nowadays − against Hellenistic poetry, foolishly regarded as a minor product of art, in an absurd classification of ancient literary works.

36. D. PAGE, *Sappho a. Alc.*, cit., 120.

37. G.S. KIRK in "Class. Quart." 57 (1963) 51 f. Kirk's interpretation has been accepted and completed by H. LLOYD-JONES in "Class. Quart." 61 (1967) 168, G. WILLS in "Gr. Rom. Byz. St." 8 (1967) 180 n. 26 and D.E. GERBER, *Euterpe*, Amsterdam 1970, 179.

bridal pair, and the invitation to the chorus to sing and utter cries of joy and good wishes. In a fragment of Euripides' *Phaethon* (fr. 781,14-31 N.²) the choral song celebrating the marriage of Phaethon constitutes a hymenaeus in the true sense, and includes the traditional praise of the bride and groom.[38]

In the final scene of Aristophanes' *Peace* the marriage of Trygaeus seems to reproduce popular forms of the wedding song. Trygaeus himself directs the ceremonies (lines 1316 ff. εὐφημεῖν χρὴ καὶ τὴν νύμφην ἔξω τινὰ δεῦρο κομίζειν / δᾷδάς τε φέρειν, καὶ πάντα λεὼν συγχαίρειν κἀπικελεύειν) and sings the hymn to Hymen. The chorus (lines 1333 ff.) does then take up and amplify the song of praise to the god with which the comedy ends: here we find typical ingredients of the wedding song, such as the μακαρισμός of the bridegroom (1333 ff.), the jesting towards the bride (1337 ff.) which indeed suggests the influence of the popular stratum of the wedding song, and the wishes for happiness and prosperity (1346). The praises of the god Hymen ring out again in the finale of the *Birds* (lines 1720 ff.) on the occasion of the wedding of Peisthetairos and Basileia, but this is the only regular feature of the *hymenaeus* proper which appears.

It was in the Hellenistic period that the wedding song had its greatest development; the best-known examples are those of Callimachus and Theocritus, but alongside their names can be cited those of Eratosthenes, Nossis of Locris, and Anyte of Tegia. The fragment of Callimachus' song for the wedding of Ptolemy and Arsinoe (*fr.* 392 Pf.)[39] – hence a song composed, like Catullus' c. 61, for a real occasion – does not allow us to determine whether Callimachus' influence extended beyond the area of narrative technique.

Of the vast Hellenistic output only the eighteenth *Idyll* of Theocritus, the epithalamium of Helen, has survived. Kaibel's theory,[40] that this poem is an imitation of a Sapphic epithala-

---

38. Cf. E.A. MANGELSDORFF, *Lyr. Hochzeitsged.*, cit., 25.

39. *Frg.* 392 Pf. Ἀρσινόης ὦ ξεῖνε γάμον καταβάλλομ' ἀείδειν. For the meaning to attribute to the fragment see R. PFEIFFER, *Callimachus*, I, Oxford 1949, 322.

40. G. KAIBEL in "Herm." 27 (1892) 249 ff.

mium, is unconvincing[41]; the scholia actually state that Theocritus used the *Helen* of Stesichorus (τοῦτο τὸ εἰδύλλιον ἐπιγράφεται Ἑλένης ἐπιθαλάμιος καὶ ἐν αὐτῷ τινα εἴληπται ἐκ τοῦ πρώτου Στεσιχόρου Ἑλένης) and besides, the tone is very different from that of the Sapphic fragments.[42] When considering possible connections between *Idyll* 18 and Catullus c. 61, we need to distinguish the various aspects of the problem: the character of Theocritus' *Idyll* is very different from that of Catullus' song, because Theocritus seems to be using the epithalamium to illustrate the αἴτιον of the cult of Ἑλένη Δενδρῖτις; the techniques too are different, narrative in Theocritus, mimetic-dramatic in Catullus. On the other hand, when one turns to the content, various motifs found in the *Idyll* appear also in Catullus: the ironic badinage to the groom (lines 9-15) — even though the tone of the reproaches addressed to Menelaus is far from the jesting of the *fescennina iocatio* —, the μακαρισμός of the bridal pair (16-20), the eulogy of the beauty and accomplishments of the bride (21-37), the wishes for a happy life (l. 49), for prosperity and offspring (50 ff.), the encouragement to savour the joys of love (l. 55), and, like Catullus c. 61, Theocritus' *Idyll* is "eine glückliche Mischung von Gelehrsamkeit und Volkstümlichkeit".[43]

In Rome the first example of marriage song occurs in the *Casina* of Plautus (lines 798 ff.); this is in fact a parody of a wedding ceremony. Olympio urges the flautist to play during the *deductio* and he joins with Lysidamus in singing the *hymenaeus*. The maid-servant Pardalisca[44] brings out the "bride" (who is really Calinus disguised as a woman) and gives advice on how to behave with her "husband". At line 839 there is a reference to a torch, a detail

41. This opinion is shared by Mangelsdorff, who is always eager to find echoes of Sappho's poetry everywhere.

42. Cf. P. MAAS in "R.E.P.W." IX 1 (1914) 134.

43. Cf. P. MAAS in "R.E.P.W." IX 1 (1914) 134. On *Idyll* 18 as a source used by Catullus see also C. CALAME, *Les choeurs de jeunes filles en Grèce archaïque*, I, Roma 1977, 162 n. 230.

44. This is what we read in the manuscripts and it is commonly accepted that they have no authority as for the attribution of cues. However, G. WILLIAMS in "Journ. Rom. Stud." 48 (1958) 18 thinks (correctly, in my opinion) that the ritual formulae (1.815 ff.) must be attributed to Cleostrata, a matron who probably fulfills the traditional functions of a *pronuba* at a wedding ceremony. But I intend to come back to this problem later in the book.

14

which recalls the traditional torchlit wedding procession. That Plautus is echoing the original *Casina* of Diphilus has to my mind been proved by Günther Jachmann[45]; but Gordon Williams has recently brought to light some elements of the ritual in the *Casina* which reproduce purely Roman customs, thus constituting an innovation on the part of Plautus.[46]

Such ardent admirers of Alexandrian poetry as the neoterics could hardly pass over a literary genre which had flourished so spectacularly in the Hellenistic world. Another probable factor affecting the neoteric poets, including Catullus, was the influence of Parthenius, a younger contemporary of Catullus. He composed hymenaei, as is proved by fr. 32 Martini ἵλαος ὦ Ὑμέναιε which must certainly have belonged to a hymn in honour of the god Hymen.[47] In addition to the wedding songs of Catullus, some fragments of Calvus and Ticidas date from the same period.[48] Calvus, in fr. 4 Morel *uaga candido / nympha quod secat ungui* is treating the same motif which recurs in Catullus 62,43: *(flos) cum tenui carptus defloruit ungui*, while in the lines *et leges sanctas docuit et cara iugauit / corpora conubiis et magnas condidit urbes* (fr. 6 Morel) he expresses, within the context of an allusion to Ceres, the theme of the sacred marriage-bonds, which occupies an emphatic position in c. 61 (lines 71-5) and is treated by Catullus with solemn imagery. The line *Hesperium ante iubar quatiens* (fr. 5 Morel), which on Priscian's evidence (*Gramm.* II 170.10 K.) also occurred in the context of an epithalamium, possibly formed part of a description of a motif comparable with that which appears in Catullus 62,34 ff., *nocte latent fures, quos idem saepe reuertens / Hespere, mutato comprendis nomine Eous.*[49] As for Ticidas, (fr. 1 Morel) he represents an "Anredeform" to the marriage bed, similar to that in Catullus 61,107 ff.

45. G. JACHMANN, *Plautinisches und Attisches*, Berlin 1931, 105 ff.
46. G. WILLIAMS in "Journ. Rom. Stud." 48 (1958) 17 ff.
47. The fragment is quoted by Choeroboscus, *Schol. in Theodos. Canon.* p. 252.21 Hilgard.
48. Of course the problem is not exclusively a literary one; M. CITRONI in "Stud. Ital. Fil. Class." 51 (1979) 19 is right when he asserts that not only does the frequency of wedding songs in the neoteric output testify a literary trend; it must also be connected with a complex courteous ritual in vogue among the members of that poetic circle.
49. On Calvus as a writer of this genre see E. CASTORINA, *Questioni neoteriche*, Firenze 1968, 92.

In Catullus we find (a) the marriage song in a mythological setting (c. 64), on the model of Theocritus, *Idyll* 18; (b) the type devoid of all reference to the actuality (c. 62 with its imaginary contest between a chorus of youths and a chorus of maidens); and, in contrast, (c) the song composed for a real occasion (c. 61).

CHAPTER II

THE CLETIC HYMN

The first part of c. 61 consists of the hymenaeus and Catullus' invitation to Junia to come out (ll. 1-113). The praises of Hymen and the invocation to the god are in lines 1-75, whereas in ll. 76-113 we find the song urging the bride to leave her father's house and reach the groom's one.

Catullus amplifies the cry invoking the god, which was typical of the hymenaeus, by developing it into a hymn; it occupies a remarkable place in the structure of c. 61, but, at the same time, it is strictly and harmoniously related to the subsequent context, where some motifs already mentioned in ll. 1-75 are resumed and dealt with more deeply. The hymn itself is also divided into two parts: lines 1-45 form the cletic hymn, while ll. 46-75 are intended for the ἐγκώμιον of the god.

The cletic hymn is constructed according to the rules of sacred hymns and, at the beginning (ll. 1-15), it shows a learned and minute description of the god's origin, provenance and outward appearance. In Wilamowitz's words "diese gelehrten Mythologeme dienen nur dem Schmucke des Einganges".[1] In my opinion, however, this view does not seem exact and his criticism not in the right perspective; in fact, not only does Catullus imitate the technique of hymns, but he also strives to reproduce the solemn and refined style characteristic of the language of prayers. His erudite references, therefore, far from being superfluous, fulfill a function in an extremely precise structure and are to be appraised in the light of the genre to which they belong.

---

1. U. v. WILAMOWITZ-MOELLENDORFF, *Hell. Dicht.*, cit., II 282.

Collis o Heliconii
cultor, Vraniae genus,
qui rapis teneram ad uirùm
uirginem, o Hymenaee Hymen,
   Hymen o Hymenaee.²

cinge tempora floribus
suaue olentis amaraci,
flammeum cape,³ laetus huc
huc ueni niueo gerens
   luteum pede soccum;   10

excitusque hilari die,
nuptialia concinens
uoce carmina tinnula
pelle humum pedibus, manu
   pineam quate taedam.   15

One of the common features of hymns is the mention of the god's
dwelling when invokating him. This is proved as early as Homer,
in old Cryses' invocation to Apollo: *Il.* 1,37 ff. κλῦθί μευ,
ἀργυρότοξ᾽ ὃς Χρύσην ἀμφιβέβηκας / Κίλλαν τε ζαθέην Τενέδοιό
τε ἶφι ἀνάσσεις.⁴ Catullus himself employs an analogous

<hr>

2. Mynors, following the *editio Aldina*, corrects the corrupt text of
manuscripts by changing it into *o Hymen Hymenaee*. But Riese observed
that there is no evidence of *o Hymen* at the beginning of the invocation,
which usually has this forms: ὑμέναι᾽ ὦ, ὑμὴν ὦ ὑμέναι᾽ ὦ, ὑμὴν ὦ Ὑμέναιε
(Theocr. 18,58), *hymen hymenaee o hymen, hymen o Hymenaee* (Catullus
in c. 62). It is safer, then, to accept *Hymen o Hymenaee* here as well as in the
other cases (l. 40; 50; 60); on the prosody of *Hymen* cf. P. MAAS in "Philol."
66 (1907) 593.
   3. I do not share Mynors' punctuation (*flammeum cape laetus, huc / huc
ueni*), which I think should be excluded on the ground of Plat. *Leg.* 4,712 b
ὁ (*sc.* θεός) ... ἵλεως εὐμενής θ᾽ὑμῖν ἔλθοι, *Hymn. Orph.* 6,10 βαῖνε
γεγηθώς. "*Laetus* si riferisce a *ueni*", F. Della Corte observes (*Catullo. Le
poesie*, Verona 1977, 289) referring to *Hymn. Orph.* 6,10; however, with
regard to both the text and the translation, he accepts Mynors' punctuation,
as Bardon does too. Agreeing with the punctuation adopted by me, PARRONI
in "Riv. Fil. Istr. Class." 101 (1973) 488 refers also to Hor. *Carm.* 3,18,3-4,
where the god's *incessus* is described *lenis incedas abeasque paruis / aequus
alumnis.*
   4. Various Greek examples are cited by C. AUSFELD in "Jahrb. class.
Philol." Suppl. XXVIII (1903) 524.

technique in a parody of lofty style in 36,11-14 *nunc o caeruleo creata Ponto, / quae sanctum Idalium Vriosque apertos / quaeque Ancona Cnidumque harundinosam / colis* (cf. Theocr. 15,100 δέσποιν᾽ ἃ Γολγώς τε καὶ Ἰδάλιον ἐφίλασας) as well as in a solemn invocation to Eros and Venus in c. 64 (ll. 95-96 *sancte puer, curis hominum qui gaudia misces, / quaeque regis Golgos quaeque Idalium frondosum*).

At the outset of the hymn, after the god has been invoked, his origin is mentioned (*Vraniae genus*); with regard to this device, Catullus follows the traditional trend, whose antecedents can be found in the Homeric hymns: cf. 4,1 f. Ἑρμῆν ὕμνει Μοῦσα Διὸς καὶ Μαιάδος υἱόν, 7,1 ἀμφὶ Διώνυσον, Σεμέλης ἐρικυδέος υἱόν, 15,1 Ἡρακλέα Διὸς υἱὸν ἀείσομαι.[5] By choosing the formula *Vraniae genus* Catullus also respects the conciseness used in similar expressions by Greek writers, for whom "mos est, ut paucis uerbis, plerumque adiectiuo uel talibus uoculis: παῖ, τέκος, κόρη, θύγατερ, gens dei aduocati explicetur".[6]

The invocation to the god and the mentioning of his origin are followed by a relative clause (l. 3): this detail, generally neglected by Catullus' annotators, is in fact of the greatest importance, because the use of "Relativstil" plays a fundamental rôle in the technique of the hymn. As the annotators' carelessness does not pertain this device only, I will expatiate upon this case and some others by citing further examples. Of course both in this occasion and in the other quotations of passages by authors who use the same expressions as Catullus are included in order to help to understand the tone and meaning of the context. As Eduard Norden asserts "der Stil war im Altertum eine Grossmacht, und richtig verhört, wird er auch Interpretationsfragen beantworten".[7] Indeed, Norden has proved that the use of relative clauses in prayers is of very ancient origins[8]: we find it in Homer, in the lines from *Iliad* quoted above (1,37 ff.). It seems that in the greatest number of cases and mainly in the earliest of them it only consisted in the definition of the god's place of worship. Even so, Homer himself offers examples of the subsequent stage of this

5. Numerous evidences of the τόπος in E. NORDEN, *Agnostos Theos*, Stuttgart 1956[4], 148.

6. C. AUSFELD in "Jahrb. class. Philol." Suppl. XXVIII (1903) 523.

7. E. NORDEN, *Agnostos Theos*, cit., 143.

8. E. NORDEN, *Agnostos Theos*, cit., 168 ff.

technique: instead of a mere definition, a relative clause was used to describe, like in Catullus, the god's δυνάμεις: cf. Hom. *Il.* 3, 277 Ἥλιός ϑ᾽ ὃς πάντ᾽ ἐφορᾷς καὶ πάντ᾽ ἐπακούεις. Alongside Greek authors,[9] Latin poets too used it frequently: in all probability the oldest example of "Relativstil" is Plaut. *Poen.* 1187 ff. *Iuppiter, qui genus colis alisque hominum / per quem uiuimus uitalem aeuom, / quem penes spes uitae sunt hominum / omnium, da diem hunc sospitem quaeso.* Later on this device was used to a great extent by Horace (cf. e.g. *Carm.* 1,2,30 ff. *uenias precamur / nube candentis umeros amictus / augur Apollo, / siue tu mauis Erycina ridens, / quam Iocus circum uolat et Cupido, / ... quem iuuat clamor,* 1,12,13 ff. *quid prius dicam solitis parentis / laudibus, qui res hominum ac deorum, / qui mare ac terras uariisque mundum / temperat horis*) and Virgil (cf. e.g. *Aen.* 11,785 ff. *summe deum, sancti custos Soractis Apollo, / quem primi colimus, cui pineus ardor aceruo / pascitur*).

The first strophe ends with the ritual invocation to the god. The wedding invocation's origin and forms have been analysed by Paul Maas;[10] he has drawn up a list of Greek and Latin instances and has come to the conclusion that the name itself of the god of nuptials derives from the cry ὑμήν.

It is interesting to point out that in Catullus, besides the traditional invocation to the god, we come across the technique of the ἀναδίπλωσις of this invocation, which is another relevant constituent of solemn prayers: the repetition helped to emphasize the cry and stress its urgency.[11] The fact that this method is ancient is proved by the use made of it by Homer (*Il.* 5,31 Ἄρες Ἄρες) and Archilocus (*Frg.* 94 D. = 174,1 Tarditi ὦ Ζεῦ, πάτερ Ζεῦ, σὸν μὲν οὐρανοῦ κράτος). Afterwards, Sophocles (*Aiax* 695 ὦ Πάν Πάν, *Ant.* 781 ι. Ἔρως ἀνίκατε μάχαν, Ἔρως ὃς ἐν κτήμασι πίπτεις) and, more frequently, Euripides (*Bacch.* 370 ff. Ὀσία, πότνα θεῶν, / Ὀσία δ᾽ ἃ κατὰ γᾶν / χρυσέαν πτέρυγα φέρεις,

9. Cf. the numerous examples cited by E. NORDEN, *Agnostos Theos*, cit., 169 ff.

10. P. MAAS in "Philol." 66 (1907) 590-596. His analyses need to be completed, and sometimes corrected, on the ground of the study of R. MUTH in "Wien. Stud." 67 (1954) 7 ff.

11. The most important instances have been collected, also in this case, by E. NORDEN, *P. Vergilius Maro. Aeneis Buch VI*, Stuttgart 1957[4], 136; ID., *Agnostos Theos*, cit., 169 and n. 1.

Hipp. 525 f. Ἔρως Ἔρως, ὃ κατ' ὀμμάτων / στάζεις πόθον, *Ion* 125 f. ὦ Παιάν, ὦ Παιάν, *Tro.* 840 f. Ἔρως Ἔρως, ὃς τὰ Δαρδάνεια / μέλαθρά ποτ' ἦλθες) both used it. In Rome a famous example of ἀναδίπλωσις is the god's name invoked in *Marmar* of the Arvals' song.

A second motif typical of the technique of hymns is the description of the god's *incessus* (ll. 9 ff.). Evidences of this τόπος[12] exist: a) in a very old prayer of women from Elis to Dionysus, quoted by Plutarch (*Quaest. Gr.* 36,299 b), b) in another prayer to Dionysus, in which he is asked to μολεῖν καθαρσίῳ ποδί, c) in Aristoph. *Ran.* 330 f. (Ἴακχε, ἐλθέ ...) θρασεῖ δ' ἐγκατακρούων ποδὶ τὰν ... τιμάν. As for Latin poetry, the theme recurs in Verg. *Georg.* 2,7 f. *huc, pater o Lenaee, ueni nudataque musto / tingue nouo mecum dereptis crura cothurnis* and in Hor. *Carm.* 3,18,1 f. *Faune, Nympharum fugientum amator, / per meos fines et aprica rura / lenis incedas.*

In addition to the god's *incessus*, a remarkable detail is the description of his attitude, which Catullus derives from ancient sources: indeed it was customary that the god should appear *laetus*, as in Plat. *Leg.* 4,712 b θεὸν ... καλούμεθα, ὁ δ' ἀκούσειε καὶ ἀκούσας ἵλεως εὐμενὴς θ'ὑμῖν ἔλθοι, *Hymn. Orph.* 6,10 βαῖνε, γεγηθώς.[13]

The use itself of devices pertaining to prayers lends gravity to the context; but, apart from the technique employed, words, *iuncturae* and structures here are such as those used in solemn speeches. Therefore I think that many critics are wrong in regarding as popular both the atmosphere at the beginning of the poem and the language; the style, in fact, is perfectly adequate to the seriousness of the invocation to the god.

The presence of an *o* at line 1 (*collis o Heliconii*) makes the apostrophe particularly emphatic.[14] Notice also that the transposition of the *o* is poetic − this seems to be the first case of a "Wortstellung" which, according to *Thes.* IX 2, 11,48, appears in prose only in Caes. Arel. *Epist. ad uirg.* 3,2. *Cultor* (l. 2) belongs

12. E. FRAENKEL dwells upon this subject in *Horace*, Oxford 1957, 204 n. 4.
13. Cf. other examples of the τόπος in LIDDELL-SCOTT-JONES s.v. ἵλαος (1).
14. Cf. E. NORDEN, *Agnostos Theos*, cit., 144.

to the aulic style, as it is rarely used with the meaning of *incola* and mainly in solemn poetic contexts: cf. e.g. Plaut. *Amph.* 1065 *et tibi et tuis propitius caeli cultor* (sc. *Iuppiter*) *aduenit*; in prose too, moreover, *cultor* recurs only in passages of elevated style.[15]

Genus explained as "metonymice de singulis personis ex genere alicuius"[16] already existed in Ennius, although the context there was not comparable with the one in Catullus (*neque ... in gremium extollas liberorum ex te genus*). After Catullus − see also his emphatic line *o nimis optato saeclorum tempore nati / heroes, saluete deum genus* (64,22 f.) − *genus* is often used by Virgil with this meaning and always in grave situations: cf. e.g. *Aen.* 6, 500 *Deiphobe ... genus alto a sanguine Teucri*; 6,792 *Augustus Caesar, Diui genus*; 6,839 *Aeaciden, genus ... Achilli*; 7,213.556 *(Aeneas) egregium Veneris genus*. An equally solemn use is in Hor. *Carm.* 1,3,27 *Iapeti genus.*[17] As for prose, the word does not seem to have occurred in any writer before Tac. *Ann.* 6,31 *(Phraates) genus Arsacis.* Catullus could find some distinguished instances for this use in Hom. *Il.* 5,544 γένος δ'ἦν ἐκ ποταμοῖο Ἀλφειοῦ, Soph. *Ant.* 1117 Διὸς γένος, Eur. *Cycl.* 104 Σισύφου γένος and principally Callim. *Hymn.* 4,109 Νύμφαι Θεσσαλίδες, ποταμοῦ γένος.[18]

With regard to l. 3, I have already stressed the function of a relative clause in the solemn style of hymns and, consequently, I cannot agree with those who see a purely colloquial tone in it. Furthermore we must take into consideration the fact that an analogous pattern (invocation to the god, relative clause, imperative) is in a fragment of *Medea* by Ennius (*Scaen.* 284 V.²) *Iuppiter tuque adeo summe Sol, qui res omnis spicis / ... inspice hoc facinus.* In Catullus it is also worth noticing the effective alliteration *uirum uirginem*, all the more so as the two words are in contrast with each other, and the accurate "Wortstellung" *teneram ad uirum uirginem*. Ronconi has already underlined that *suaue olentis (amaraci)* (l. 7) is a learned graecism.[19]

15. Cf. *Thes.* IV 1318,77 ff.
16. *Thes.* VI 1890,70 ff.
17. On Horace cf. R.G.M. NISBET - M. HUBBARD, *A Commentary on Horace: Odes. Book 1*, Oxford 1970, 55.
18. Cf. E. NORDEN, *Aen.*, cit., 324; F. BÖMER, *P. Ouidius Naso. Die Fasten*, II, Heidelberg 1958, 368 f.
19. A. RONCONI, *Studi catulliani*, Brescia 1971², 171.

I would not include the repetition of *huc* (ll. 8-9) among the instances of anaphora, a common feature of colloquial language; on the contrary, it is a case of ἀναδίπλωσις, typical of the solemn style of prayers: cf. Catull. 64,195 *huc huc aduentate* (in a pathetic invocation to the Eumenides), Hor. *Carm.* 3,26,6 f. *hic hic ponite lucida funalia* (immediately before the invocation to Venus in the style of hymns, with a relative clause and the mentioning of the place where the goddess is worshipped: *o quae beatam diua tenes Cyprum et / Memphim*). *Huc huc* is an example of ἀναδίπλωσις of a detail considered relevant in the progress of the ceremony; in the same category one can include the ἑκὰς ἑκάς of mysteries (cf. Verg. *Aen.* 6,258 *procul o procul*) and, on the other hand, the εὐφημεῖτε εὐφημεῖτε of Aristoph. *Ach.* 237.241; *Pax* 434; sim. Eur. *Bacch.* 83.152 ἴτε βάκχαι ἴτε βάκχαι or the well-known ἀναδίπλωσις of χαῖρε.[20]

The imperative *ueni*, like ἐλθέ, βαῖνε, ἰκοῦ, μόλε is frequent in the style of prayers[21]; Catullus could find a distinguished source for his *huc ueni* in Sapph. 1,5 L.-P. ἀλλὰ τυίδ' ἔλθε and Aristoph. *Ach.* 665 δεῦρο Μοῦσ' ἐλθέ, *Equit.* 559 δεῦρ' ἔλθ' ἐς χορόν, *Thesm.* 319 ἐλθὲ δεῦρο; see also, always in contexts of serious prayers, Soph. *Oed. Tyr.* 167 ἔλθετε καὶ νῦν, Callim. *Hym.* 5,33.43 ἔξιθ' 'Αθαναία.

Credit must be given to La Penna[22] for highlighting that, even in his learned poems, Catullus tends to match refined and colloquial styles, in order to obtain new stylistic effects from the contrast itself, as if it were. The origin of this method is recognizable especially in the complex stylistic nature of the Alexandrian epyllion. What we can draw from Catullus, then, is an example of stylistic ποικιλία, achieved through the union of aulic expressions and colloquialisms.

In the cletic hymn such a technique is less evident due to the

20. Cf. E. NORDEN, *Aen.*, cit., 136 f.; ID., *Aus altrömischen Priester-büchern*, Lund/Leipzig 1939, 145. On the repetition of adverbs cf. J. ÉVRARD-GILLIS, *La récurrence lexicale dans l'oeuvre de Catulle. Étude stylistique*, Paris 1976, 136-137. The remarkable study made by Mrs. Évrard-Gillis should be read and completed with the help of the enlightening recension by A. TRAINA in "Riv. Fil. Istr. Class." 106 (1978) 363-74.
21. Cf. the Greek examples cited by C. AUSFELD in "Jahrb. class. Philol." Suppl. XXVIII (1903) 516 f.
22. A. LA PENNA in "Maia" 8 (1956) 155.

solemnity of the invocation; and yet, even in this part of the poem, Catullus does not disdain to include images that have definitely nothing to do with everyday language (as many critics would have it). As a matter of fact, they are peculiar to a stylistic level quite different from that of prayers. They are set, however, in the section of the hymn where Catullus stresses the picturesque sides of the representation of the god and his qualities, and in the description of the bride, rich in grace and delicacy. *Amaracus* (1.7) appears in Catullus for the first time; later on it is almost always used by technical writers, like Plinius or Palladius; but Virgil too, in his *Aeneid*, employs it in a passage overflowing with grace and refinement: 1,693 *mollis amaracus (Ascanium) ... floribus et dulci adspirans complectitur umbra*; in Lucretius there is evidence of the adjective *amaracinus* (or the noun derived from the neuter gender) in not too elevated contexts; besides 6,973 *amaracinum fugiat sus*,[23] cf. 2,847 *amaracini blandum stactaeque liquorem et nardi florem*, 4,1179 *postis ... unguit amaracino (amator)*. The adjective *niueus* was probably a new creation,[24] at that time — there seems to be no mention of it before *Rhet. Herenn.* 4,44 and Catullus.[25] *Luteus* is surely not a feature pertaining to a solemn style: apart from Plautus, it is to be found in Lucretius and in one of Horace's *Epodes* (10,16). It is very frequent in prose, above all in Pliny the Elder. *Soccus* too, although common in comedies, is avoided in poetry in the literal sense of the word, whereas it is used as a metaphor to indicate 'comedy'. An innovation by Catullus is represented by the use of *excitus* "fere pro

23. The reference to Lucr. 6,973 is in A. RONCONI, *Studi catulliani*, cit., 149.

24. On the adjectives ending in —*eus* Norden's notes are always substantial (*Aen.*, cit., 218); see also D.O. ROSS, *Style and Tradition in Catullus*, Cambridge/Mass. 1969, 60 ff.

25. E. BEDNARA in "Arch. Lat. Lexik. u. Gramm." 15 (1908) 224 believes that *niueus* probably sprang from dactylic poetry, prior to the *auctor* of the *Rhetorica ad Herennium*, "weil dieser Prosaiker seine Redeweise mit dichterischen Wörtern zu schmücken sucht und das Adjektiv *niueus* sich sonst nur bei Daktylikern findet ... ausserdem nur noch bei dem Prosaiker Seneca, der die Sprache der daktylischen Dichter sehr haüfig nachahmt." Cf. also D.O. ROSS, *Style and Tradition*, cit., 62. *Niueus*, however, is an adjective dear to Catullus, who uses it also in 58b,4; 63,8; 64,240.303.309.364; 68,125.

adi., i.q. laetus, bono et erecto animo"[26]; according to Rehm in *Thes.* V 2,1247,36 ff. the only example, in addition to Catullus, is Stat. *Silu.* 4,3,101 *illic flectitur excitus viator.* By choosing *hilaris dies*, Catullus changed the sacral formula *bonus dies* (see *Thes.* II 2092,68 ff. and Norden, *Agnostos Theos*, cit., 148; but *hilaris* was a recent form and never before Cicero and Catullus was it used instead for *hilarus*; with the active meaning of *laetitiam praestans, hilaris* (or *hilarus*) belongs to the *sermo familiaris* (cf. Cic. *Att.* 5,20,5 *hilara Saturnalia*) and to prose.[27] Most likely, there is only one indication of *tinnulus* (1.13) being used before Catullus, that is, in a fragment of an atellana by Pomponius (*Com. Frg.* 57 R.[3]). Finally, it is significant that Catullus (l. 14) does not use elevated *iuncturae*, such as *pulsare pedibus* (see Enn. *Ann.* 1 V.[2]), or *plaudere pedibus* (see Verg. *Aen.* 6,644), but *pellere pedibus*, which is also employed by Lucr. 5,1402 and Hor. *Carm.* 3,18,15.[28]

From these, as well as from other view-points, it is possible to underline, in the first few lines, the chief characteristic of c. 61 and some of the basic qualities of Catullus' art. A proof of his being close to Alexandrian poetry is the search for rare myths and erudite details: as early as Pindar, Hymen had been traditionally defined as the Muses' child (*Frg.* 139 Snell); the main sources mention Calliope or Terpsichore or Clio as his mother; the only reliable evidences of Urania as Hymen's mother are in Catullus and Nonn. 24,88 Οὐρανίη δ' Ὑμέναιον ... / παιδὸς ἑοῦ γονόεντος ἐπώνυμον, 33,67 f. Ὑμέναιος ... τεκούσης / Οὐρανίης. Wilamowitz[29] believed that this erudite mark might have come from an

26. Wrongly W. KROLL, *C. Valerius Catullus*, Stuttgart 1960[4], 108 interprets it with the meaning of ἀνακληθείς.
27. Cf. J. SVENNUNG, *Catulls Bildersprache*, Uppsala 1945, 140, *Thes.* VI 3,2786,74 ff.
28. Cf. E. NORDEN, *Aen.*, cit., 297.
29. U. v. WILAMOWITZ-MOELLENDORFF, *Hell. Dicht.*, cit., II 283. V.A. ESTEVEZ in "Maia" 29-30 (1977-78) 103-105 has recently resumed an old interpretation by R. ELLIS, *A Commentary on Catullus*, Oxford 1889, 210, according to whom "it is not impossible that Urania is selected as a name of a good omen with which to begin a hymeneal; pure love was under the protection of Cypris Urania, as impure of Pandemus". Estevez refers to the numerous allusions to *bonum omen* in c. 61 and also suggests that the choice in this poem might have been facilitated by metrical reasons. On the contrary, I am not convinced by the rather impressionistic explanation given

25

Hellenistic source; his hypothesis is now corroborated by Callim. *Frg.* 2a,42 ff. Pf. καὶ Οὐ[ρανίας ὀ] Ὑμένα[ιω]ς λέσχης [ὀ]μιλία[ς].[30] Again, the description of a child of a Muse as an inhabitant of Helicon dates back to an unusual Hellenistic piece of information.[31]

Catullus' debts to the literary tradition are evident, as regards his use of the conventional techniques of hymns as well as the description of Hymen, which follows well-known examples. Hymen is described *pulchritudine muliebri*, with bridal clothes and attributes[32]: he wears a garland of flowers (cf. Paul. *ap.* Fest. 56,1 L. *corollam noua nupta de floribus, uerbenis herbisque a se lectis sub amiculo ferebat*, Ouid. *Her.* 21,165 f. *proicit ipse sua deductus fronte coronas, / spissaque de nitidis tergit amoma comis*), a *flammeum* and a *luteus soccus*[33]; his foot is *niueus* and his voice is *tinnula*.[34] Hymen's feminine traits recur in the

by PUTNAM in "Class. Phil." 71 (1976) 372: "since its author is part officiant, part master of ceremonies, the poem also becomes concerned as well as with the literal details of an *epithalamium*".

30. Cf. R. PFEIFFER, *Callimachus*, cit., II 104.

31. Cf. U. v. WILAMOWITZ-MOELLENDORFF, *Hell. Dicht.*, cit., II 283 n. 1.

32. Of course the description of Hymen in bridal clothes is not simply literal, but it is connected with the representation of the god with proper attributes, such as the torch, the garland and the *flammeum*: LIEBERG in "Gnom." 47 (1975) 356 refers to SCHMIDT, *De Hymenaeo et Talassio*, diss. Kiel 1886, 57-58. Mrs. MANTERO has rightly pointed out in *Crocina candidus in tunica (Cat. 68,134)*, in "Studi Traglia", I, Roma 1976, 190 that also the *Hymenaeus* depicted on the fresco of the "house of Meleagros" wears a garland of flowers: cf. W. HELBIG, *Untersuchungen über die Campanische Wandmalerei*, Leipzig 1873, 171 n. 855 and on wedding-garlands J. KOECHLING, *De coronarum apud antiquos ui atque usu*, diss. Giessen 1914, 61-62.

33. Cf. DAREMBERG-SAGLIO III 1655 and n. 9; E. PERNICE in GERCKE-NORDEN, *Einleitung i.d. Altertumswiss.*, II³, Leipzig 1922, 57. On the cromatic value of the adjective *lūteus* cf. T. MANTERO in "Studi Traglia", cit., I 182, according to whom the *lūteum soccum* in Catull. 61,10 must be regarded as an expressive change made by the poet, because when related to wedding ceremonies, sometimes the adjective designates a reddish colour. Mrs. Mantero points out that here *luteum* stands for *croceum* and mentions further instances of the god's clothes (Ouid. *Met.* 4,393; 10,1; *Her.* 21,162) as well as the famous representation of the "Aldobrandini wedding", where the colour of the *soccus* verges on orange.

34. Cf. Pompon. *Com. Frg.* 57 ff. R.³ *uocem deducas oportet, ut uideantur mulieris / uerba. Iube modo adferatur munus: uocem reddam ego /*

rhetoricians' description of Gamos[35]: cf. Menand. *Rhet. Gr.* III
404,29 ff. Spengel ἐξέσται δέ σοί ποτε καὶ φιλοτιμουμένῳ τὸν
Γάμον τὸν θεὸν ἐκφράσαι ... ὅτι νέος ἐστὶν ἀειθαλὴς ὁ Γάμος,
λαμπάδα φέρων ἐν ταῖν χεροῖν, ῥοδινὸς ἐν ἐρυθήματι τὸ
πρόσωπον καταλαμπόμενον, ἵμερον ἀποστάζων ἐκ τῶν ὀμμάτων
καὶ τῶν ὀφρύων; cf. also Corn. Balb. *ap.* Seru. *ad* Verg. *Aen.*
4,127 *Cornelius Balbus Hymenaeum ait ... pulchritudine muliebri.*
Catullus' image of Hymen was partially resumed by Seneca, *Med.*
67-70, who also repeats some stylistic structures of the hymn:
*et tu, qui facibus legitimis ades / noctem discutiens auspice
dextera, / huc incede gradu marcidus ebrio / praecingens rosea
tempora uinculo.*

In addition to Catullus' debts to tradition it is necessary to
point out his effort to change the traditional ingredients of the
Greek hymenaeus: *rapere* (l. 3) is a typical verb indicating the
utterly Roman custom of the *raptio*[36]; *amaracus* is not present
anywhere else as one of the flowers in the bride's garland. The
motif of a dance in connection with the singing of the hymenaeus
might appear conventional: see Hes. *Scut.* 277 τῇσιν δὲ χοροὶ
παίζοντες ἕποντο, Aristoph. *Pax* 1316 ff. εὐφημεῖν χρὴ καὶ τὴν
νύμφην ἔξω τινὰ δεῦρο κομίζειν / δᾳδάς τε φέρειν ... καὶ τὰ
σκεύη πάλιν εἰς τὸν ἀγρὸν νυνὶ χρὴ πάντα κομίζειν /
ὀρχησαμένους καὶ σπείσαντας, Theocr. 18,2 f. παρθενικαί
... πρόσθε νεογράπτω θαλάμω χορὸν ἐστάσαντο. Some rhetoricians, moreover, classify it among the usual components of a
hymenaeus: see Menand. *Rhet. Gr.* III 409,8 ff. Spengel ἕως
αὐτοὶ τελοῦσι τὰ ὄργια τοῦ γάμου καὶ τελοῦνται, ἡμεῖς ῥόδοις
καὶ ἴοις στεφανωσάμενοι καὶ λαμπάδας ἀνάψαντες περὶ
τὸν θάλαμον παίξωμεν καὶ χορείαν στησώμεθα, καὶ τὸν
ὑμέναιον ἐπιβοώμεθα, τὸ δάπεδον πλήττοντες τοῖς ποσίν, ἐπικρο-
τοῦντες τὼ χεῖρε, ἐστεφανωμένοι πάντες; Catullus' innovation,
then, consists in this, that he shifts the dance motif from choruses
of youths and maidens — who must only sing praises to Hymen —
to the god himself.

The wedding torch (l. 15) constitutes another peculiar feature:
it is only in Catullus, anyway, that a *pinea taeda* is mentioned: in

tenuem et tinnulam.
35. Gamos is the name attributed to Hymen by the rhetoricians.
36. Cf. l. 56.

Rome, as a matter of fact, the torch in Ceres' honour that they used to light in the bride's house and carry during the *deductio* was made of hawthorn: see Fest. 282,22 ff. L. *patrimi et matrimi pueri praetexti tres nubentem deducunt; unus, qui facem praefert ex spina alba*, Varr. *ap.* Non. 112 M. *quae noctu fieri initia solita etiam nunc spinea fax indicat*, Plin. *Nat. Hist.* 16,75 *spinea, nuptiarum facibus auspicatissima.* [37]

A further ingredient typical of Catullus and added by the poet to enliven the conventional subject is his love for colour effects[38]: it is recognizable in the description of the god's attributes, in which the stress is laid on *flammeum* (1. 8), *luteus soccus* (ll. 9-10) and *niueus pes* (ll. 9-10).

*

The invocation to the god is followed by the explanation of the reason of the cry: Junia is going to marry Manlius under propitious auspices. To take auspices by looking at some birds' flight was proper to the ritual of archaic Roman wedding ceremonies: but in the time of Catullus this phase of the celebration had been practically abolished, according to what we read in Cic. *Diuin.* 1,28 *nihil fere quondam maioris rei nisi auspicato ne priuatim quidem gerebatur, quod etiamnunc nuptiarum auspices declarant, qui re omissa nomen tantum tenent.* [39] It is therefore a detail without correspondence in the actual ritual of the ceremony and Catullus introduced it in relation with archaic traditions.

Junia is similar to Venus, when the goddess appeared in front of Paris for the famous judgement, and she shines like myrtle nourished by dew. Ferrero has rightly observed that the bride is introduced at the very moment she approaches the groom: she looks beautiful and shy, sublime and humble as if she were coming

---

37. On the nuptial torch in Ceres' honour see also Seru. *ad* Verg. *Buc.* 8, 29 and J. HECKENBACH in "R.E.P.W." VIII 2 (1913) 2133. On the motif of *quatere taedam* during the ceremony and its Greek forerunners cf. A. GRILLI, *Nota a un frammento adespoto e Catullo, carme 61*, in "Studi classici in onore di Q.Cataudella", III, Catania 1972, 95-97.

38. On chromatism in Catullus cf. H. BARDON, *Propositions sur Catulle*, Bruxelles 1970, 57, T. MANTERO in "Studi Traglia", cit., I 176 and n. 56.

39. Cf. E. PERNICE in GERCKE-NORDEN, cit., 57, DAREMBERG-SAGLIO III 1655.

· before a judge. Frequent mythical allusions are put into the personal theme, which starts from the ritual cletic hymn and adds to it a precise link with the concreteness of the historical event.[40]

Namque Iunia[41] Manlio
qualis Idalium colens
uenit ad Phrygium Venus
iudicem, bona cum bona
    nubet alite uirgo,

floridis uelut enitens
myrtus Asia ramulis
quos Hamadryades deae
ludicrum sibi roscido
    nutriunt umore.[42]

Also in this part of the cletic hymn Catullus takes up the traditional pattern of the genre. It is typical of the technique of hymns to put a sentence beginning with *nam* (γάρ) after the invocation to the god and the invitation for him to come[43]; in a prayer the

40. L. FERRERO, *Interpretazione di Catullo*, Torino 1955, 293.

41. I accept the form *Iunia*, instead of *Vinia*, only to conform to Mynors' text; but in this case, since there is no further mentioning of the name of the character dealt with, both solutions are possible. With regard to *uinctos/iunctos* of 58b,7 cf. G. JACHMANN in "Gnom." 1 (1925) 207, who asserts that "über *ui* und *iu* gibt es keine andere Entscheidung als die des Sinnes (daher dann auch über *Vinia* und *Iunia Aurunculeia* keine)". F. DELLA CORTE, *Personaggi catulliani*, Firenze 1976, 87-88 has recently resumed Syme's hypothesis, published by CH.L. NEUDLING, *A Prosopography to Catullus*, Oxford 1955, 185, in the light of which we should read *Vibia* because the manuscript tradition may have made the frequent mistake of confusing −*b* with −*v*−.

42. *Nutriunt umore* in the manuscripts is the only example of substitution of a dactyl with a spondee in a pherecratean verse. C.J. FORDYCE, *Catullus*, Oxford 1961, 241 proved that this case is not to be placed on the same level as analogous substitutions at the second foot of the phalaecian hendecasyllable. J.A. Maehly, taking the corrupt text into consideration, proposed *nutriuntur honore*; but the correction of *umore* is unlikely, the more so as the same "iunctura" is in Plin. *Nat. Hist.* 9,38 *roscido ... umore uiuentes*. A more probable theory is the one suggested by U. v. WILAMOWITZ-MOELLENDORFF, *Sappho and Simonides*, Berlin 1913, 308, who thinks that Catullus might have altered a line like Anacreon's συρίγγων κοῖλώτερα (Frg. 11 D.= 17 Gentili).

43. Cf. E. NORDEN, *Agnostos Theos*, cit., 152 ff.

reason for calling the god must be given, and in this case it is represented by the imminent start of the wedding ceremony. Catullus reproduces a technique already used by Pindar, *Olymp.* 4,1 ff. ἐλατὴρ ὑπέρτατε βροντᾶς ἀκαμαντόποδος / Ζεῦ. τεαὶ / γὰρ Ὧραι / ὑπὸ ποικιλοφόρμιγγος ἀοιδᾶς ἐλισσόμεναί μ᾽ ἔπεμψαν κτλ., *Isthm.* 5,1 ff. μᾶτερ Ἀελίου πολυώνυμε Θεία / σέο ἕκατι καὶ μεγασθενῆ νόμισαν / χρυσὸν ἄνθρωποι περιώσιον ἄλλων. / καὶ γὰρ ἐριζόμεναι / νᾶες ἐν πόντῳ καὶ ⟨ὑφ᾽⟩ ἅρμασιν ἵπποι / διὰ τεάν, ὤνασσα, τιμὰν ὠκυδινά- / τοις ἐν ἁμίλλαισι θαυμασταὶ πέλονται and Aristoph. *Ran.* 403-410 Ἴακχε φιλοχορευτά, συμπρόπεμπέ με. / σὺ γὰρ κατεσχίσω μὲν ἐπὶ γέλωτι / κἀπ᾽ εὐτελείᾳ τόδε τὸ σανδαλίσκον / καὶ τὸ ῥάκος ... / Ἴακχε φιλοχορευτὰ συμπρόπεμπέ με. / καὶ γὰρ παραβλέψας τι μειρακίσκης / νῦν δὴ κατεῖδον καὶ μάλ᾽ εὐπροσώπου, 875 ff. ὦ Διὸς ἐννέα παρθένοι, ἀγναί / Μοῦσαι ... / ἔλθετ᾽ ... · / νῦν γὰρ ἀγὼν σοφίας ὁ μέγας χωρεῖ πρὸς ἔργον ἤδη.[44] Although Kiessling and Heinze do not mention it in their commentary on Horace, the same device is present in Hor. *Carm.* 4,14,5-13, in a context where the poet addresses Augustus as if he were a god, and, consequently, his language is that of sacred hymns: *o qua sol habitabilis / inlustrat oras maxime principum, / quem legis expertes Latinae / Vindelici didicere nuper / quid Marte posses: milite nam tuo / Drusus Genaunos, implacidum genus, / Breunosque uelocis et arcis / Alpibus impositas tremendis / deiecit.*

Following the rules of the technique of hymns, lines 16-20 explain the reason for the invitation to the god and draw a comparison between the bride and Venus; the style is aulic, as the seriousness of the topic requires. Svennung defines the simile as being of Homeric style,[45] only used by Catullus in emphatic or solemn contexts: the same technique of instituting a parallel is a) in the description of Ariadne when she first met Theseus, in 64,89 ff. *quales Eurotae praecingunt flumina myrtus / auraue distinctos educit uerna colores* ...; b) in the famous simile, taken from Hom. *Il.* 4,422 ff., in 64,269 ff. *hic, qualis flatu placidum mare matutino / horrificans Zephyrus procliuas incitat undas* ...

44. W.B. Stanford and other commentators say nothing about either case in Aristophanes.
45. J. SVENNUNG, *Cat. Bildersprache,* cit., 44.

sic tum uestibuli linquentes regia tecta / *ad se quisque uago passim pede discedebant*; c) in the pathetic comparison between his own song and Ity's cry in 65,12 ff. *semper maesta tua carmina morte canam,* / *qualia sub densis ramorum concinit umbris* / *Daulias, absumpti fata gemens Ityli*; d) in the one, of epic origin too,[46] between the *riuus* that quenches the traveller's thirst and tears of love in 68,57 f. *qualis in aerii perlucens uertice montis* / *riuus muscoso prosilit e lapide* ...

Idalium colens (l. 16) recalls the aulic *collis ... Heliconii cultor* (ll. 1-2): the various examples in *Thes.* III 1672,3-41 of *colere* meaning *custodire*[47] and referred to a god prove that this expression belongs to the style of prayers; in Catullus the same *iunctura* is in the prayer to Venus in 36,12 ff. (*quae sanctum Idalium ... colis*). As for *iudex* used to designate Paris, it recurs in Juno's speech to the gods in Hor. *Carm.* 3,3,18 ff. *Ilion, Ilion fatalis incestusque iudex* / *et mulier peregrina uertit* / *in puluerem.*

Bona cum bona (l. 19) constitutes in Kroll's opinion[48] an instance of "volkstümliche Paranomasie": but the polyptoton does not always belong to the same stylistic range; it is accepted in elevated contexts too, especially when the "iunctura" has an ancient and noble literary tradition.[49] In this case, *cum bona alite* reproduces Hesiod's σὺν οἰωνοῖς ἀγαθοῖσιν (*Frg.* 240,11 Merkelbach-West), and it is an expression of the language of prophecies.[50]

---

46. Cf. C.J. FORDYCE, *Catullus*, cit., 350.

47. G. LIEBERG in "Gnom." 47 (1975) 356 does not approve of such a meaning, but he maintains that the verb here is synonimous with *habitare*.

48. W. KROLL, *Cat.*, cit., 109.

49. Cf. J.B. HOFMANN - A. SZANTYR, *Lat. Syntax u. Stilistik*, 707 f. and A. RONCONI, *Studi catulliani*, cit., 56. J. ÉVRARD-GILLIS, *La récurrence lexicale dans l'oeuvre de Catulle*, cit., 115 observes that "l'adjectif répété peut également déterminer des mots dépendant syntaxiquement l'un de l'autre et dans un rapport étroit de proximité. Dans l'épithalame 61, le poète souligne le caractère parfaitement heureux du mariage". On the "Wortstellung" in similar cases cf. J. ÉVRARD-GILLIS, op. cit., 132.

50. Cf. *Thes.* I 1526,66 ff., F. BÖMER, *Die Fasten*, cit., II 58. This may be corroborated by the prophetic quality of the examples in Horace (*Ep.* 10,1 *mala soluta nauis exit alite*, 16,13-14 *secunda ... alite, Carm.* 1,15,5 *mala ducis aui domum*) cited by R.G.M. NISBET - M. HUBBARD, *A Commentary on Horace: Odes Book 1*, cit., 192.

The Alexandrian refinement of rare details is evident in the mentioning of Idalium, in the isle of Cyprus, as a place of worship of Venus. Such a piece of information does not exist in historians and among geographers it is only found in Stephen of Byzantium.[51] In poetry, on the other hand, its fortune is possibly due to Theocritus (15,100 Δέσποιν' ἃ Γολγώς τε καὶ Ἰδάλιον ἐφίλασας), on whose model Latin poets from Catullus on took up the erudite particular.[52] The term Phrygius associated with Paris is another detail that occurs before Catullus in Callim. *Hym.* 5,18 οὐδ'ὅκα τὰν Ἴδᾳ Φρὺξ ἐδίκαζεν ἔριν κτλ. After Catullus see Verg. *Aen.* 7,363 *at non sic Phrygius penetrat Lacedaemona pastor.*

I think that there are further traces of alexandrinism in the choice of myrtle to draw a comparison with the bride. Catullus' annotators do not give weight to this,[53] but the poet must have chosen this plant in his parallel for a definite reason: myrtle was sacred to Venus and symbolised virginity.[54] It is significant that Catullus mentions Venus at l. 18 and the word *uirgo* referred to Junia at l. 20. Moreover, the association myrtle-worship of Venus is very old and is given ample evidence in literary sources.[55] In this context, however, a special rôle is played by the hint at Paris' verdict, before the parallel bride-myrtle: it suggests that Catullus may be following a rare Alexandrian myth, found in Nicander,[56]

51. Cf. also Plin. *Nat. Hist.* 5,130.
52. Cf. E. OBERHUMMER in "R.E.P.W." IX I (1914) 869 f.
53. Only FORDYCE, *Catullus*, cit., 241 hints that "the connexion of the myrtle with Venus gives it special point here."
54. Cf. V. HEHN, *Kulturpflanzen und Hausthiere*, Berlin 1902[7], 223 f., E. FEHRLE, *Die kultische Keuschheit im Altertum*, im "Religionsgeschichtliche Versuche u. Vorarbeiten" VI (1910) 126 ff., 239 ff.
55. As regards the myrtle's double attribution to verginity and Venus, Mrs. TARTARI CHERSONI in "Paideia" 28 (1973) 220 brings forward the hypothesis that the plant may have been considered as a symbol and the ideal "trait d'union" between the two stages of women's evolution, different from each other but necessarily consequent in the harmonic development of personality.
56. Nic. *Alex.* 618 f. πρὸς δ'ἔτι (that is, in addition to myrtle) τοῖς Δίκτυννα τεῆς ἐχθήρατο κλῶνας / Ἥρη τ' Ἰμβρασίη μούνη στέφος οὐχ ὑπέδεκτο, / κάλλεος, οὕνεκα Κύπρω, ὅτ' εἰς ἔριν ἠέρθησαν / ἀθάναται, κόσμησεν ἐν Ἰδαίοισιν ὄρεσσι. Maybe the passage is interpolated: cf. O. SCHNEIDER, *Nicandrea*, Leipzig 1856, 157, who is followed by A.S.F.

for which at Paris' judgement the victorious goddess was adorned with myrtle.

Neoteric refinement is evident in the following strophe (ll. 21-25), as for both imagery and style; surely a different literary atmosphere from that of the cry to the god was suitable for the delicate comparison between the bride and myrtle. Notice a sign of refinement immediately at the beginning, in the use of *enitere* (l. 21), a verb which is employed by Plautus and Cicero as a metaphor (i.e. "clarum esse, excellere"), whereas it is only found in Accius, *Trag.* 234 b R.[3] *probae etsi in segetem sunt deteriorem datae fruges, tamen ipsae suapte natura enitent*, besides Catullus, with the meaning "de nitore uel ubertate frugum, florum".[57]

Floridus (l. 21), an adjective dear to Catullus, is never used before Cicero; the fact that it belongs to the neoteric poetic language is proved by examples such as Lucr. 5,785 *florida fulserunt uiridanti prata colore, Culex* 70 f. *florida cum tellus, gemmantes picta per herbas / uere notat dulci distincta coloribus arua, Priap.* 86,10 *florido mihi* (sc. *Priapo*) *ponitur picta uere corolla* and by its recurrence in late imitators of neoteric poetry (*Peruig. Ven.* 13, Auson. 384,6 Peiper). The "iunctura" *floridis ramulis*, in which an adjective is joined with a diminutive, removes any doubt about the stylistic worth of the expression. On the presence of diminutives in Catullus' *carmina docta* see Ronconi's remarks[58]; he underlines with great efficacy their function in Catullus, and in neoteric poetry in general, when he says[59] that a diminutive mirrors an affectionate disposition of the subject who depicts things of a poetic world, transforming them into something caressed. In c. 61 diminutives are frequent with regard to Junia, and it is noteworthy that, from the very first image of the young bride, Catullus wants to emphasize her grace and delicacy by using a stylistic device of affective language.

The "iunctura" *roscido umore* appears in Plin. *Nat. Hist.* 9,38 *roscido ... umore uiuentes*; on the basis of Forcellini's evidence, *roscido umore* seems to be common in poetry of the first century B.C. and in prose.

GOW and A.F. SCHOLFIELD in their edition (Cambridge 1953). Cf. also the scholia *ad loc.* (p. 110 f. SCHNEIDER).

57. *Thes.* V 2,594,53.
58. A. RONCONI, *Studi catulliani*, cit., 122 ff.
59. A. RONCONI, *Studi catulliani*, cit., 129 f.

The Alexandrian love for erudite details recurs in *myrtus Asia*, where the adjective is probably[60] not referred to the well-known province, but to the region of Lydia, mentioned by Hom. *Il.* 2, 461 'Ασίῳ ἐν λειμῶνι (cf. Verg. *Aen.* 7,701 f. *Āsia palus, Georg.* 1,383 *Āsia prata*); when Catullus means the province of Asia, he always employs *ă*; cf. 46,6; 66,36; 68,89 and Seru. *ad* Verg. *Georg.* 1,383 *de palude Asia a longa est; nam de prouincia corripit a. Āsius* is only found in Catullus and in two passages by Virgil (cf. E. Diehl in *Thes.* II 787,1 ff.); this adjective is rare in Greek writers too; apart from the above-quoted line by Homer, Liddell-Scott-Jones cites only Strab. 14,1,45 and Steph. Byz. 131,7.

As regards *Hamadryades deae*, Dryads, Adryads and Hama-dryads are often confused in poetry: a famous indication of this confusion is in Prop. 1,20,12 ff. Sometimes Hamadryads simply stand for sylvan nymphs: besides Catullus see Verg. *Buc.* 10,62, Prop. 2,32,37; 34,76; Ouid. *Fast.* 2,155; *Met.* 14,621. It is highly likely that it was a Hellenistic habit, if we consider that the same use is present in Nonnus and often in epigrams of *Anthologia Palatina.*[61]

The Alexandrian ποικιλία is evident if we take into account the imagery and themes employed by Catullus: ll. 16-25, for instance, are a mixture of conventional elements and echoes of Sappho, Callimachus and Theocritus.

The comparison between the bride and Venus belongs to the traditional motifs of wedding-songs, in which the εἰκάζειν is a fixed rule[62]; when discussing the presence of εἰκάζειν in epithalamia, Himerius the rhetorician attributes the custom of using it to Sappho: *Or.* 9,16 Colonna Σαπφοῦς ἦν ἄρα μήλῳ μὲν εἰκάσαι τὴν κόρην ... τὸν νυμφίον τε 'Αχιλλεῖ παρομοιῶσαι καὶ εἰς ταὐτὸν ἀγαγεῖν τῷ ἥρῳ τὸν νεανίσκον ταῖς πράξεσιν. Particularly frequent in hymenaei was the comparison with divinities (see the parallel Junia-Venus in c. 61) or mythical characters,[63] this too

60. Cf. C.J. FORDYCE, *Catullus*, cit., 241.
61. Cf. W. ROSCHER, *Lex. d. Myth.*, I 2, 1826 f. and W. SÜSS in "R.E. P.W." VII 2 (1912) 2287 ff.
62. Cf. E.A. MANGELSDORFF, *Lyr. Hochzeitsged.*, cit., 17 f. I will deal with this subject more in detail in connection with 1.102.
63. Menand. *Rhet. Gr.* III 402,10 ff. Spengel; cf. B. SNELL, *Ges. Phil. Schr.*, 83. J. SVENNUNG, *Cat. Bilderspr.*, cit., 61 ff. does not distinguish usual parallels men-gods from the comparisons typical of wedding-songs.

recommended by the rhetoricians: see Sappho's fragment 111, 5-6 L.-P. γάμβρος †εἰσέρχεται ἴσος† Ἄρευι / ἄνδρος μεγάλω πόλυ μέζων and the famous φαίνεταί μοι κῆνος ἴσος θέοισιν κτλ. (31,1 ff. L.-P.), if it is an epithalamium,[64] as Wilamowitz[65] and Snell[66] believed. In the long Sapphic fragment on Hector and Andromache's wedding (44 L.-P.), ll. 31 ff. are relevant from this point of view: γύναικες δ'ἐλέλυσδον ὄσαι προγενέστεραι, / πάντες δ'ἄνδρες ἐπήρατον ἴαχον ὄρθιον / Πάον'ὀγκαλέοντες ἐκάβολον εὐλύραν, / ὔμνην δ'Ἔκτορα κ'Ἀνδρομάχαν θεοϊκέλοις.

The parallel between the bride and natural elements, furthermore, is one of the τόποι of epithalamia. It is as well recommended by writers on rhetoric: see Menand. *Rhet. Gr.* III,404,5 Spengel κάλλος δὲ παρ'ἀμφοῖν κατὰ ἀντεξέτασιν, πάντως οὐχ ἡ μὲν φυτῶν καλλίστω ἐλαίᾳ, ὁ δὲ φοίνικι παραπλήσιος; καὶ ὅτι ὁ μὲν ῥόδῳ προσέοικεν, ἡ δὲ μήλῳ. Himerius for his part states that one needs a poetic language to describe the beauty of the bride's face, similar to a flower: *Or.* 9,19 Colonna εἰ δὲ καὶ τὸ ἄνθος τῆς ὄψεως γράφειν ἐθέλοιμι, τὰ ποιητῶν ἀνάγκη φθέγγεσθαι.

In order to find a possible source for this τόπος in Catullus, vague comparisons women-plants, such as the one in Hom. *Od.* 6,163 concerning Nausicaa[67] or the numerous examples collected by Svennung,[68] do not count so much as the presence of this motif in the poetic tradition of wedding-songs: in this case the origin of the τόπος is probably Sapphic. In addition to the rhetoricians' explicit reference to Sappho, see some well-known fragments of her epithalamia; 105a L.-P. οἶον τὸ γλυκύμαλον ἐρεύθεται ἄκρῳ ἐπ'ὔσδῳ, / ἄκρον ἐπ' ἀκροτάτῳ, λελάθοντο δὲ μαλοδρόπηες, / οὐ μὰν ἐκλελάθοντ', ἀλλ' οὐκ ἐδύναντ'ἐπίκεσθαι, 105c L.-P. οἶαν τὰν ὑάκινθον ἐν ὤρεσι ποίμενες ἄνδρες / πόσσι καταστείβοισι, χάμαι δέ τε πόρφυρον ἄνθος. Theocritus, too, however,

---

64. Significant objections against the identification of fr. 31 L.-P. with an epithalamium have been raised by G. JACHMANN in "Rhein. Mus." 107 (1964) 1 ff. and by G. WILLS in "Gr. Rom. Byz. Stud." 8 (1967) 174 ff.

65. U. v. WILAMOWITZ-MOELLENDORFF, *Sappho und Simonides*, cit., 56 ff.

66. B. SNELL, *Ges. Phil. Schr.*, 82 ff.

67. The comparison is cited by C.J. FORDYCE, *Catullus*, cit., 241.

68. J. SVENNUNG, *Cat. Bilderspr.*, cit., 73 f.

used the same τόπος in his epithalamium when comparing Helen with a cypress: πιείρᾳ μεγάλα ἅτ'ἀνέδραμε κόσμος ἀρούρᾳ / ἢ κάπῳ κυπάρρισος ἢ ἅρματι Θεσσαλὸς ἵππος (18,29-30).

Reinhold Merkelbach[69] attracted the reader's attention on the echo of a Sapphic description of Venus' place of worship at lines 21-25 of c. 61 (see 2,5 f. L.-P. ἐν δ'ὕδωρ ψῦχρον κελάδει δι' ὔσδων / μαλίνων and Catull. 61,23-25 quos ... umore, Sapph. 2,9-10 L.-P. ἐν δὲ λείμων ἱππόβοτος τέθαλεν / ἠρίνοισιν ἄνθεσιν and Catull. 61,21-22 floridis ... ramulis. In all probability, Sappho's lines inspired the theme present in Catullus, but in expressing it he must have also remembered Callimachus; in Kroll's opinion,[70] ludicrum sibi referred to the Hamadryads recalls Callim. Hym. 4,323 f. ἃ Δηλιὰς εὔρετο νύμφῃ / παίγνια κουρίζοντι καὶ 'Απόλλωνι γελαστύν. At the same time, even the description of a plant nourished by dew is associated with Sappho as well as Callim. Hym. 2,80 ff. σεῖο δὲ βωμοί / ἄνθεα μὲν φορέουσιν ἐν εἴαρι τόσσα περ Ὧραι / ποικίλ'ἀγινεῦσι ζεφύρου πνείοντος ἐέρσην. On Callimachus' influence in these lines of the poem consider the above-mentioned definition of Paris as Φρύξ.

With regard to the technique itself of comparing a virgin with a flower, serious doubts could be entertained about Sappho as Catullus' direct source; in support of a different theory, E. Rohde showed with a wealth of examples that such a parallel was frequent in the love poetry of the Hellenistic age: therefore he posited that this kind of poetry may have exerted a decisive influence upon imitations of the genre by Latin poets.[71]

*

Following a conventional technique of hymns, Catullus asks the god (who knows by now the reason why he has been called) to hasten to leave his dwelling and persuade the bride to reach the groom's house.

69. R. MERKELBACH in "Philol." 101 (1957) 26 f.
70. W. KROLL, Cat., cit., 109.
71. E. ROHDE, Der griechische Roman und seine Vorläufer, Leipzig 1900², 161 ff. For Catullus see p. 164 n. 3.

quare age, huc aditum ferens,
perge linquere Thespiae
rupis Aonios specus,
nympha quos super irrigat
    frigerans Aganippe.   30
ac domum dominam uoca
coniugis cupidam noui,
mentem amore reuinciens
ut tenax hedera huc et huc
    arborem implicat errans.   35

A completely different "Stimmung" would be expressed in ll.31-35 if we accepted the punctuation suggested by Wilamowitz.[72] He inserts a comma after *uoca* and not after *noui*: in this case the husband's mind would be *cupida* instead of the bride herself. But, as Eduard Fraenkel pointed out,[73] the punctuation suggested by

72. U. v. WILAMOWITZ-MOELLENDORFF, *Hell. Dicht.*, cit., II 285.
73. E. FRAENKEL, *Kl. Beitr.*, II 93. With regard to my comment, G. LIEBERG in "Gnom." 47 (1975) 356 notes that "bei den Versen 31-33 fehlt die Erklärung von *cupidam* als Prolepsis und der Hinweis auf die in V. 33 liegende Begründung für das proleptische *cupidam*". The interpretation given by Lieberg is not new: it appears, for example, in some commentaries (cf. F. GUGLIELMINO, *Catullo. Carmi scelti*, Catania 1945[6], G.B. PIGHI, *Il libro di Gaio Valerio Catullo e i frammenti dei "poeti nuovi"*, Torino 1974) and it is accepted by E.D'ARBELA in his translation (Milano 1957). I do not believe that there is any possibility of a prolepsis nor am I convinced by the objection raised against Fraenkel's interpretation of *cupidam* by G.G. BIONDI, *Semantica di "cupidus"*, Bologna 1979, 14: "se la *domina* è già *cupida*, *amore reuinciens* diventa ozioso" (Biondi cites D'Arbela) and moreover: "aggiungiamo che il *munus* di Imeneo (v. 43) si ridurrebbe a quello di semplice accompagnatore, compito inadeguato al *boni coniugator amoris*". Cf. moreover pp. 72-74 of Biondi's work, in which there are, in fact, some interesting points. On the function of Hymen cf. F. DELLA CORTE in "Maia" 29-30 (1977-78) 79 n. 11. Biondi himself (p. 14) supports the punctuation assumed by me when he says that it "sembra avallata sul piano del significante, dalla iunctura allitterante del v. 32 (*coniugis cupidam*), che fa riscontro alla figura etimologica *DOMum DOMinam* del v. 31 (...), un parallelismo che suggerisce unità anche sintattica tra i due versi". On reviewing Biondi's book, GRANAROLO in "Rev. Ét. Lat." 57 (1979) 417 hints at another possibility, maybe a little too adventurous: one should consider *uoca* as in zeugma or in ἀπὸ κοινοῦ and attribute to the verb at l. 31 the meaning of "invite, attract", and to the verb at l. 32 that of "urge to be" in a passional attitude towards the husband.

Wilamowitz destroys the link between *mentem amore reuinciens* and the rest of the strophe; on the contrary, it is the bride who is compared to ivy winding itself round a tree and it is not disrespectful to define her *coniugis cupidam noui*: that love in c. 61 is also regarded as the satisfaction of the senses is quite clear in the final part of the poem. One must notice, however, that as a counterpart to the parallel between the bride and ivy winding round a tree there is a parallel between the groom and vine that *adsitas implicat arbores* (ll. 102-103).

Solemn language and Alexandrian imagery, expressions of neoteric tone and neologisms alternate and co-exist in ll. 26-35. The "iunctura" *quare age* belongs to elevated poetry; according to *Thes.* I,1406,55 ff. it is found here for the first time and reappears in epic poetry (Verg. *Aen.* 7,429; Sil. It. 16,208; Val. Fl. 5,538; Petronius too in 120,94 uses it in a grave invocation to Fate when dealing with the civil war in his verses) or, anyway, in emphatic poetic contexts (*Laus Pison.* 81; Stat. *Sil.* 1,4,31; Colum. 10,230. 294). The solemnity of l. 26 is increased by the "iunctura" *aditum ferre* – present again in Catullus at l. 43, always with reference to Hymen – a serious periphrasis which was appreciated by Apuleius (see *Met.* 4,19; 6,12; 8,16; sim. *reditum ferre* in 63,47.79 and 66, 35).

The structure *pergo* + infinitive (l. 27) is employed by Ennius (*Scaen.* 202 V.[2] *heu me miseram, interii: pergunt lauere sanguen sanguine*) and later on by Lucretius (1,932) in an emphatic and solemn situation in which he announces the content and meaning of his poetry: *religionum animum nodis exsoluere pergo. Linquo* seems to be a typical verb of sacral language: it is present in the invocation to Pan at the beginning of the Georgics, l. 16 f. *ipse nemus linquens patriam saltusque Lycaei / Pan ... adsis*; its use in sacral language sprang by analogy from λείπω, employed in hymns to express the conventional technique of inviting the god to leave his dwelling: it is therefore the same motif of lines 25-30 of Catullus' epithalamium (cf. Alcm. 35 D. = *Poetae Melici Graeci* 55 Page Κύπρον ἱμερτὰν λιποῖσα καὶ Πάφον περιρρύταν). In addition, the simple *linquo* is chosen rather than *relinquo* because the former conveys an idea of ancientness.[74]

74. Cf. J.B. HOFMANN - A. SZANTYR, *Lat. Syntax u. Stilistik*, 298 f. On expressions like *perge linquere* in cletic hymns cf. the evidences in

As far as *ac domum dominam uoca* (l. 31) is concerned, I would not agree with Ronconi, who perceives in it a matching of words connected by a colloquial etymological relation[75]; in contrast with him, Hofmann in *Thes.* V 1,1955,82 ff. defines solemn both the opposition *domus ... dominus (domina)* and Catullus' juxtaposition: see *Trag. inc. frg.* 184 R.[3] *o domus antiqua, heu quam dispari dominare domino!*, Cic. *Verr.* 2,4,5 *domus erat non domino magis ornamento quam ciuitati* and other examples of the same stylistic level, among which Catull. 68,68 *isque domum nobis isque dedit dominae* and 68,156 *et domus ⟨ipsa⟩ in qua lusimus et domina*, quoted by Hofmann.[76]

Even the use made of the conjunction *ac* can be significant, in order to establish the stylistic character of the line. Ross has recently analysed the presence of *ac* in *carmina docta* and has come to the conclusion that *ac* is employed in contexts where epic and Alexandrian tones co-exist. In c. 61, as well as c. 64 and c. 66 "*ac* may be safely assumed to be a connective of archaic formality, fitting epic solemnity and useful to a neoteric poet in lending dignity to contexts either learned or of mock loftiness".[77] The use of *reuincio* as a metaphor (l. 33) belongs to the poetic language elevated by Enn. *Ann.* 5 V.[2] *somno leui placidoque reuincius.*

Alongside these solemn structures there are images of neoteric kind and neologisms invented by Catullus: the adjective *Thespius* (l. 27), which Wilamowitz thinks[78] is a "falsche Form" instead of ϑεσπικός, appears in Catullus for the first time and is only found in Valerius Flaccus[79] after him. Another creation of Catullus is the verb *frigero* (l. 30), derived, perhaps, from the more common *refrigero*; an innovation that did not turn out very lucky, since there is no evidence of this verb until the 5th century A.D., in Celius Aurelianus' medical works.[80]

R.G.M. NISBET - M. HUBBARD, *A Commentary on Horace: Odes. Book 1*, cit., 345.

75. A. RONCONI, *Studi catulliani*, cit., 62.

76. F. DELLA CORTE, *Catullo. Le poesie*, cit., 290 cites rightly Cic. *Fin.* 1,58 *neque ... beata esse potest ... in discordia dominorum domus.*

77. D.O. ROSS, *Style and Tradition*, cit., 28 f.

78. U. v. WILAMOWITZ-MOELLENDORFF, *Hell. Dicht.*, cit., II 283 n. 1.

79. Θέσπιος is attested in Hes. *Frg.* 310,2 Merkelbach-West.

80. *Acut.* 1,15,142; 2,37,192.197; 3,21,208; *Chron.* 4,1,9; 5,7,84; cf. *Thes.* VI 1,1323,48 ff.

The imagery in ll. 34-35 has neoteric origin: the comparison with ivy has its antecedents in Alexandrian poetry: cf. Theocr. 20, 21 ff. ἐμοὶ ἐπάνθεεν ... ὡς κισσὸς ποτὶ πρέμνον. But it is from Catullus on that it penetrates Latin poetry and is employed in love-contexts: cf. Hor. *Carm.* 1,36,18 ff. *nac Damalis nouo / diuelletur adultero / lasciuis hederis ambitiosior, Ep.* 15,5 f. *artius atque hedera procera adstringitur ilex / lentis adhaerens bracchiis*, Gallien. *Anth. Lat.* 711,2 f. Riese *non murmura uestra columbae, / brachia non hederae, non uincant oscula conchae.*[81]

Like in the imagery used, there are traces of neoterism in the words too: the "iunctura" *tenax hedera* is probably of neoteric tone. The adjective *tenax* is frequent in the poetic output of Augustus' days and in the 1st century A.D.; in prose it is rarely found and with reference to people, not to natural elements. On *arborem implicat* see note to l. 103. *Errans*, meaning *passim uagans* and referred to natural elements, recurs in the fourth Bucolic of Virgil, in lines pervaded by neoteric grace and delicacy (ll. 18-20 *at tibi prima, puer, nullo munuscula cultu / errantis hederas passim cum baccare tellus / mixtaque ridenti colocasia fundet acantho*) and in an eclogue by Calpurnius Siculus, in a similar poetic atmosphere (1,12 *fagus ... ramis errantibus implicat umbras*). As for *huc et huc,*[82] according to *Thes.* VI 3,3070,46 ff. the "iunctura" is never found before Catullus and afterwards it is present in Virgil (*Aen.* 11,601), Horace (*Ep.* 4,9), Seneca (*Herc. Fur.* 953; *Med.* 385; *Oed.* 343; *Tro.* 970; 1092), Valerius Flaccus (4,266) and Avienus (*Ora Marit.* 127).

Lines 25-30 present an Alexandrian component, in addition to the neoteric one: *Aonius* (l. 28) is an original creation, on the part of Catullus, based on the adjective Ἀόνιος. Never before the Hellenistic age, however, did Ἀόνιος, Ἀονία begin to be employed to replace Βοιωτιακός, Βοιωτία: the first few evidences are Callim. *Hym.* 4,75 φεῦγε καὶ Ἀονίη, *Frg.* 572 Pf. κύματος Ἀονίου, Apoll. Rhod. 3,1178 Ἀονίοιο δράκοντος and 3,1185 Ἀονίοισιν ... πεδίοισιν; as an adjective, it is more frequent in Nonnus[83]; in Rome there are instances of *Aonius* in Verg. *Georg.*

81. Cf. H. HAFFTER in *Thes.* VI 3,2588,48 ff.
82. On the formula *huc atque huc* cf. Verg. *Aen.* 9,56; 12,558 and Sil. Ital. 9,360.614.
83. Cf. PAPE-BENSELER, *Wörterb. d. griech. Eigennamen*, s.v. Ἀόνιος;

3,11, Prop. 1,2,28 and later, always in poetry until Cassiodorus, who is the first author to choose it when writing prose. The use of *nympha* instead of *lympha* is an instance of stylistic refinement. It has been analysed by Moriz Haupt[84] and Jacob Wackernagel[85]: it is true what they state, that Latin poets (including Catullus as the first to do it) derived this use from Greek examples (Haupt and Wackernagel cite Euen. 2,3 D. χαίρει κιρνάμενος δὲ τρισὶν νύμφαισι τέταρτος). But it became widespread in Hellenistic poetry, as it is proved by the indication in *Anth. Pal.* 9,258,1 f. (Antiphan.) ἡ πάρος εὐΰδροισι λιβαζομένη προχοαῖσι / πτωχὴ νῦν νυμφῶν μέχρι καὶ εἰς σταγόνα)[86]; from there it reached Latin poetry. In Rome besides Catullus, *nympha* seems to be used with the meaning of *limpha* by Lucr. 6,1178[87]; Hor. *Carm.* 3,13,15; Prop. 3,16,4; Martial. 6,43,2; 47,1; Stat. *Sil.* 1,3,37.46.

The whole strophe (ll. 26-30), anyway, is permeated with Alexandrian grace; possibly Catullus found inspiration in some description frequent in the Idylls of Theocritus: cf. e.g. 22,37 ff. εὗρον δ᾽ ἀέναον κρήνην ὑπὸ λισσάδι πέτρη, / ὕδατι πεπληθυῖαν ἀκηράτῳ· αἱ δ᾽ ὑπένερθε / λάλλαι κρυστάλλῳ ἠδ᾽ἀργύρῳ ἰνδάλλοντο / ἐκ βυθοῦ· ὑψηλαὶ δὲ πεφύκεσαν ἀγχόθι πεῦκαι / λευκαί τε πλάτανοί τε καὶ ἀκρόκομοι κυπάρισσοι / ἄνθεά τ᾽ εὐώδη, λασίαις φίλα ἔργα μελίσσαις, / ὅσσ᾽ ἔαρος λήγοντος

A. ARDIZZONI, *Apollonio Rodio. Le Argonautiche, Libro III*, Bari 1958, 225.

84. M. HAUPT, *Opusc.*, II 169 n. 1.

85. J. WACKERNAGEL, *Kl. Schr.*, II 1226.

86. The example of Meleagros (*Anth. Pal.* 9,331) cited by LIDDELL-SCOTT-JONES is not pertinent, as it concerns the nymphs themselves.

87. C. Bailey accepts *multi praecipites lymphis putealibus alte* etc. and says nothing more on the matter in his commentary. But both Oblongus and Quadratus have *nymphis*, whereas *lymphis* is in Laurent. 35,31, in Vatican. Barber. Lat. 154 and in Cantabrigensis; MARTIN in his Teubner edition rightly puts *nymphis*. Also in the passage by Horace cited immediately afterwards (*Carm.* 3,13,15) *nympha* is attested only in some manuscripts; editors prefer *lympha* which could be supported by the alliteration (*loquaces/lymphae*) as PARRONI in "Riv. Fil. Istr. Class." 101 (1973) 489 assumes. The identification *nympha-lympha* is not accepted in Catullus' context by LIEBERG in "Gnom." 47 (1975) 356 according to whom "das Bild von der die Grotten des Helikon bewässernden Nymphe Aganippe sollte nicht zerstört werden".

ἐπιβρύει ἄν λειμῶνας. Although words are definitely different, the poetic atmosphere remains the same; in my opinion, however, it is not a case of imitation of particular lines, but at attempt to reproduce a poetic pattern typical of Theocritus.

Finally, some learned details have Alexandrian origins: the mentioning of the spring Aganippe – on the description of which in Hellenistic poets see E. Maass in "Herm." 31 (1896) 375 ff. – and of the Muses' antrum near Thespis; Wilamowitz[88] observes that the latter mention implies the poet's interest in the Muses' shrine near the spring Aganippe, which was built with the money of a Fileterus, Eumene's son.[89] The Helicon, where Callimachus relates he was carried in a dream, belonged to Thespis, "aber die Erwähnung bei dem Römer zeugt doch für geborgte Gelehrsamkeit".[90]

*

At lines 36-45 Catullus invites a chorus of maidens to invoke Hymen, so that the god, urged to his duty, will go and patronize the wedding. For Kroll "um Hym. recht wirksam herbeizulocken, werden auch die Mädchen aufgefordert, ihn durch Einstimmen in den Refrain zu rufen, den bisher nur die Jünglinge gesungen hatten"[91]; but which detail proves a participation of a chorus of youths in Catullus' hymenaeus? The only evidence of *pueri* is at l. 114: in that case, however, they are παῖδες προπέμποντες who accompanied the phases of the *deductio* with their songs, besides fulfilling the function of torch-bearers. In c. 61, therefore, they are present in that stage of the ceremony only, because the *fescennina iocatio* was certainly not suitable for a chorus of maidens. On the other hand, the poet addresses the chorus of maidens in the final strophe of the epithalamium itself (l. 224

88. U. v. WILAMOWITZ-MOELLENDORFF, *Hell. Dicht.*, cit., II 283.
89. Cf. U. v. WILAMOWITZ-MOELLENDORFF, *Hell. Dicht.*, cit., I 46 and n. 3. On the link between caves and Muses and poetry cf. Pind. *Pyth.* 6,49; Hor. *Carm.* 2,1,39; 3,4,40; Prop. 2,30,26; 3,1,5; 3,3,14 and R.G.M. NISBET - M. HUBBARD, *A Commentary on Horace: Odes. Book 2*, Oxford 1978, 31.
90. U. v. WILAMOWITZ-MOELLENDORFF, *Hell. Dicht.*, cit., II 283.
91. W. KROLL, *Cat.*, cit., 110.

claudite ostia uirgines): as the function of *claudere ostia* concerned the παράνυμφος in Greece and the *pronuba* in Rome, it is probable that the poet's invitation is referred to the maidens, who have assisted and accompanied him in the various phases of the ceremony; it is probably too that *lusimus satis* (l. 225) is related to the poet as well as the chorus of *puellae integrae*, rather than being a plural *maiestatis*.

The incentive to put a chorus of maidens in his wedding-song may have been supplied to Catullus by the situation in Theocritus' epithalamium: 18,1 ff. ἔν ποκ ἄρα Σπάρτᾳ ξανθότριχι πὰρ Μενελάῳ / παρθενικαὶ θάλλοντα κόμαις ὑάκινθον ἔχοισαι / πρόσθε νεογράπτω θαλάμω χορὸν ἐστάσαντο, / δώδεκα ταὶ πρᾶται πόλιος, μέγα χρῆμα Λακαινᾶν, / ἀνίκα Τυνδαρίδα κατεκλάζετο τὰν ἀγαπατάν / μναστεύσας Ἑλέναν ὁ νεώτερος Ἀτρέος υἱῶν. / Ἄειδον δ'ἄρα πᾶσαι ἐς ἓν μέλος ἐγκροτέοισαι / ποσσὶ περιπλέκτοις, περὶ δ'ἴαχε δῶμ'ὑμεναίῳ.

Another influence on this aspect of c. 61 might have been exerted by a *genus* belonging to the Greek tradition, the parthenion, which already existed in ritual and literary expressions.

> uosque item simul, integrae
> uirgines, quibus aduenit
> par dies, agite in modum
> dicite, o Hymenaee Hymen,
> Hymen o Hymenaee. 40
>
> ut lubentius, audiens
> se citarier ad suum
> munus, huc aditum ferat
> dux bonae Veneris, boni
> coniugator amoris. 45

While in the strophe referred to the *integrae uirgines* the poetic language does not reach a particular loftiness (although it would be wrong to consider it a colloquial style), in the strophe dedicated to the god, which preludes a new series of praises in the style of hymns (ll. 46 ff.), aulic and refined expressions lend a solemn character to the context.

With regard to ll. 36-40, Axelson[92] asserts that *item* (l. 36)

92. B. AXELSON, *Unpoetische Wörter*, Lund 1945, 94.

could be defined an "unpoetical" term. Truly *item* is common in theatrical authors and avoided by poets of Augustus' time[93]; but I do not believe that in Catullus' days it was considered "unpoetical", otherwise there would be no reason for the frequent use made of it by Lucretius (more than 60 examples). There is evidence of *item* also in the Georgics (1,187; 2,248) and in *Culex* (1. 402). Then, we may accept the theory that it was the elegiac poets who banned *item* from their poetry and established its "unpoetical" character; they were followed on this track by the poets of the 1st century A.D. In Catullus, moreover, it is necessary to take the "iunctura" *item simul* into consideration and not merely analyse the word *item*.

Integer (1. 36) is the conventional adjective to express the *castitas* of a *uirgo*: see Plaut. *Cas.* 832; Ter. *Hec.* 150. In hymns it was required to mention this condition clearly, as it was indispensable for the success of the cry: Catullus, in his hymn to Diana, invites *puellae et pueri integri* to join his song (34,2). The expression *aduenit ... dies* (1. 37 f.) is conventional too (see *Thes.* I 833,3 ff.); whereas the connection *agite* + imperative (ll. 38-39) is frequent in the dialogues of comedies.[94]

The language in the subsequent strophe is very different: the verb *cito* (1. 47) meaning *deum aduoco* belongs to the style of prayers: see Cic. *De orat.* 1,251 *quam totiens, quotiens praescribitur, Paeanem aut Nomionem citarimus*, Hor. *Sat.* 1,3,7 *ab ouo usque ad mala citaret "io Bacche"*, Ouid. *Fas.* 5,683 f. *falsoue citaui / non audituri numina magna Iouis.* On *munus* in relation to the god's activity see the numerous examples in *Thes.* VIII 1644,35-59 and on the solemn periphrasis *aditum ferre* what has been observed above apropos of 1. 26. *Bonus* is an epithet typical of gods[95]; it is worth stressing that Catullus repeats the same technique employed at 1. 19: *bonus* is used at the penultimate line of the strophe, with reference to two different nouns: the paronomasia serves the purpose of underlining emphatically the identity *bona Venus − bonus* (i.e. *legitimus*) *amor.*[96]

93. Cf. *Thes.* VII 2,532,58 ff.
94. Cf. *Thes.* I 1405,44 ff.
95. Cf. the examples cited in *Thes.* II 2086,15 ff. and G. APPEL, *De Romanorum precationibus*, in "Religionsgeschichtliche Versuche und Vorarbeiten" VII (1909) 99.
96. Mrs. ÉVRARD-GILLIS, *La récurrence lexicale dans l'oeuvre de*

The present infinitive in the passive form *–ier* (l. 42) contributes to increase the aulic character of the strophe: such forms are often found in comedies and in the prose of the archaic period,[97] but it would be rash to deduce their pertaining to "Umgangssprache", as Wölfflin does.[98] Catullus' behaviour, as a matter of fact, is significant: except for 68,141 where it is impossible to express a stylistic appraisal of *componier*, since this word is a mere conjecture and it is followed by a lacuna – passive forms ending in *–ier* only exist in the first 75 lines of c. 61 (l. 42; 65; 68; 70; 75), therefore only in the hymn to Hymen. Most likely Catullus used also the archaic infinitive form *–ier* to achieve the effect of gravity required by the hymn to the god.[99]

In this atmosphere of stylistic refinement and elegance Catullus placed the word *coniugator*, created by him and never used again either by him or by any other author of the time. Fordyce[100] cites the use of the verb *coniugare* in Cicero; but in Cicero the only reliable mentions are past participles with a technical meaning in contexts of rhetorical subjects (*Top.* 11.12.71), while the passage from *De officiis* (1,58) cited by *Thes.* IV 325,81 seems to have been interpolated.[101] *Coniugare* acquires the meaning of *matrimonio iungere* only from Apuleius onwards, and only after Solinus it becomes synonymous with *coniungere*. It is rather on the basis of *coniugium* and terms such as *Iuno Iuga* and *Hera Zygia* that Catullus coined the word *coniugator*.[102]

Catulle, cit., 113-114 draws the same conclusion: she includes this in a series of other cases, all found in Catullus, where the adjective repeated is referred to words with common origin and syntactically equivalent. She observed that semantic affinity and grammatical parallelism give sufficient correlation to nouns, because "les occurrences de l'adjectif répété ne se dispersent pas au point de vue de la signification, mais se renforcent". Cf. also 64,69-70 *illa (...) toto ex te pectore, Theseu, / toto animo, tota pendebat perdita mente*, 68,34-35 *illa domus, / illa mihi sedes.*

97. Cf. F. SOMMER, *Handbuch der lateinischen Laut- und Formenlehre*, Heidelberg 1948³, 599.

98. E. WÖLFFLIN in "Philol." 34 (1876) 146.

99. On the infinitives ending in *–ier* in Catullus see also H. HEUSCH, *Das Archaische in der Sprache Catulls*, Bonn 1954, 109 ff.

100. C.J. FORDYCE, *Catullus*, cit., 243.

101. Cf. P. FEDELI in "Ciceroniana" 3-6 (1961-64) 74 f. K.B. Thomas, the latest champion of the integrity of *De officiis*, does not give his opinion on the subject.

102. Cf. W. KROLL, *Cat.*, cit., 111.

CHAPTER III

THE ENCOMIUM OF THE GOD

Lines 46-75 present the encomium of the god, another traditional motif of hymns, in which the praises of the divinity occupied a prominent place. The fact that Catullus owes much to Greek patterns is evident both in his technique and in the rhetorical devices employed by him; but alongside these components handed down from the past, some typically Roman themes occur in this poem. In the first part of the encomium (ll. 46-60), where some important structures of the language of prayers are used, we find two Roman motifs: *raptio* and *conuentio in manum*.

> quis deus[1] magis est ama-
> tis petendus amantibus?
> quem colent homines magis
> caelitum, o Hymenaee Hymen,
>   Hymen o Hymenaee? 50
>
> te suis tremulus parens
> inuocat, tibi uirgines
> zonula soluunt sinus,
> te timens cupida nouos
>   captat aure maritus. 55
>
> tu fero iuueni in manus
> floridam ipse puellulam
> dedis a gremio suae
> matris, o Hymenaee Hymen,
>   Hymen o Hymenaee. 60

1. Against the old school prejudice asserting that *quis* is only used as a pronoun and *qui* as an interrogative adjective cf. E. LÖFSTEDT, *Syntactica*, II, Lund 1933, 79-86. The phrase *quis deus*, moreover, is exactly what interrogative sentences normally present: cf. Catull. 40,3; 66,31 and the numerous

The manuscripts have *quis deus măgĭs ămatis / est petendus amantibus* at ll. 46-47, which is metrically impossible. I accept Bergk's transposition, whereas Haupt[2] puts *anxiis* instead of *amatis* and interprets the lines as follows: "Quis deus dignus est quem magis anxie, h.e. magis sollicite et studio feruidiore petant amantes?". As a matter of fact, both conjectural readings are liable to adverse criticism. As for Bergk's interpretation, doubts consist in this, that in order to explain *amatis ... amantibus* no better evidences exist than Catull. 45,20 *mutuis animis amant amantur* and Caes. Bass. *Gramm.* VI 263,13 K. *uiuis, ludis, habes, amas, amaris.* But the objections one may raise against *anxiis* are even weightier; they concern the meaning itself of the poem. Theodor Bergk[3] rightly observes: "Ich kenne wenigstens kein analoges Beispiel, wo *anxius* die Unruhe bezeichnet, welche das Gemüth bei einem bevorstehenden Glück überfällt". It is indeed true that *anxius* is sometimes used with reference to lovers (cf. e.g. Cic. *Tusc.* 4,70; *Att.* 2,24,1): in this case, however, the adjective designates the lovers' obvious fear that their love may not last for ever and their beloved must turn out faithless. If we accepted *anxiis ... amantibus*, we should be led to attribute to Catullus the ridiculous advice, given to the *anxiis amantibus*, that they should get married to avoid such fears.

It is preferable, then, to accept Bergk's suggestion and suppose that, by using *amatis amantibus*, Catullus meant reciprocal love, a more suitable feeling for the description of the wedding than the lovers' *anxietas*. Bergk's conjectural text also explains the reason for the mistake: in all probability it was caused by some copyist trying to avoid the division of a word in two lines. Not knowing the metrical system of c. 61, the author of this change was only concerned with the number of syllables and not with their quantities; therefore he thought that the only remedy was to transpose *est* to the following line.

Lines 46-50 contain two interrogative sentences[4] expressing a

examples in LÖFSTEDT, *Syntactica*, II, cit., 83 n. 2. *Quis deus* seems to be employed only in prose and very rarely too.

2. M. HAUPT, *Opusc.*, I 16 f.

3. T. BERGK in "Philol." 16 (1860) 619.

4. The precisely planned structure of the strophe is underlined by Évrard-Gillis who points out (p. 211) that the parallelism between the two interrogative sentences (*quis ... amantibus? quem ... caelitum*) is emphasized by

theme well known in the rhetorical tradition of the epithalamium: the exaltation of Hymen as the greatest god: on this τόπος cf. Liban. VI 516,11 Förster ... τὸν Γάμον ... θεὸν ὄντα καὶ θεῶν μέγιστον, Menand. *Rhet. Gr.* III 400,31 ff. Spengel τὰ δὲ μετὰ τὰ προοίμια ἔστω περὶ τοῦ θεοῦ τοῦ γάμου λόγος ὑπερθετικὸς ... · γενόμενος δὲ ὁ θεὸς οὗτος συνάπτει μὲν οὐρανὸν τῇ γῇ, συνάπτει δὲ Κρόνον τῇ Ῥέᾳ ... · εἶτα ἐφεξῆς ἐρεῖς ὅτι ἡ τῶν ὅλων διακόσμησις διὰ τὸν γάμον γέγονεν, ἀέρος, ἀστέρων, θαλάσσης κτλ.

The repetition of rhetorical questions too has been considered an example of *sermo communis*: even in Hofmann-Szantyr this case is included in the list of repetitions of interrogative sentences recurring "hauptsächlich im Dialog der Alltagsrede".[5] But it is possible that the solemn encomium of the god should be based on patterns typical of everyday language? On the contrary, Catullus is probably imitating a technique present in completely different sources: series of rhetorical questions appear, for instance, in the serious ending of Callimachus' hymn to Zeus (1,92 ff. τεὰ δ' ἔργματα τίς κεν ἀείδοι; / ... τίς καὶ Διὸς ἔργματ'ἀείσει; or in equally serious contexts in the hymn to Artemis (3,113 ff. ποῦ δέ σε τὸ πρῶτον κερόεις ὄχος ἤρξατ'ἀείρειν; / ... ποῦ δ'ἔταμες πεύκην, ἀπὸ δὲ φλογὸς ἥψαο ποίης; / ... ποσσάκι δ'ἀργυρέοιο, θεή, πειρήσαο τόξου; and 183 ff. τίς δὲ νύ τοι νήσων, ποῖον δ'ὄρος εὔαδε πλεῖστον, / τίς δὲ λιμήν, ποίη δὲ πόλις; τίνα δ'ἔξοχα νυμφέων / φίλαο, καὶ ποίας ἡρωίδας ἔσχες ἑταίρας). Horace also employs the same technique in elevated contexts: cf. *Carm.* 1,2,25 ff. *quem uocet diuum populus ruentis / imperi rebus? prece qua fatigent / uirgines sanctae minus audientem / carmina Vestam? / cui dabit partis scelus expiandi / Iuppiter?* (notice that in Horace, as well as Catullus, interrogative pronouns are used in different cases and the subject changes); 1,12,1 ff. *quem uirum atque heroa lyra uel acri / tibia sumis celebrare Clio?* [6] */ quem deum? cuius recinet iocosa / nomen imago ...?*

The archaic and solemn *caelitum* (l. 49) is perfectly suitable for the atmosphere of the encomium. The plural *caelites* is a neologism

the presence of *magis* in both of them.
5. J.B. HOFMANN - A. SZANTYR, *Lat. Syntax u. Stilistik*, 311.
6. Cf. Pind. *Olymp.* 2,2 τίνα θεόν, τίν' ἥρωα, τίνα δ'ἄνδρα κελαδήσομεν; and E. FRAENKEL, *Horace*, cit., 291.

invented by Ennius[7] on the model of *οὐρανίωνες* (*Scaen.* 316 V.[2] *ego deum genus esse semper dixi et dicam caelitum*; cf. Charis. *Gramm.* I 32,17 K. *hi caelites οὐρανίωνες*), and it only occurs in elevated contexts[8]: in Plautus too it is only found at the beginning of *Rudens*, in the prologue spoken by the star *Arcturus*, the messenger of the gods: l. 2 *(Iouis) sum ciuis ciuitate caelitum*. In Catullus *caelites* is also used at line 190 and in the grave part of c. 11 (ll. 13-14 *omnia haec, quaecumque feret uoluntas / caelitum temptare simul parati* ...).

In the next strophe we find the words *tibi uirgines / zonula soluunt sinus* (ll. 52-53), which represent Catullus' alteration of an important detail of the wedding ceremony: according to Paul. *ap.* Fest. 55 L. *cingillo noua nupta praecingebatur quod uir in lecto soluebat* ...; *initio coniugii solutio erat cinguli, quod noua nupta erat cincta*; Catullus than refers to the maidens themselves an action which is in fact performed by the groom in the thalamos. Anyway, this apparent incoherence is not relevant, because with regard to ll. 51-55 Catullus is not interested in obsolete particulars, but, as Riese asserted, he "folgt griechischem Ausdruck".[9] *Ζώνην λύειν* was the fixed phrase to indicate, with an image taken from reality, the actual definitive marriage-contract; as early as Homer[10] the deed is attributed to the groom. But Catullus follows other literary sources that, in contrast with these, refer the act to the bride: cf. Eur. *Alc.* 177 f. *ὦ λέκτρον, ἔνθα παρθένει' ἔλυσ' ἐγώ / κορεύματα*, *Anth. Pal.* 7,324 (anon.) *ἅδ'ἐγὼ ἁ περίβωτος ὑπὸ πλακὶ τῇδε τέθαμμαι, / μούνῳ ἐνὶ ζώναν ἀνέρι λυσαμένα*. Riese[11] pointed out: "Also ist Catullus auch hier nicht antiquarisch genau"; but his words have been neglected by subsequent annotators, usually inclined to seek only the connections between Catullus' description and the real celebration of the ceremony.

Another conventional feature of the imagery of wedding-song is probably the representation of the groom's *timor* mixed with *cupiditas,*[12] while waiting for the bride in the bedchamber (ll. 54-

---

7. Cf. A. RONCONI, *Studi catulliani*, cit., 175.
8. Cf. *Thes.* III 66,76 ff.
9. A. RIESE, *Die Gedichte des Catullus*, cit., 171.
10. *Od.* 11,245; *Hym.* 3,165.
11. A. RIESE, *Die Gedichte des Catullus*, cit., 117.
12. *Timor noui mariti* should not be confused with the *anxietas* supposed

50

55): indeed the same motif is in Statius' epithalamium for Arruntius Stella and Violentilla: *Sil.* 1,2,31 ff. *tu tamen attonitus, quamuis data copia tantae / noctis, adhuc optas promissaque numine dextro / uota paues.*[13]

The style of the strophe is the solemn one required by sacral topics: the "Du-Stil" actually belongs to the highest expressions of religious language, and Eduard Norden's remarks on it are never to be forgotten.[14] The ἀρεταὶ θεοῦ are mentioned in sentences with asyndeton, beginning with the second person singular personal pronoun; such an anaphora is very frequent in Greek sacred hymns and in religious contexts[15] of the Hellenistic age, whereas in the archaic period it is rarely found and never in asyndetic form.[16] As for Catullus, one could not regard this as a case of anaphora caused by the alleged popular character of the poem: it will suffice to remember that the first two indications of "Du-Stil" in Rome are in Lucretius, in the proem of *De rerum natura* and in the eulogy of Epicurus: 1,6-8 *te, dea, te fugiunt uenti, te nubila caeli / aduentumque tuum, tibi suauis daedala tellus / summittit flores, tibi rident aequora ponti,* 3,9 f. *tu pater es, rerum inuen-*

by Haupt at l. 46. E. ENSOR in "Hermath." 12 (1903) 108 ff. maintains that a parody of this strophe is in Hor. *Carm.* 2,8,21-24 *te suis matres metuunt iuuencis / te senes parci miseraeque nuper / uirgines nuptae, tua ne retardet / aura maritos.* His conclusions are shared by R.G.M. NISBET - M. HUBBARD, *A Commentary on Horace: Odes. Book 2,* cit., 132, according to whom "Horace keeps the tricolon and the anaphora of his model, and seems to echo the concluding cadence *aure maritus,* but he wittily transfers the anxiety from the young husband to the old fathers and the newly married *uirgines".* On *cupidus* see G. PERROTTA, *Cesare, Catullo, Orazio ed altri saggi,* Roma 1972, 98.

13. Cf. the commentary by F. VOLLMER, *P. Papinii Statii Siluarum libri,* Leipzig 1898, 242: "Der Bräutigam glaubt noch nicht an sein Glück, an dem er so lange gezweifelt ... und das ihm erst der Göttin persönliches Eingreifen gewährt hat; obwohl er die Möglichkeit, die Aussicht auf eine so genussreiche Nacht heute durch die Vollziehung der Vermählung bekommen und ihm die Erfüllung seiner Wünsche im Beisein der Venus versprochen ist, besorgt er noch, es könnte ein Hindernis dazwischentreten". The fact that Statius' epithalamium has its origin in Alexandrian sources has been in my view proved by VOLLMER, op. cit., 234 f.

14. E. NORDEN, *Agnostos Theos,* cit., 143-163.

15. Cf. the numerous examples cited by E. NORDEN, *Agnostos Theos,* cit., 158 ff.

16. Cf. A.D. NOCK in "Class. Quart." 18 (1924) 185.

tor, tu patria nobis / suppeditas praecepta. In Virgil we find it in the hymn sung by the Salii in Heracles' honour, in *Aen.* 8,293 ff. *tu nubigenas inuicte, bimembris / Hylaeumque Pholumque manu, tu Cresia mactas / prodigia et uastum Nemeae sub rupe leonem. / Te Stygii tremuere lacus, te ianitor Orci.* Horace often employs the "Du-Stil" and always in contexts either of religious character or rich in the stylistic patterns of the language of prayers: cf. e.g. *Carm.* 1,10,9 ff.; 3,21,13 ff. Catullus uses the same technique in the solemn hymn to Diana: 34,13-17 *tu Lucina dolentibus / Iuno dicta puerperis, / tu potens Triuia et notho es / dicta lumine Luna. / Tu cursu, dea, menstruo ...*

The verb *inuocare* also pertains to sacral language: for further evidences of this verb in the style of prayers see the numerous examples in *Thes.* VII 2,254,52 ff.[18]

How can the presence of the diminutive *zonula* be justified in a solemn context? Possibly *zonula* belongs to everyday language, as Ronconi believes[19]: in this case one could explain it by considering that, referred to the *uirgines*, it lends them a note of delicacy and grace, in contrast with the image and attitude of the *nouus maritus.* Since *zonula* is very seldom used,[20] however, it may be a neologism derived from the equivalent Greek diminutive: *zona* is a coinage suggested by ζώνη, commonly accepted in Latin lexicon, and, similarly, *zonula* would represent Catullus' attempt to reproduce the Greek diminutive ζώνιον mentioned in Aristoph. *Lys.* 72, Aristot. *Mir.* 832b 23 and *Anth. Pal.* 5,158,2 (Asclep.).

Cupida aure is a refined *iunctura*: for *Thes.* IV 1427,82 ff. *cupidus* in relation to parts of the body recurs only in poetry from Catullus on (the only exception being a passage by Porphyrion). On *captare aure* cf. *Thes.* III 376,78 ff.

In lines 56-60, starting with the pronoun *tu*, which recalls the "Du-Stil" of the previous strophe, Catullus possibly alludes to two typically Roman motifs: the legal procedure of the *conuentio*

---

17. Cf. R.G.M. NISBET - M. HUBBARD, *A Commentary on Horace*, cit., 131.

18. Cf. also G. APPEL, *De Romanorum precationibus*, cit., 68.

19. A. RONCONI, *Studi catulliani*, cit., 96.

20. Forcellini states that after Catullus it is only to be found in Seren. *ap.* Non. 539,13 M. and in Script. Hist. Aug. *Alex. Seu.* 52.

in manum and the archaic habit of the *raptio*. In the progress of the ceremony, the *raptio* is a moment at the beginning of the *deductio*: the procession of relatives and guests, who will accompany the bride to the groom's house, pretend that they snatch the girl out of the mother's arms: cf. Fest. 364 L. *rapi simulatur uirgo ex gremio matris, aut si ea non est ex prima necessitudine, cum ad uirum traditur.* A proof of this typically Roman practice[21] is in Macrob. *Sat.* 1,15,21 *nuptiae, in quibus uis fieri uirgini uidetur*[22]; Catullus hints at it with the words *a gremio suae matris.*

On the other hand, Catullus alludes to the ancient custom of marriage *in manum*, in the expression *fero*[23] *iuueni in manus (dedis puellulam)*. Fordyce prefers to recognize in it the *ardor uiolentus* of love and refuses to accept it as a reminiscence of the ancient habit and a legal allusion, because "*a gremio* is a natural phrase, which does not need that explanation, and the principle of the marriage *in manum* was obsolescent or obsolete in Catullus' time, when the wife did not normally pass into the legal *manus* of her husband but remained in the *potestas* of her father or, if he was not alive, was *sui iuris*".[24] But, as for the former objection, it is significant that in Festus there is the same formula *e gremio*; as for the latter, we have already stated that, luckily, Catullus does not aim at appearing antiquated[25]; what he really cares about are the picturesque elements of the ceremony and those details, such as the *raptio*, that may be useful to set the reader's imagination afire; in this circumstance his merit consists in avoiding a drily juridical language and inserting legal formulae into images full of life.

In lines 56-60 our attention is attracted by the drama of the girl on the point of leaving her father's house: no wonder, therefore, that Catullus does not use, like in the previous strophe, any phrases of solemn style, but chooses elements of affectionate

21. As for Greece, there is something analogous in Sparta: cf. Plut. *Lyc.* 15.
22. Cf. DAREMBERG-SAGLIO III and G. WILLIAMS in "Journ. Rom. Stud." 48 (1958) 18 n. 13.
23. On *ferus* used with erotic meaning cf. M. PUELMA in "Mus. Helv." 34 (1977) 167 and n. 42.
24. C.J. FORDYCE, *Catullus*, cit., 244.
25. See what has been observed with regard to *amaracus, cum bona alite, zonula soluunt.*

language: the diminutive *puellula* is typical of this stylistic range, clearly employed to create an atmosphere of grace and delicacy around the image of the young bride and to increase the contrast with the *ferus iuuenis*. Ronconi has acutely underlined that Catullus attributes to the groom words implying passion and desire, whereas to the bride delicate feelings of modesty and hesitation. It is natural, then, that the diminutives pertain to Junia: she is a *puellula*, her *pedes* are *aureoli*, her *brachiolum* is *teres*, her *os* is *floridulum*. All these diminutives do not modify the ideas of the original forms, but they add a connotation to the context by means of affectionate style sprung from everyday language.[26] Not even *floridus*[27] belongs to elevated poetic language: used with a metaphorical meaning ("fere i.q. florens, uigens, pulcher", *Thes.* VI 925,45) and referred to people, it is found here for the first time and, later on, in Ouid. *Met.* 13,790 *(Galatea) floridior pratis*, Sil. Ital. 12,482 *aeui floridior Fabius* and in the prose written by Christian authors.

*

In the next three strophes (ll. 61-75), linked by the refrain *quis huic deus compararier ausit?*, the δύναμις θεοῦ and the usefulness of marriage are exalted.

> nil potest sine te Venus,
> fama quod bona comprobet,
> commodi capere, at potest
> te uolente. quis huic deo
> > compararier ausit?   65
>
> nulla quit sine te domus
> liberos dare, nec parens
> stirpe nitier; at potest

26. A. RONCONI, *Studi catulliani*, cit., 122 f.
27. As regards the meaning that Catullus intends to attribute to the word *floridus*, a most valuable remark is made by G. GIANGRANDE in "Ant. Class." 47 (1978) 544; in his opinion, *flos*, "when referred to a girl who marries, entails the notion of her virginity"; he also cites 17,4 *quoi cum sit uiridissimo nupta flore puella*. M.C. PUTNAM in "Class. Phil." 71 (1976) 372, for his part, is right, when he thinks that the mentioning of *alba parthenice* at l. 187 serves the same purpose.

te uolente. quis huic deo
compararier ausit?   70

quae tuis careat sacris
non queat dare praesides
terra finibus: at queat
te uolente. quis huic deo
compararier ausit?   75

With regard to *queat* (l. 73), Kroll wonders: "*At queat* wo der
Indikativ logisch wäre, durch eine Art von Attraktion, oder
futurisch?".[28] Fordyce, for his part, cautiously says nothing on
the problem, which in fact is worth discussing: in this strophe,
actually, while *non queat* at l. 72 is perfectly understandable and
motivated, one would imagine to find *at quit*, and not *at queat*, at
l. 73, when the same verb is repeated. Hofmann-Szantyr's syntax
deals with the matter[29] and classifies this case as an attraction
between two subordinate clauses; but the way Catullus uses it is
not comparable with Plaut. *Mil.* 369 *numquam hercle deterrebor
quin uiderim id, quod uiderim*, cited by Hofmann-Szantyr. Jacob
Wackernagel had already dealt with the problem of assimilation,
pointing out that "die beiden Sätze, zwischen denen Angleichnung
stattfindet, brauchen nicht im Abhängigkeitsverhältnis zu ein-
ander zu stehen"[30]; as an example, he mentions, besides Catullus,
the well-known iamb against women of Semonides of Amorgos
(*Frg.* 7 D. ll. 81-82): πᾶσαν ἡμέρην βουλεύεται, / ὅκως τιν' ὡς
μέγιστον ἔρξειεν κακόν. Wackernagel observes that the future
indicative is what the reader would expect, therefore the optative
mood is utterly without motivation and inexplicable; but it
becomes understandable if we consider that at l. 80 the same
optative is employed, in that case in the regular and normal way:
οὐδ' ἄν τιν' εὖ ἔρξειεν. In Semonides, like in Catullus, the expression present in a sentence and echoed in the following one
justifies the irregular use of the same mood and the same tense in
the second phrase. Notice also that nowhere else in this poem does
Catullus change, in three parallel strophes (ll. 61-75), *at potest te
uolente*, which is closely connected with the refrain.[31]

28. W. KROLL, *Cat.*, cit., 122.
29. J.B. HOFMANN - A. SZANTYR, *Lat. Syntax u. Stilistik*, 547.
30. J. WACKERNAGEL, *Vorlesungen über Syntax*, I², Basel 1950, 58.
31. An interesting, and probably right, explanation is the one proposed

Besides the praises of the δύναμις θεοῦ, the three strophes present as a common denominator the exposition of some basic principles of Roman ethics. In the first strophe (ll. 61-65) the benefit of marriage for the bridal couple is exalted: Venus needs Hymen, otherwise love would not be approved of by *bona fama*; in the second (ll. 65-70) the poet praises the value of marriage for the whole family: without Hymen the newly married pair cannot have children and multiply their offspring; finally, in the third strophe (ll. 71-75), the importance of marriage for the State itself is celebrated: without Hymen the country would have no one to defend its territories.

Truly the motif of the usefulness of marriage to propagate one's family and nation represented in Greece an element of folk-philosophical literature, included by the rhetoricians among the themes of the ἐπιθαλάμιος λόγος[32]: cf. the eulogy of Γάμος in Menand. *Rhet. Gr.* III 401,22 ff. Spengel ἐμπλεονάσεις δὲ τούτῳ τῷ μέρει δεικνὺς ὅτι δι᾽ αὐτὸν θάλαττα πλεῖται, δι᾽ αὐτὸν γεωργεῖται γῆ, ὅτι φιλοσοφία καὶ γνῶσις τῶν οὐρανίων δι᾽ ἐκεῖνόν ἐστι καὶ νόμοι καὶ πολιτεῖαι καὶ πάντα ἁπλῶς τὰ ἀνθρώπινα and the panegyric of Γάμος in Himer. *Orat.* 9,8 Colonna (δι᾽αὐτοῦ) τίκτεται δὲ καὶ φυτὰ καὶ ζῷα καὶ γῆ οἰκεῖται καὶ τὸ νηχόμενον λαμβάνει θάλασσα καὶ ἀὴρ ἐφάνη πτερῷ πορεύσιμος. ἀφῆκε δὲ ὁ Γάμος καὶ φυτὰ φυτοῖς καὶ ποταμοὺς πηγαῖς καὶ χάλαζαν καὶ ὄμβρους τῇ γῇ. The same notion is in Gregory of Nazianzius, *Carm. Mor.* 1,249 ff. (= Migne III 522 ff.) τίς σοφίην ἐδίδαξε φίλην καὶ βένθε᾽ ἀνεῦρεν / ὅσσα χθών, ὅσα πόντος, ὅσ᾽οὐρανὸς ἐντὸς ἐέργει; / τίς πτολίεσσιν ἔθηκε νόμους; καὶ τῶνδε πάροιθεν / τίς πτόλιας δ᾽ἀνέγειρε καὶ εὕρετο μήδεσι τέχνας; / τίς πλῆσεν δ᾽ ἀγορὰς καὶ δώματα; καὶ τίς ἀγῶνας; / τίς στρατὸν ἐν πολέ'οισι καὶ ἐν θαλίῃσι τραπέζας; /

by ÉVRARD-GILLIS, *La récurrence lexicale dans l'oeuvre de Catulle*, cit., 53; according to her, this case is to be included among the "reprises qui visent à opposer une affirmation à sa négation". To support her theory, she mentions 61,139-141 (= 146-148) and 91,8-9 *non satis id causae credideram esse tibi. / Tu satis id duxti.* Her view has been shared by A. TRAINA in "Riv. Fil. Istr. Class." 106 (1978) 367. In connection with the commentary by M. LENCHANTIN DE GUBERNATIS (Torino 1965, 111), G. LIEBERG in "Gnom." 47 (1975) 356 (but cf. also "Latinitas" 22 [1974] 219-220) interprets the subjunctive as the apodosis of a potential conditional sentence.
    32. Cf. R. REITZENSTEIN in "Herm." 35 (1900) 93.

τίς χορὸν ὑμνητῆρα θυώδεϊ πήξατο νηῷ; / τίς θηρῶν κατέλυσε
βίον καὶ γαῖαν ἀράσσειν / καὶ φυτοεργείην ἐδιδάξατο, καὶ
πελάγεσσι / νῆ᾽ ἐπαφῆκε μέλαιναν ἐπειγομένην ἀνέμοισι; /
τίς γαῖαν καὶ πόντον ὑγρῇ ἀνέδησε κελεύθῳ / νόσφι γάμου, τὰ
δὲ πολλὸν ἀπόπροθεν εἰς ἓν ἀγείρει;. By that time, anyhow,
this view had been accepted and shared by the Romans, and
Catullus derives it from the local tradition: it is relevant that the
sequence itself of ideas expressed by Catullus resounds in Cicero's
sublime words on the origin of the State (*Off.* 1,54) *prima societas
in ipso coniugio est, proxima in liberis, deinde una domus, com-
munia omnia: id autem est principium urbis et quasi seminarium
rei publicae.*[33]

Another indication of the theory of giving birth to children for
the good of one's own country is in Prop. 2,7,13 *unde mihi patriis
gnatos praebere triumphis?*, although Propertius gives a curt
answer to the question: *nullus de nostro sanguine miles erit* –
proving, for this as well as for other reasons, that he was not
committed to the Augustan regime. The above-cited fragment
of an epithalamium by Calvus, belonging to the same period as
Catullus, states that Gamos' partner Ceres *et leges sanctas docuit
et cara iugauit / corpora conubiis et magnas condidit urbes.*

These ideas permeated legal formula too: according to Riese,
in ll. 66-69 Catullus does not discriminate between legitimate and
spurious children; he merely asserts "den Gegensatz ehelicher
Kinder ... gegen Kinderlosigkeit".[34] But if it is so, it is not clear
why marriage should represent the guarantee that the couple will
have children; the contrast *legitimi-spurii*, however, recurs in
Gaius (1,64) *si quis nefarias atque incestas nuptias contraxerit,
neque uxorem habere uidetur neque liberos.*

The co-existence of these two motifs (encomium of the δύναμις
θεοῦ, praises of the marriage for its meaning with relation to the
institutions of family and State) causes the mixture – easily
detectable in ll. 61-75 – of formulae of the official and traditional

33. On the motif of *liberos dare* as the aim of marriage in Rome, cf.
E. BENVENISTE in "Rev. Ét. Lat." 14 (1936) 57, resumed by M. MANSON
in "Mél. Éc. Fr. Rome" 90 (1978) 251-253. See also another work by
BENVENISTE: *Il vocabolario delle istituzioni indoeuropee*, trad. ital., I,
Torino 1976, 247-250.
34. A. RIESE, *Die Gedichte des Catullus*, cit., 118; his point of view has
been resumed by C.J. FORDYCE, *Catullus*, 244.

language and expressions of the style of prayers. The phrase *liberos dare* belongs to the first category: although it is not present in prose, it probably repeats, as Fordyce believes,[35] an ancient formula: cf. Verg. *Aen.* 1,274 *geminam partu dabit Ilia prolem*, Ouid. *Her.* 6,122 *pignora Lucina bina fauente dedi*, Hor. *Carm.* 3,6,47 f. *mox daturos / progeniem uitiosiorem*, Tib. 2,5,9 *fetus matrona dabit* and other examples in *Thes.* V 1,1696,37 ff.; in addition, the *iunctura* recurs at l. 204, in the solemn finale of the poem. *Stirpe nitier* (l. 68), reproducing the metaphor of children as pillars of the house, is characteristic of the same type of language: cf. Cic. *Cael.* 79 *qui hoc unico filio nititur*, Sen. *Contr.* 2,1, 7 *non tibi per multos fulta liberos domus est*, Prop. 4,11,69 *et serie fulcite genus*. A similar comment can be made on the allusion to the approval by *bona Fama*: instances of *fama* being "quasi personata" (*Thes.* VI 1,211,37) are frequent in Latin as early as the archaic period: cf. J. Svennung, *Cat. Bilderspr.*, cit., 13 and 136 and for the "iunctura" Ter. *Phorm.* 724 *non satis est tuum te officium fecisse, id si non fama approbat*, Colum. 3,2,30 *genus uitium ... fama probatum*, CIL VIII 24787,3 *orta, ut fama probat, ... diuite Roma.*

Typical expressions of sacral contexts, on the contrary, are *nil potest sine te Venus*, at l. 61 (slightly changed at ll. 66 f. and 71 f.) and *at potest* (l. 63); *sine te* is actually a formula recurrent in the style of prayers.[36] The oldest indications of this are in Aeschylus and Pindar: cf. Aesch. *Suppl.* 823 f. (the chorus' prayer to Jove) τί δ᾽ ἄνευ σέθεν / θνατοῖσι τέλειόν ἐστιν;, *Agam.* 1485 ff. διαὶ Διός / παναιτίου πανεργέτα . / τί γὰρ βροτοῖς ἄνευ Διὸς τελεῖται;, Pind. *Nem.* 7,1 ff. Ἐλείθυια, πάρεδρε Μοιρᾶν βαθυφρόνων, / παῖ μεγαλοσθενέος, ἄκου- /σον, Ἥρας, γενέτειρα τέκνων . ἄνευ σέθεν / οὐ φάος, *Olymp.* 14,10 ff. (an invocation to the Charites) οὐδὲ γὰρ θεοὶ σε- / μνᾶν Χαρίτων ἄτερ / κοιρανέοντι χορούς οὔτε δαῖτας. Later evidences testifying that the formula belongs to the sacral sphere are in Ariphr. *Poet. Mel. Gr.* 813,10 Page (to Hygieia) σέθεν δὲ χωρὶς οὔτις εὐδαίμων ἔφυ, in Chlean's hymn to Zeus (*Collect. Alex.* 1,15 f., p. 227

35. C.J. FORDYCE, *Catullus*, cit., 244.
36. The formula has been discussed, as usual, by E. NORDEN, *Agnostos Theos*, cit., 157, 159 n. 1, 349; cf. also R.G.M. NISBET - M. HUBBARD, *A Commentary on Horace*, cit., 307.

58

Powell) οὐδέ τι γίγνεται ἔργον ἐπὶ χθονὶ σοῦ δίχα, δαῖμον, / οὔτε κατ᾽αἰθέριον θεῖον πόλον, οὔτ᾽ἐνὶ πόντῳ and in *Hymn. Orph.* 16,5 (referred to Hera) χωρὶς γὰρ σέθεν, 60,9 (concerning the Charites) ὑμῶν χωρίς, 68,8 (referred to Hygieia) σοῦ γὰρ ἄ-τερ πάντ᾽ ἐστὶν ἀνωφελέ᾽ ἀνθρώποισιν.

In Rome the most ancient mentionings are in Catullus and in the solemn hymn to Venus, in the proem of Lucretius' *De rerum natura*: ll. 21 ff. *quae quoniam rerum naturam sola gubernas / nec sine te quicquam dias in luminis oras / exoritur*; cf. then Hor. *Carm.* 1,26,9 f. (to the Muse) *nil sine te mei / prosunt honores.* But the phrase is also used when addressing a mortal being; in that case, its presence helps to understand that the poet is deifying the character in question: see, for instance, the eulogy to Maecenas in Verg. *Georg.* 3,40 ff. *interea Dryadum siluas saltusque sequamur / intactos, tua, Maecenas, haud mollia iussa: / te sine nil altum mens incohat.* Propertius employs the same device with reference to Cynthia in 2,30,40 *nam sine te nostrum non ualet ingenium*, and it is significant that in the elegy Cynthia is described like a Muse.

Analogous remarks are possible about *at potest*: the δύναμις θεοῦ[37] was already expressed by Homer, in the prayer to Apollo, in *Il.* 16,514 f. δύνασαι δὲ σὺ πάντοσ᾽ ἀκούειν / ἀνέρι κηδομένῳ. Cf. also Hes. *Theog.* 420 (referred to Hecates) καί τέ οἱ ὄλβον ὀπάζει, ἐπεὶ δύναμίς γε πάρεστιν, Pind. *Nem.* 7,96 ff. (invocation to Heracles) δύνα- / σαι δὲ βροτοῖσιν ἀλκὰν / ἀμαχανιᾶν δυσβάτων θαμὰ διδόμεν, Callim. *Hym.* 2,29 (with reference to Apollo) δύναται γάρ, ἐπεὶ Διὶ δεξιὸς ἧσται,[38] 4,226 f. (with reference to Hera) ἀλλὰ φίλη, δύνασαι γάρ, ἀμύνεο πότνια δούλους / ὑμετέρους, *Anth. Pal.* 6,76,5 (Agathias) ἀλλά, θεά (scil. Κύπρι), δύνασαι γάρ, ἢ ἡβητῆρά με τεῦξον / ἢ καὶ τὴν πολιὴν ὡς νεότητα δέχου, Procl. *Hymn.* 1,46 (to Helios) δός, ἄναξ, δύνασαι δὲ τελέσσαι ἄπαντα.[39] Once again, there

37. On the motif cf. G. APPEL, *De Romanorum precationibus*, cit., 153; E. NORDEN, *Agnostos Theos*, cit., 154; R.G.M. NISBET - M. HUBBARD, *A Commentary on Horace*, cit., 334.

38. Cf. F. WILLIAMS, *Callimachus Hymn to Apollo. A Commentary*, Oxford 1978, 37.

39. On Proclus' line cf. U. v. WILAMOWITZ-MOELLENDORFF, *Die Hymnen des Proklos und Synesios*, Sitzungsber. Berlin. Akad. Wiss., 1907, 275 f.

seems to be no earlier evidence of this in Rome than Catullus[40]; after him cf. Hor. *Carm.* 3,11,13 f. *tu potes tigris comitesque siluas / ducere et riuos celeres morari, Ep.* 17,45 *et tu, potes nam, solue me dementia,* Verg. *Aen.* 6,117 (invocation to Apollo priestess) *alma precor miserere, potes namque omnia* and Prop. 3,17,1 ff. *nunc, o Bacche, tuis humiles aduoluimur aris: / da mihi pacatus uela secunda, pater. / Tu potes insanae Veneris compescere fastus.*[41] Among the above-quoted instances, the same antithesis *nil potest sine te ... at potest te uolente* is present at the beginning of Pindar's *Nemea* 7 and *Olympic* 14 and in Aesch. *Agam.* 1448.

The formula *te uolente* too is peculiar to sacral fields, because the term *uolens* belongs to religious language: cf. Plaut. *Mil.* 1351 *agite, ite, cum dis bene uolentibus,* Hor. *Carm.* 3,30,16 *lauro cinge uolens, Melpomene comam* and Liu. 1,16,3 *uti uolens propitius suam semper sospitet gentem.*[42]

The elevated style of the context justifies the use conveniently made of archaic present infinitives in the passive (or deponent) form: cf. *compararier* (ll. 65, 70, 75), *nitier* (l. 68) and what has been previously said with respect to *citarier* (l. 42). The same observation is valid for *ausit,* on which cf. F. Sommer, *Latein. Laut- und Formenlehre,* cit., 584-587. Notice also that Catullus chooses *queo* − regarded by him as an archaism − instead of *possum* at ll. 66, 72, 73; the form *quit,* except for Sall. *Iug.* 14, 11 (where the text is uncertain) is only used in poetry.[43]

40. Plaut. *Amph.* 139 *facile meus pater quod volt facit* is not to be placed on the same stylistic level as Catullus, as in fact R.G.M. NISBET - M.HUBBARD, *A Commentary on Horace,* cit., 334 would have it.

41. Propertius' elegy, meant to exalt Bacchus' virtues, presents other themes of sacral language: above all cf. lines 5-8.

42. The formula *uolens propitius* is dwelt upon by E. NORDEN, *Aus altrömischen Priesterbüchern,* cit., 19 f.

43. Cf. E. NORDEN, *Aen.,* cit., 254 and H. HEUSCH, *Das Archaische i. d. Sprache Catulls,* cit., 121. On the refrain cf. J. VAHLEN, *Opusc.,* II 215.

CHAPTER IV

THE SONG BEFORE THE BRIDE'S HOUSE

The hymn to the god ends, at l. 75, with the repetition of the refrain *quis huic deo compararier ausit*. The sudden exhortation to open the door introduces the second part of the poem, containing the song in front of the bride's house before the *deductio*.

Because of her *pudor*, the bride hesitates to come out and the poet-coryphaeus tries to persuade her: in order to avoid the conflict between *amor* and *pudor* and to show her that, in fact, it has no reason to exist, the poet first (ll. 76-91) praises the *pudor* of the bride — who is crying as she does not want to leave her old home — and her incomparable beauty; this section ends with the formula of invitation *prodeas noua nupta*.

After a strophe, in which again the girl is urged to come out, Catullus expresses, to make his exhortation more convincing, the motif of the certainty of the husband's faithfulness; this section (ll. 92-106) starts and finishes with the refrain (*prodeas noua nupta*). The third phase of the attempt to persuade Junia is based on the exaltation of the erotic joys of the married state (ll. 107-113); a further invitation to come out (*prodeas noua nupta*) ends this part of the poem, which shows clear influences of themes present in Greek poetry, as Ellis[1] rightly observes.

> claustra pandite ianuae.
> uirgo ades! uiden ut faces
> splendidas quatiunt comas?
>
> . . . .
> . . . .   (80)

---

1. R. ELLIS, *A Commentary on Catullus*, cit., 221.

<pre>
. . . .
. . . .
</pre>

tardet ingenuus pudor,

quem tamen magis audiens,   80

flet quod ire necesse est.   (85)

flere desine. Non tibi Au-

runculeia periculum est

ne qua femina pulchrior

clarum ab Oceano diem   85

uiderit uenientem.   (90)

talis in uario solet

diuitis domini hortulo

stare flos hyacinthinus.

sed moraris, abit dies.   90

⟨prodeas noua nupta.⟩   (95)

Manuscripts read *adest* at 1. 77, and Schrader's *ades* (an obvious correction, in my opinion) has had hardly any success, although E. Fraenkel, *Kl. Beitr.*, II 98 n.3 admonishes: "The conservative obstinacy of Ellis, who at 1. 77 clings to the final stroke of the MS reading *adest* ... is now repeated in Schuster's Teubner edition of 1949". Mynors and Fordyce too prefer *adest*: but both the frequently repeated invocation *prodeas noua nupta* (1. 91 f., 106, 113) and the statement at 1. 115 (*flammeum uideo uenire*) make the present indicative *adest* at 1. 77 improbable. As for Fordyce's defence of *adest* (*ades* would be too peremptory and in contrast with the respectful *prodeas* of ll. 91-113), Zicàri has pointed out in "Riv. Fil. Istr. Class." 90 (1962) 77 (= *Scritti catulliani*, Urbino 1978, 257) how insubstantial this hypothesis is with regard to the presumed greater imperiousness of an imperative in comparison with a subjunctive expressing a command. Parroni, for his part, in "Riv. Fil. Istr. Class." 101(1973) 489 advances a new argument in favour of *ades*: he underlines that ll. 92-95 *prodeas noua nupta (...) / uiden? faces aureas quatiunt comas* repeat with *uariatio* ll. 77-78.

The integration of 1. 91 is certain: the refrain is necessary, since it is the end of each section of the song before the bride's house; in this case, it has been left out because it is also repeated at the beginning of the next section.

At line 77 Catullus addresses the bride for the first time: in order to convince her to come out he shows her the flaring torches of the wedding procession[2]; by mentioning this, Catullus makes us understand that the evening star is already shining in the sky and it is time for the *deductio*: cf. the beginning of c. 62 *Vesper adest, iuuenes consurgite: Vesper Olympo / expectata diu uix tandem lumina tollit. / Surgere iam tempus, iam pinguis linquere mensas, / iam veniet virgo, iam dicetur hymenaeus.*

It is difficult to state what was expressed in the missing part after line 78: Kroll[3] thinks there must have been the τόπος of the *desiderium mariti*, a motif, then, in contrast with the bride's *pudor*; but it is present in ll. 97 ff. and would be definitely premature here, if one considers the sequence of the topics. Wilamowitz supposes that there was an allusion to the evening star, whose appearance determined the beginning of the *deductio*[4]; it seems more probable to me, as Fordyce[5] believes too, that in the missing part there must have been the bride's intimate conflict between her natural *pudor* and the equally spontaneous call of love. The bride's *pudor* is, indeed, exalted in the last three lines of the strophe, where, in a sudden dramatic movement, Junia is described in tears in her father's house. We find here the descriptive element, which will play a relevant rôle in subsequent sections of the poem.

Catullus depicts himself and the people taking part in the wedding procession while they are all waiting for the bride in trepidation: one obviously sees the affinity between this theme and the situation described at the outset of Callimachus' hymn to Apollo (*Hymn.* 2,4-8): οὐχ ὁράᾳς; ἐπένευσεν ὁ Δήλιος ἡδύ τι φοῖνιξ / ἐξαπίνης, ὁ δὲ κύκνος ἐν ἠέρι καλὸν ἀείδει. / Αὐτοὶ νῦν κατοχῆες ἀνακλίνασθε πυλάων, / αὐταὶ δὲ κληΐδες . ὁ γὰρ θεὸς οὐκέτι μακρήν . / οἱ δὲ νέοι μολπήν τε καὶ ἐς χορὸν

---

2. F. DELLA CORTE, *Catullo. Le poesie*, cit., 291 points out that torches so shaken as to be ablaze bring good luck (cf. Plin. *Epist.* 4,9,11).

3. W. KROLL, *Cat.*, cit., 113.

4. U. v. WILAMOWITZ-MOELLENDORFF, *Hell. Dicht.*, cit., II 283 n. 3, who proposes, *exempli causa*, the following glyconics: *ecce lampada noctifer / tollit Hesperus Oeta / uirginem ut Venus e domo / excitet bona, neu pedem / tardet* etc.

5. C.J. FORDYCE, *Catullus*, cit., 245.

ἐντύναοθε. It is highly likely – Kroll asserts[6] – that the representation of the waiting in front of the temple's door for the epiphany of the god may have suggested to Catullus the waiting before the bride's door; this could help to determine the function of *ianuae* better: it would be a vocative and not genitive case,[7] if we admit that Callimachus exerted a great influence on Catullus and compare l. 7 of the hymn to Apollo.

It is interesting to notice that the end of the hymn also marks the passage to another stylistic level: on the other hand, colloquial tones, and not expressions of solemn language, are suitable for the lively invitation to the bride. Surely in Virgil (*Aen.* 6,779 *uiden ut geminae stant uertice cristae*) *uiden ut* + indicative may represent an archaism.[8] But the situation is different for Catullus: Wackernagel[9] and Pascucci[10] prove that Catullus, who handed the formula down from writers of comedies to the poets of the Augustan age, chose it for its presence in dialogues of comedies[11] and employed it in colloquial contexts: besides the passage in question, cf. 62,8 (during the contest between the two choruses of youths and maidens) *sic certest; uiden ut perniciter exsiluere?*

The metaphor of the torches' *comae* (l. 78) is traditional, although in Rome there seems to be no evidence of it before Catullus[12]; the metaphor, which has Greek origin and was frequent in Greek prose,[13] was used as early as Aesch. *Agam.* 306

6. W. KROLL, *Cat.*, cit., 112.
7. Compare also my observations on *claudite ostia uirgines* (l. 224).
8. Cf. E. NORDEN, *Aen.*, cit., 112. In Greek cf. Hom. *Il.* 7,448 οὐχ ὁράᾳς; (see also *Od.* 17,545, Callim. *Hymn.* 2,4), Alcm. 1,50 ἦ οὐχ ὁρῇς; (cf. A. GRIFFITHS in "Quad. Urb. Cult. Class." 14 [1972] 13), *PMG* 7,5 οὐκ εἰσορῇς, quoted by R.G.M. NISBET - M. HUBBARD, *A Commentary on Horace: Odes. Book 1*, cit., 118.
9. J. WACKERNAGEL, *Vorlesungen über Syntax*, cit., I^2, 244.
10. G. PASCUCCI in "St. Ital. Fil. Class." 29 (1957) 187 ff.; cf. also J. GRANAROLO, *L'oeuvre de Catulle. Aspects religieux, éthiques et stylistiques*, Paris 1967, 339.
11. On the *correptio iambica* in *uiden* cf. F. SOMMER, *Latein. Laut- und Formenlehre*, cit., 236. It is worth considering that *tersus atque elegans* Tibullus employs *uiden ut* in connection with a subjunctive (2,1,25).
12. *Thes.* III 1752,50 ff.
13. Cf. J. SVENNUNG, *Cat. Bilderspr.*, 103 and on the image of the *coronae* of a torch see also the instances mentioned by E.A. HAHN in "Am. Journ. Phil." 81 (1960) 75-77.

φλογὸς μέγαν πώγωνα, *Prom. uinct.* 1044 πυρὸς ἀμφήκης βόστρυχος.

Presumably the "iunctura" *pudor ingenuus*, recurring almost only in prose, had no particular high poetic value: cf. Val. Max. 9, 10 ext. 2, Sen. *Const. Sap.* 15,1, Quintil. *Decl. min.* 298 p. 178,10 Ritter, Iust. 16,5,4 and, in poetry, Iuuenal. 11,154. The use of *audire* "ferc i.q. oboedire alicui" is mainly prosaic: cf. the numerous examples cited in *Thes.* II 1288,26 ff. It is finally worth observing that Catullus uses the simple form *ire* instead of the compound *abire*, frequently found before him in Plautus (cf. e.g. *Cist.* 112, *Epid.* 72, *Mil.* 1339) and also in Ter. *Eun.* 593, Varr. *R.R.* 2,8,1 and Val. Aedit. *Epigr.* 2,2 Baehrens.[14]

The invitation to Junia becomes more intimate in ll. 82 ff.: resuming the motif expressed at the end of the previous strophe (*flet*), Catullus asks her to put an end to her crying (*flere desine*) and praises her beauty which is beyond comparison. The value of *tibi* at l. 82 and the meaning of the strophe have been underlined with great efficacy by Leonardo Ferrero, who has written impressive pages on c. 61. He emphasizes that not any bride's modesty, not the conventional woman's crying is described, but 'this' woman's, whom the poet calls by her name and exhorts: *non tibi, Aurunculeia, periculum est.* Ferrero notices that the use of the pronoun is not aimless; for her, and not for any other woman, no danger exists, because she excels in beauty, with which she rises to enlighten the long day of the married life. Not even after her nuptial night will any woman more beautiful than her have ever seen the daylight coming from the Ocean.[15]

In order to stress the idea of Junia's beauty, Catullus adds a delicate comparison with a natural element, the hyacinth flowering in the many-coloured garden *diuitis domini.* But the poet realizes that, while time is going by, the bride still hesitates: therefore he interrupts with an adversative sentence (*sed moraris*) the imagery developing around the central motif of Junia's beauty, and encourages her again to come out.

Catullus' originality does not consist, in this case either, in creating new themes and new images. None of the motif expressed in ll. 82-91 represents an innovation: the emphatic eulogy

14. Cf. *Thes.* V 2,630,10 ff.
15. L. FERRERO, *Interpretazione di Catullo*, cit., 294.

of the bride, who excels any other woman in beauty, is a settled theme of wedding-songs, in addition to which the intellectual qualities and other gifts of the *noua nupta* can be praised.

The first motif appears in a fragment of an epithalamium by Sappho: 113 L.-P. οὐ γὰρ ἦν ἀτέρα πάις ὦ γάμβρε τεαύτα[16]; instances of it in Rome before Catullus are in Titin. *Com. Frg.* 106 R.[3] *accede ad sponsum audacter: uirgo nulla est talis Setiae* and then in Statius' epithalamium, in the description of the bride's look after the first night of marriage (242 ff.): *quantum nosse licet, sic uicta sopore doloso / Martia fluminea posuit latus Ilia ripa, / non talis niueos tinxit Lauinia uultus, / cum Turno spectante rubet, non Claudia talis / respexit populos mota iam uirgo carina.*

Also in this case the parallel with Sappho should not lead to draw hasty conclusions concerning the influence exerted by Sappho on Catullus, because both themes are employed by Theocritus, in his epithalamium: 18,20 f. οἶα ᾿Αχαιϊάδων γαῖαν πατεῖ οὐδεμί᾿ ἄλλα, 32 ff. οὔτε τις ἐν ταλάρῳ πανίσδεται ἔργα τοιαῦτα, / οὔτ᾿ ἐνὶ δαιδαλέῳ πυκινώτερον ἄτριον ἱστῷ / κερκίδι συμπλέξασα μακρῶν ἔταμ᾿ ἐκ κελεόντων. / Οὐ μὰν οὐδὲ λύραν τις ἐπίσταται ὧδε κροτῆσαι / ῎Αρτεμιν ἀείδοισα καὶ εὐρύστερνον ᾿Αθάναν, / ὡς ῾Ελένα, τᾶς πάντες ἐπ᾿ ὄμμασιν ἵμεροι ἐντί. / ῏Ω καλά, ὦ χαρίεσσα κόρα, τὺ μὲν οἰκέτις ἤδη. Moreover, the ἔκφρασις τῆς νύμφης was recommended by the rhetoricians in their theories on the epithalamium as a genre: for Menander it is the third part of the scheme of the λόγος ἐπιθαλάμιος: *Rhet. Gr.* III 404,11 f. Spengel τῆς παρθένου γὰρ φυλάξῃ διὰ τὰς ἀντιπιπτούσας διαβολὰς κάλλος ἐκφράζειν, πλήν εἰ μὴ συγγενὴς εἴης, 405,28 ff. Spengel ἐροῦμεν δὲ ἐγκώμιον τῆς νύμφης διὰ βραχέων, οὐ τὸ ἀπὸ τῆς σωφροσύνης οὐδὲ ἀπὸ φρονήσεως οὐδὲ τῶν λοιπῶν ἀρετῶν τῆς ψυχῆς, ἀλλὰ τὸ ἀπὸ τῆς ὥρας καὶ τοῦ κάλλους.

With respect to the image of sunlight rising from the Ocean and contemplating Junia's beauty, Catullus imitates another conventional motif of Greek poetry: he varies and adapts to Junia's situation the well-known motif of the Sun, ὃς πάντ᾿ ἐφορᾷ (cf. e.g. Hom. *Il.* 3,277), also employed by Greek poets to

---

16. ῟Ην ἀτέρα, however, is Blomfield's conjectural reading; codices of Dion. Hal. *Comp.* 201-2 (VI 1, p. 127-8 Usener-Radermacher), which hand the fragment down, have ἑτέρα νῦν.

express the absolute perfection of somebody or something: so Euripides (*Hec.* 635) defines Helen τὰν καλλίσταν ὁ χρυσοφαής / Ἅλιος αὐγάζει. Catullus' source is probably Callimachus, who used the same image to describe the wonderful temple of Artemis in Ephesus:*Hymn.*3,249 τοῦ δ'οὔ τι θεώτερον ὄψεται ἠώς. Compare besides this *Anth. Pal.* 9,58,7 f. (Antipat.) νόσφιν Ὀλύμπου / Ἥλιος οὐδέν πω τοῖον ἐπηυγάσατο. The traditional image is also "rinnovata dalla *callida iunctura*, dalla suggestione che essa esercita e riflette su tutto il passo; ché serale è il corteggio di Imeneo allo splendore delle fiaccole e notturni i gaudi che attendono gli sposi".[17]

The comparison between the bride and a flower was a conventional feature of wedding-songs: we have already ascertained its presence in the rhetorical scheme of epithalamia[18] apropos of l. 21. As concerns, in particular, the parallel Junia-hyacinth, the majority of critics have no doubts; following Kaibel,[19] Mangelsdorff[20] states: "Dieses Lob hält sich ganz in Sapphischem Stil", and his opinion is commonly shared; the fragment 105 c L.-P. οἵαν τὰν ὑάκινθον ἐν ὤρεσι ποίμενες ἄνδρες / πόσσι καταστείβοισι χάμαι δέ τε πόρφυρον ἄνθος is usually cited on this subject and, due to the simile with the hyacinth, it is regarded as Catullus' source. Fordyce[21] is more cautious, and rightly so, when he asserts that, on the contrary, the context in Catullus might echo Hom. *Od.* 6,231 οὔλας ἧκε κόμας ὑακινθίνῳ ἄνθει ὁμοίας, just as the allusion to the garden *diuitis domini* might be an imitation of Hom. *Il.* 11,68, where in an analogous comparison, there is the mentioning ἀνδρὸς μάκαρος κατ'ἄρουραν. The wild

17. L. FERRERO, *Interpretazione di Catullo*, cit., 294; on the traditional motif cf. K.J. McKAY in "Rhein. Mus." 114 (1971) 191 f.; G. LIEBERG in "Gnom." 47 (1975) 356 (but already in "Latinitas" 22 [1974] 218-9) does not think that here Catullus varies, owing to Hellenistic refinement, the conventional image of the sun that sees everything; he is rather convinced, on the grounds of Hom. *Il.* 18,61, Eur. *Alc.* 151.395, that the poet uses *diem uidere* with the meaning of *uiuere*: therefore, in this case Catullus consoles the bride by assuring her that no woman more beautiful than her has ever seen the sun rising from the Ocean (that is, no woman more beautiful than her has ever lived).

18. Cf. Menand. *Rhet. Gr.* III 404,5 Spengel.

19. G. KAIBEL in "Herm." 27 (1892) 252.

20. E.A. MANGELSDORFF, *Lyr. Hochzeitsged.*, cit., 39.

21. C.J. FORDYCE, *Catullus*, cit., 246.

hyacinth trodden upon ἐν ὤρεσι, however, is quite different from the flower grown with great care *in hortulo diuitis domini!*

A Sapphic motif imitated by Catullus could in fact be present in c. 62,39 ff. *ut flos in saeptis secretus nascitur hortis, / ignotus pecori, nullo conuolsus aratro, / quem mulcent aurae, firmat sol, educat imber; / multi illum pueri, multae optauere puellae: / idem cum tenui carptus defloruit ungui / nulli illum pueri, nullae optauere puellae.* Page[22] is definitely in favour of this hypothesis and even strives to reconstruct the meaning of the missing part of the Sapphic fragment by means of Catullus' poem. But Eduard Fraenkel, in a paper published in the same year[23] demonstrated that this method is rather unreliable: according to Fraenkel, if Catullus really imitated Sappho, he did it with great originality, because both the atmosphere and character of the context and the ideas expressed are very different from the ones in Sappho; it is more probable, in fact, that the fragment 105 c L.-P. was imitated by Catullus in the final strophe of c. 11 (ll. 21-24 *nec meum respectet, ut ante, amorem, qui illius culpa cecidit uelut prati / ultimi flos, praetereunte postquam / tactus aratro est*). Therefore, also in respect of c. 61, a greater caution would be more useful than the certainty about Sapphic influences: besides, a mere look at Städler's article (Ὑάκινθος) in "R.E.P.W." IX 1 (1914) 4 can be sufficient to understand how common this imagery was in Greek and Latin poetry.[24]

How can a new comparison between the bride and a vegetable element be justified, after the simile of ll. 21-25? Is it a sheer repetition of the motif already expressed in the ὕμνος κλητικός, as Kroll[25] would have it? Probably it is not as simple as that: while in ll. 16-25 the simile is included in the description of

22. D. PAGE, *Sappho a. Alc.*, cit., 121 n. 4.

23. E. FRAENKEL, *Vesper adest*, in "Journ. Rom. Stud." 45 (1955) 1-8 = *Kl. Beitr.* II 87-101.

24. P. PARRONI in "Riv. Fil. Istr. Class." 101 (1973) 489-90 underlines that in a papyraceous fragment by Anacreon (*P. Oxy.* 2321 = 60 Gentili) the unrestrained abandon to the joys of love of a most beautiful girl, who conceals her ardour, is symbolically represented by ὑακίνθιναι ἄρουραι where Cypris ties up mares free from their jokes (ll. 7-9). Consequently, he maintains that, if also in the passage by Catullus hyacinth symbolizes sensual love, the gradation with myrtle, a symbol of virginity, is perfect.

25. W. KROLL, *Cat.*, cit., 113.

Junia's beauty before the wedding celebration, here — Ferrero[26] rightly perceived it — the poet's imagination goes even further and he depicts Junia, as usual ablazing with beauty, after her first night of love with Manlius; the mentioning of dawn in the previous strophe suggests this, as well as the sudden *sed moraris* seems to put an end to an idea contemplated with the imagination rather than to the description of what the poet represents as being in progress. It is remarkable, moreover, that a hint at the newly married pair waking up at the rising of the sun is also present in Theocritus' epithalamium, in which the chorus of maidens urges the couple to remember to wake up at sunrise (18,55 ἐγρέσθαι δὲ πρὸς ἀῶ μή᾽ πιλάθησθε), and in the above-quoted lines of Statius' epithalamium (*Sil.* 1,2,242 ff.). On this grounds the allusion to *diues dominus* too is understandable: *diues dominus* is the groom, who has picked the hyacinth grown by him with love for a long time.

It is possible that all this is based on literary reminiscences, but the atmosphere created by Catullus is new, due to the delicacy of his imagery and the choice of the right stylistic tone, as well as the absolutely original adaptation of his sources.

The style swings, in this circumstance too, from refined expressions to more intimate and familiar tones. Propertius will remember the exhortation *flere desine* (l. 82) in the pathetic beginning of the last elegy of book IV. *Femina* (l. 84) was a less prosaic term than *mulier* at Catullus' time, and therefore it was more suitable for poetry of high stylistic level.[27] The use of *dies* instead of *sol* is refined and poetic from Lucretius (1,47) on: cf. *Thes.* V 1,1027, 56 ff.[28]; the stylistic value of the context, anyway, becomes evident if we consider the "iunctura" *clarus dies*: Catullus invented it, or at least it is mentioned here for the first time[29] and after him it is frequently accepted in elevated poetry: cf. e.g. Verg. *Aen.* 5,43; Hor. *Carm. Saec.* 23; Ouid. *Her.* 18,34; Sen.

26. L. FERRERO, *Interpretazione di Catullo*, cit., 294.
27. Cf. B. AXELSON, *Unp. Wört.*, cit., 56.
28. K. PFLUGBEIL, the author of the article in *Thesaurus*, does not mention Catullus' passage among the examples of *dies* used in the sense of *sol*: but the imperfections of the article *dies* in *Thesaurus* have been pointed out by E. FRAENKEL, *Das Geschlecht von "Dies"*, in "Glotta" 8 (1917) 24-68 = *Kl. Beitr.* I 27-72.
29. Cf. *Thes.* III 1272,15 ff.

Herc. Fur. 586.821; *Med.* 5; *Octau.* 4; Lucan 7,787; 9,839; Sil. It. 6,452; Stat. *Theb.* 7,224. Notice also the alliteration of the pherecratic at the end of the strophe (*uiderit uenientem*).

In the following strophe the atmosphere of grace and delicacy is conveyed also through the style: the diminutive *hortulus*, to be sure, was frequently employed in prose too, by then, without any particular stylistic connotation[30]; but Catullus may have used it with a definite purpose in a context where the diminutive well contributes to stress the familiar and affectionate tone of the comparison between Junia and the hyacinth. The search for rare "iuncturae" and images reappears in the periphrasis *flos hyacinthinus* (l. 86) instead of the normal *hyacinthus*: Ronconi[31] believes that it has "un'intonazione culta"; it is actually a coinage derived from the neoteric ὑακίνθινον ἄνθος (*Od.* 6,231), which is also used, but in the plural, by Eur. *Iph. Aul.* 1299; afterwards the "iunctura" is only present in Sidon. Apoll. *Carm.* 24,62 *narcissos hyacinthinosque flores*.

Another influence exerted by Callimachus is detectable, on the other hand, in the refrain *prodeas noua nupta* (l. 91). Catullus' debts towards Alexandrian poetry in general and Callimachus in particular, as concerns the ὕμνος κλητικός, have already been underlined; with regard to the refrain in this section of the poem, there is a singular coincidence with Callimachus' hymn V, in which the poet, waiting for Athena's epiphany, repeats three times the invocation for the goddess to come out: ἔξιθ' 'Αθαναία, at ll. 33 and 43, πότνι' 'Αθαναία, τὺ μὲν ἔξιθι, at l. 55.

Noua nupta, on the contrary, is the conventional expression to designate the bride: compare, for example, the use of the same formula in the comic wedding ceremony of Plautus' *Casina* (ll. 798 and 815). In *Casina*, although in a different context, we find the detail of the bride's delay before going out, emphasized by Lysidamus, who loses his patience and exclaims: *nam quid illaec nunc tam diu intus remorantur?* (l. 804). One might infer that the motif of the delay too was conventional in the progress of wedding ceremonies and songs. Similarly, *prodeas* seems to echo a traditional formula: the verb is indeed used by Plautus, with the

---

30. Cf. A. RONCONI, *Studi catulliani*, cit., 96 f.
31. Cf. A. RONCONI, *Studi catulliani*, cit., 150.

same meaning and in the same situation: *Cas.* 806 *quid si etiam suffundam hymenaeum, si qui citius prodeant?*

At the beginning of the next strophe Catullus repeats the final statement of the previous one — a technique used some other times in the same poem[32] —, almost to highlight its urgency and importance: the bride is kindly asked (*si iam uidetur*) to come out and listen to the poet-coryphaeus, who for the second time calls her attention to the sparkling torches.

This strophe of transition precedes the mentioning of the second motif chosen by Catullus to persuade the bride to come out: Junia can be sure that never will her husband be unfaithful or leave her; on the contrary, Manlius will be bound up with her as vine is fastened to trees. The assertion that time goes quickly, together with another invitation to the bride, ends this part of the poem, containing the eulogy of the groom's faithfulness.

prodeas noua nupta, si		
iam uidetur, et audias		
nostra uerba. uiden? faces		
aureas quatiunt comas:	95	
prodeas noua nupta.	(100)	
non tuus leuis in mala		
deditus uir adultera,		
probra turpia persequens,		
a tuis teneris uolet	100	
secubare papillis,	(105)	
lenta sed uelut adsitas		
uitis implicat arbores		
implicabitur in tuum		
complexum. sed abit dies:	105	
prodeas noua nupta.	(110)	

The parallel groom/vine (l.102 ff.) belongs to the series of similes between the bridal pair and natural elements that represent a fixed theme of wedding-songs [33]; the origin of the comparisons

32. Ll. 81-82 *flet ... flere desine*; 123-125 *concubinus ... concubine*; 128-130 *concubine ... concubine*; 193-194 *ne remorare ... non diu remoratus es*; 203-204 *multa milia ludi ... ludite ut lubet*; 218-220 *matris ... matre.*
33. On the parallel between the bride and an element of the vegetable

is the ancient habit of the εἰκάζειν, which apart from being frequent in the New Comedy, was also a parlour game quite widespread in Greece.[34] As for the influence on Catullus of the techniques, as well as the custom, of the εἰκάζειν, it is relevant that the noun *uitis* is connected with the adjective *lenta:* this is another frequent detail of the εἰκάζειν, where the thing compared is usually in connection with an adjective or, more often, with a past participle. The reason for this, in Fraenkel's opinion, is the fact that the mere mentioning is not considered sufficient, so it is also necessary to point out that the thing in question happens to be in a particular situation.[35]

With regard to the content of the parallel, the Greek rhetoricians who theorize the λόγος ἐπιθαλάμιος never cite a comparison identical with the one drawn by Catullus. The basic idea, however, must be Greek: Menander[36] advises the authors of epithalamia to mention the links between trees and to compare them with marriage: ὥσπερ καὶ ὑμεῖς ἐν ὥρᾳ καὶ ἀκμῇ τοῦ κάλλους τυγχάνετε, καὶ δένδρα δένδρεσιν ἐπιμίγνυται, ἵνα τοῦτο γένηται τελετὴ καὶ γάμος·[37] Catullus himself develops the parallel between marriage and other kinds of relations taken from the vegetable world in the famous lines (49-58) of c. 62: *ut uidua in nudo uitis quae nascitur aruo, / numquam se extollit, numquam mitem educat uuam, / sed tenerum prono deflectens pondere corpus / iam iam contingit summum radice flagellum; / hanc nulli agricolae, nulli coluere iuuenci: / sic uirgo, dum intacta manet, dum inculta senescit; / cum par conubium maturo tempore adepta est, / cara uiro magis et minus est inuisa parenti.* It is impossible not to compare Catullus' simile in c.61 and the one in an epithalamium by Sappho between the groom and a delicate twig: 115 L.-P. τίῳ σ᾽, ὦ φίλε γάμβρε, κάλως ἐικάσδω; / ὄρπακι βραδίνῳ σε μάλιστ᾽ ἐικάσδω.

The image itself of vine appears, as it seems, in Alexandrian

kingdom, compare what has been said with regard to l. 23.
    34. Cf. E. FRAENKEL, *Elementi plautini in Plauto*, transl. by F. Munari, Firenze 1960, 162 ff.; ID., *Aeschylus. Agamemnon*, III, Oxford 1950, 773. The first evidence of the motif in Rome is in a fragment of Lucilius' *iter Siculum* (117 M.), imitated by Horace (*Sat.* 1,5,56).
    35. E. FRAENKEL, *Elementi plautini*, cit., 163 n. 4.
    36. Menand. *Rhet. Gr.* III 408,14 ff. Spengel.
    37. Cf. A.L. WHEELER in "Amer. Journ. Phil." 51 (1930) 211.

poetry; but as concerns its presence in epithalamia there is only one reference to Heratosthenes in *Etymol. gen.* s.v. Αὐροσχάς· ἡ ἄμπελος · μέμνηται Παρθένιος ἐν Ἡρακλεῖ "αὐροσχάδα βότρυν Ἰκαριωνίης". Ἐρατοσθένης δὲ ἐν Ἐπιθαλαμίῳ τὸ κατὰ βότρυν κλῆμα.[38] It is more logical, then, to suppose that in choosing vine as the element of comparison with the groom, Catullus was influenced by a typically Roman view, which had its origin in old rural customs: Svennung observes that "ein Spezialausdruck römischer Bauernsprache ist die Metapher *maritus* von Bäumen, an welche nach italischer Sitte Weinreben angebunden werden"[39]; cf. Cat. *Agr.* 32,2 *arbores facito ut bene maritae sint uitesque satis multae asserantur*, Hor. *Ep.* 2,9 f. *ergo aut adulta uitium propagine / altas maritat populos, Carm.* 4,5,30 *uitem uiduas ducit ad arbores*, Ouid. *Her.* 5,47 f. *non sic adpositis uincitur uitibus ulmus, / ut tua sunt collo bracchia nexa meo, Am.* 2,16,41 *ulmus amat uitem, uitis non deserit ulmum.*[40] And it is indeed Catullus who says about the *vine*: *si forte eadem est ulmo coniuncta marito* (62,54): apropos of this line of c. 62 Eduard Fraenkel comes to the same conclusion, in contrast with the hypothesis of a Greek model.[41]

Lines 102-105 of c. 61 are therefore another proof of a technique frequently used by Catullus; he imitates a traditional pattern of Greek poetry — in this case, the parallels between the

38. Cf. R. REITZENSTEIN in "Herm." 35 (1900) 96. On the content of the comparison cf. R.G.M. NISBET - M. HUBBARD, *A Commentary on Horace: Odes. Book 1*, cit., 406 and on the metaphor of marriage F. DELLA CORTE in "Maia" 29-30 (1977-78) 79-80; he emphasizes how Catullus understood that the simile upset the traditional relation *uitis / uirgo, ulmus / uir* and ended the parallel by repeating the verb *implicare* in the semi-passive form, in order to lend it a certain meaning of reciprocity. On the use of the same verb in comparisons cf. ÉVRARD-GILLIS, *La récurrence lexicale dans l'oeuvre de Catulle*, cit., 49-50, who cites 8,4-5; 72,3-4; 87, 1-2.

39. J. SVENNUNG, *Cat. Bilderspr.*, cit., 76.

40. On the motif of embrace as a proof of faithfulness cf. Hor. *Ep.* 15, 3-6 *cum tu magnorum numen laesura deorum / in uerba iurabas mea, / artius atque hedera procera adstringitur ilex / lentis adhaerens bracchiis.*

41. E. FRAENKEL, *Kl. Beitr.*, II 99: "There can be no doubt that in Greek lands, even in λεπτόγεως Attica, the vines were sometimes fastened to trees ...; but the custom of 'wedding the vines to a tree' ... was and is far more common in the rich plains of Italy. It is therefore unlikely that this feature in the poem should be derived from a Greek model".

groom and a plant, and between marriage tie and a union relating to the vegetable kingdom – but he employs an imagery derived from Roman traditions to express it.

In the new exhortation to Iunia a formula of prayers follows an expression of everyday language, motivated by the intimate character of the call. According to Kroll[42] *si iam uidetur* pertains to the "Umgangssprache"; but this opinion should be modified: it is rather a polite formula peculiar of the most refined familiar language, as it is proved by Hofmann.[43] The words *si uidetur* (*uidebitur*) are actually found, besides Plautus (*Capt.* 218), in polite expressions of some of Cicero's correspondents (Pomp. *ap.* Cic. *Att.* 8,6,2; Balb. *ap.* Cic. *Att.* 9,7 b,2) and in a letter from Fronto to Marcus Aurelius (*Epist.* 84,6 van den Hout). *Audias nostra uerba* belongs to the language of prayers: *audio* is the verb "quo precantes deum rogant, ut ipsos audiant animosque ad preces intendant"[44]; analogous is the use of κλῦθι, κλύε, ἄκουσον, ἄκουε, et sim.[45] *Aureas quatiunt comas* (l. 95) is a *uariatio* of *splendidas quatiunt comas* (l. 78); also in this circumstance, to attract Junia's attention, Catullus mentions a colour element.[46]

Refined structures and colloquial expressions co-exist in the next strophe (ll. 97-101), in which Catullus expresses the opposition adultery – faithful love; the disdain of adultery is stressed by the "iuncturae" *in mala adultera* and *probra turpia persequens*; to make the context more effective from a stylistic point of view he employs: a) a refined structure (*deditus + in* and the ablative) only used in two lines of Lucretius (3,647; 4,815); b) a noun (*probrum*), typical of the language of comedies and prose and re-inforced by *turpia*; c) finally, to indicate the act of abandon, the verb *secubo*, of which there is no evidence before him and very

42. W. KROLL, *Cat.*, cit., 114.

43. J.B. HOFMANN, *Lateinische Umgangssprache*, Heidelberg 1951[3], 134: "Gewählter und vornehmer, daher kaum der gewöhnlichen Alltagssprache angehörig sind die vielfach an Höherstehende gerichteten Formeln *si lubet ...*, *si (modo) tibi est commodum ...*, *si (tibi) uidetur*. Cf. also J. GRANAROLO, *L'oeuvre de Catulle*, cit., 31.

44. G. APPEL, *De Romanorum precationibus*, cit., 119, who cites numerous examples of similar sentences.

45. Cf. the evidences mentioned by C. AUSFELD in "Jahrb. class. Philol." Suppl. XXVIII (1903) 516.

46. On *aureus* used in connection with the idea of bright colour cf. T. MANTERO in "Studi Traglia", cit., I 173 nn. 48-49.

few in most uncommon occasions after him. But in the only reference to Junia in this strophe the tone becomes intimate again, by means of the delicate expression *a tuis ... teneris papillis.*

Analogous stylistic devices appear in the following strophe (ll. 102-106): the postposition of *sed* is typically neoteric, as all such transpositions of particles usually are, in imitation of an Alexandrian technique[47]; the first instance of *sed* postponed is in Catullus 51,9 *lingua sed torpet.* Catullus probably employed this Hellenistic technique, which Augustan poets amply developed,[48] to confer dignity to a metaphor that — we have pointed out — was traditionally Roman.

The search of unusual expressions is attested by the presence of *adsitas ... arbores: adsero* was a rare verb, pertaining to the specific language of agriculture: cf. Cat. *Agr.* 32,2 *facito ... uites ... uti satis multae adserantur,* Varr. *R.R.* 1,16,6 *uitis adsita ad holus,* 1,26,1 *neque propter eos* (scil. *ordines cupressorum*) *ut adserant uites;* later evidences of the verb are in Agroec. *Gramm.* VII 125,5 K., Bed. *Gramm.* VII 276,17 K. and in Ulpian *Dig.* VII 1,7,3; for *Thes.* II 863,38 ff. *adsero* recurred in poetry, besides Catullus' line, only in one of Horace's epistles (2,2,170 *populus adsita*). *Lentus* meaning *flexibilis* was more successful in poetry and Virgil used it often.[49] Another indication of refinement is *implico* with reference to plants et sim.: *Thes.* VII 1,642,63 ff. cites, apart from the two examples in Catullus' c. 61,[50] Ser. Sammon. 1073 (= *Poet. Lat. Min.* III 157 Baehrens), Paul. *ap.* Fest. 331 L. and Colum. 2,2,28. Nowhere else, finally, does the "iunctura" *implicari in complexum* occur.[51]

---

47. Compare, with regard to this, the famous pages written by M. HAUPT, *Opusc.,* I 115 ff. on *et* being postponed and, on the usual procedure, E. NORDEN, *Aen.,* cit., 402-404; valuable observations can be found also in D.O. ROSS, *Style and Tradition,* cit., 68. In this case I accept the *lenta sed* of the Oxoniensis; G. FRIEDRICH, *Catulli Veronensis Liber,* Leipzig/Berlin 1908, 271, followed by W. KROLL, *Cat.,* cit., 114, prefers, on the contrary, *lenta quin* (Avantius), on the basis of the disputable view that *lentaque* of G R "ist Unsinn, bringt also das Richtige".

48. Cf. E. NORDEN, *Aen.,* cit., 404.

49. Cf. e.g. the same "iunctura" *lenta uitis* in *Buc.* 3,38.

50. The other one is at l. 35, in a context of neoteric type.

51. On the motif of embraces in Catullus' poetry cf. M. MANSON in "Mél. Éc. Fr. Rome" 90 (1978) 257-58.

The use of paranomasia (ll. 103-104 *implicat ... implicabitur*), frequent in c. 61, is perfectly suitable for the context, in which both the familiar tone and neoteric style are evident. On the basis of the instances found by Ronconi[52] one can assert that the function of paronomasia is different according to the various part of the poem: the examples present in the ὕμνος κλητικός have a different character and a different function: cf. ll. 3-4, where *uirum uirginem* are connected to produce an alliteration and a contrast between the bride's delicacy and the husband's *cupiditas*; l. 19, where the polyptoton *bona cum bona* cannot be distinguished from the elevated "iunctura" *cum bona alite* (σὺν οἰωνοῖς ἀγαθοῖσιν); l. 31, where the opposition *domum dominam* belongs to solemn language; and, in the end, l. 46, where the refined *amatis ... amantibus* is inserted in a stylistically elevated context.

The function of paronomasia in the second part of the poem is not the same: here it is used to emphasize either Junia's (ll. 81-82 *flet ... flere*) or, like in this circumstance, the couple's attitude; it recurs frequently in the *fescennina iocatio* (ll. 124-126 *nuces ... nucibus*; 136 *abstinere sed abstine*; 145-146 *petet ... petitum*); in the final part of the poem, the stylistic device reappears in the poet's advices to the bride and groom (l. 156 *omnia omnibus*; 193-194 *remorare ... remoratus*; 197 *quod cupis cupis*; 205-206 *liberos ... liberis*), in a context, then, similar to lines 97-106, from a stylistic point of view.

The transitional part between the hymn to the god and the beginning of the *deductio* ends with the praises of the erotic joys of marriage: before urging Junia for the last time to come out, Catullus addresses the nuptial bed and exalts the delights of love, which the husband will be given *uaga nocte* and *medio die*.

> o cubile, quod omnibus
> . . . .
> . . . .
> . . . .
> candido pede lecti,   (115)
> quae tuo ueniunt ero,
> quanta gaudia, quae uaga   110

52. A. RONCONI, *Studi catulliani*, cit., 78.

nocte, quae medio die
gaudeat! sed abit dies:
prodeas noua nupta. (120)

Catullus' annotators seem to agree on the cause of the lacuna after
l. 107: Kroll[53] posits that "die Strophe ist durch mittelalterliche
Prüderie zerstört", and his opinion is generally accepted.[54] One
should wonder then what sort of indecencies may have been
described in a strophe that did celebrate the pleasures of sensual
love, but with respect to a married couple: a particularly obscene
content would not match the delicate description of Junia, neither
would it be the best way to win her modesty and convince her to
come out. And why should the copyists have been scandalized
here, considering that they left untouched, both in c. 61 and in
the rest of Catullus' output, lines that were certainly not too
chaste? It is more logical, therefore, to suppose that the reason
for the lacuna is occasional and not intentional; all the more so
as the lacuna after l. 78 is definitely not due to "mittelalterliche
Prüderie".

As it always happens in such circumstances, erudite versifiers
strived to supply the missing lines *exempli gratia*[55]; but none of
them, I think, grasped the probable content of the strophe, which
in fact can be reconstructed. The most important of the traditional motifs of epithalamia all appear in c. 61, except for a τόπος
of great significance in wedding-songs, namely the μακαρισμός,
which was present, in my view, exactly after l. 107, though
expressed in a special way.

53. W. KROLL, *Cat.*, cit., 114.

54. PIGHI in "Humanitas" 2 (1948/49) 42 does not share the *communis
opinio*, and rightly so, in my view.

55. Cf. G. FRIEDRICH, *Catulli Veronensis liber*, cit., 272 *o cubile quod
omnibus* / ⟨*gaudiis aderis mariti,* / *o quam saepe, simul bonum* / *patrat munus,
id argues*⟩ / *candido pede lecti*, U. v. WILAMOWITZ-MOELLENDORFF,
Hell. Dicht., cit., II 283 n. 3 *o cubile quod omnibus* / ⟨*molle strauit amoribus* /
ueste purpurea Tyros, / *fulsit Indus eburnei*⟩ / *candido pede lecti* and G.B.
PIGHI, *Catulli Veronensis liber*, II, Verona 1961, 37 *o cubile quod omnibus* /
⟨*strauit illecebris Venus,* / *tempus est prope, cum toros* / *illa tangat e burnei*⟩ /
candido pede lecti.

56. On the μακαρισμός in general cf. above all G. LEJEUNE DIRICHLET,
De ueterum macarismis, in "Religionsgeschichtliche Versuche und Vorarbeiten" XIV (1914) 1 ff.; see also E. NORDEN, *Agnostos Theos*, cit., 100

It is well known that the μακαρισμός – a device consisting in the exaltation of bliss through adjectives like μάκαρ μακάριος ὄλβιος εὐδαίμων felix beatus was employed in the most various situations and for the most various reasons (riches, military and sports glories, love, the capability to govern etc.). One of the characteristic uses of the μακαρισμός is in wedding-songs, where the eulogy of the bridal couple's beauty is often joined to words of admiration and praises of their happiness[57]; as early as Homer the theme, referred to the lucky man who will marry Nausicaa, occurs in *Od.* 6,158 f. κεῖνος δ᾽αὖ περὶ κῆρι μακάρτατος ἔξοχον ἄλλων / ὅς κέ σ᾽ἐέδνοισι βρίσας οἶκόνδ᾽ ἀγάγηται and in the words that Agamemnon, an unfortunate husband, says to Ulysses, whose marriage is far more successful, in *Od.* 24,192 f. ὄλβιε Λαέρταο πάι, πολυμήχαν᾽ Ὀδυσσεῦ, / ἦ ἄρα σὺν μεγάλῃ ἀρετῇ ἐκτήσω ἄκοιτιν. Hesiod employs the μακαρισμός in the description of Peleus and Thetis' wedding (*Frg.* 211,6 ff. Merkelbach-West): τοῦτ᾽ἔπος εἶπαν ἅπαντες · / τρὶς μάκαρ, Αἰακίδη, καὶ τετράκις, ὄλβιε Πηλεῦ, / ... ὃς τοῖσδ᾽ἐν μεγάροις ἱερὸν λέχος εἰσαναβαίνων κτλ.[58] Other famous examples are in the hymenaei of Aristophanes' Peace and Birds (*Pax* 1333 f. ὦ τρίσμακαρ, ὡς δικαί- / ως τἀγαθὰ νῦν ἔχεις, *Aues* 1721 ff. περιπέτεσθε / μάκαρα μάκαρι σὺν τύχᾳ . / ὦ φεῦ φεῦ τῆς ὥρας, τοῦ κάλλους . / ὦ μακαριστὸν σὺ γάμον τῇδε πόλει γήμας, 1740 f. (Ἔρως) Ζηνὸς πάροχος γάμων / τῆς τ᾽εὐδαίμονος Ἥρας, 1759 f. ὄρεξον, ὦ μάκαιρα, σὴν χεῖρα) and in Euripides, in the wedding-song that the delirious Cassandra sings for herself (*Troad.* 311 ff. μακάριος ὁ γαμέτας, / μακάρια δ᾽ἐγὼ βασιλικοῖς λέκτροις / κατ᾽ Ἄργος ἁ γαμουμένα), or in the chorus praising Phaeton, Venus' husband to-be (*Frg.* 781, 27 N.² ὦ μακάρων βασιλεὺς μείζων ἔτ᾽ὄλβον ὃς θεὰν κηδεύσεις). In Euri-

n. 1 and now, on the parody of μακαρισμός in the Cyclops by Euripides (l. 495 ff.) the fine analysis made by L.E. ROSSI in "Maia" 23 (1971) 19 f.

57. Cf. B. SNELL, *Ges. Phil. Schr.*, 84 ff.

58. Today we know for a certainty that Hesiod's fragment does not belong to an epithalamium: but the mistake made by Tzetzes (Schol. *ad* Lycophr. p. 4,13 Scheer) on the subject attests the fact that the μακαρισμός was a τόπος of the epithalamium: ἐπιθαλαμιογράφοι δὲ ποιηταὶ ὅσοι πρὸς τοὺς νυμφίους ἐν γάμοις ἐγκώμια ἔγραφον, οἷος ἦν ὁ Ἀγαμήστωρ ὁ Φαρσάλιος καὶ ἕτεροι καὶ Ἡσίοδος αὐτὸς γράψας ἐπιθαλάμιον εἰς Πηλέα καὶ Θέτιν τρὶς μάκαρ κτλ.

pides compare also Menelaus' words in *Hel.* 637 ff. ἔχω τὰ τῆς Διός τε λέκτρα Λήδας θ᾽ / ἃν ὑπὸ λαμπάδων κόροι λεύκιπποι / ξυνομαίμονες ὤλβισαν, ὤλβισαν / τὸ πρόσθεν, ἐκ δόμων δὲ νοσφίσας σ᾽ἐμοῦ / πρὸς ἄλλαν ἐλαύνει / θεὸς συμφορὰν τᾶσδε κρείσσω.[59] The vitality of the motif is proved by its presence in the Hellenistic novel, in Longus[60] and Chariton[61].

Inevitably the μακαρισμός, become a conventional formula for wishing the newly married couple well, ended by playing a permanent rôle in the literary epithalamium[62], as evidences in Sappho, and Theocritus show: cf. the exaltation of the groom in Sappho *Frg.* 112, 1-2 L.-P. ὄ λ β ι ε γάμβρε, σοὶ μὲν δὴ γάμος ὡς ἄραο / ἐκτετέλεστ᾽ ἔχῃς δὲ πάρθενον †ἄν† ἄραο and in Theocritus' epithalamium (18, 16 f. ὄλβιε γάμβρ᾽ ἀγαθός τις ἐπέπταρεν ἐρχομένῳ τοι ἐς Σπάρταν. It is understandable why the μακαρισμός recurs in Statius' epithalamium (*Sil.* 1,2,236 f.) *felices utrosque uocant, sed in agmine plures / inuidere uiro.*

The absence of this motif in Catullus is even more surprising since the μακαρισμός was considered of good wish in the wedding ceremony: cf. the words with which the chorus addresses Peleus, complaining that he has been left ἄτεκνος and ἔρημος, in Eur. *Androm.* 1218: μάτην δέ σ᾽ἐν γάμοισιν ὤλβισαν θεοί and also in Ouid. *Met.* 12,215 ff. (with regard to Pirithous and Hippodamia) *ecce canunt Hymenaeum et ignibus atria fumant, / cinctaque adest uirgo matrum nurumue caterua / praesignis facie; felicem diximus*

59. Cf. the comment of R. KANNICHT, *Euripides. Helena*, II, Heidelberg 1969, 189; following G. Zuntz, however, he attributes ll. 639 ff. to Helen.

60. *Erot. Gr.* IV 33, p. 177, 47 Hirschig (with regard to Daphne and Cloe's wedding) ὅλη γὰρ ἐκίττα ἡ πόλις ἐπὶ τῷ μειρακίῳ καὶ τῇ παρθένῳ καὶ εὐδαιμόνιζον μὲν ἤδη τὸν γάμον· ηὔχοντο δὲ καὶ τὸ γένος ἄξιον τῆς μορφῆς εὑρεθῆναι τῆς κόρης.

61. *Erot. Gr.* I 1, p. 416, 69 Hirschig (with regard to Chaireas and Callirhoes's wedding) πάντες δὲ Χαιρέαν μὲν ἐθαύμαζον, Καλλιρρόην ἠ᾽ἐμακάριζον.

62. On the passage of the μακαρισμός to the epithalamium cf. LEJEUNE DIRICHLET, *De ueterum macarismis*, cit., 34: "Apparet usitatum fuisse praedicare sponsum et sponsam in ipsis nuptiis ob pulchritudinem, generis nobilitatem, cetera bona quibus matrimonium felix ac faustum redditur. Quibus praedicationibus uulgus palam testatur admirationem suam, nouae nuptae et mariti laetitiae participem se praebet. Hac consuetudine factum est, ut macarismi formula transiret in genus carminum, quae in nuptiis cantabantur, epithalamii sive hymenaei."

illa / *coniuge Pirithoum, quod paene fefellimus omen* and the right conclusions of Dirichlet[63].

Catullus' annotators traditionally cite a fragment of the neoteric poet Ticidas as parallel with ll. 107 ff., but they do not draw the necessary conclusion: *Frg.* 1 Morel *felix lectule talibus* / *sole amoribus:* it is significant that the exaltation of the bed appears in a fragment that, according to Priscian. *Gramm.* II 189,2 K., belonged to a hymenaeus and, moreover, in glyconics: in Ticidas' epithalamium, then, whose fragment still existing has certainly exerted some influence on Catullus, there was the μακαρισμός of the nuptial bed. Such a motif pertains to the category of μακαρισμοί, frequently employed by Hellenistic poets and by their Latin imitators, of things related to one's beloved: cf. *Anth. Pal.* 5, 171 (Meleag.) τὸ σκύφος ἀδὺ γέγηθε · λέγει δ'ὅτι τᾶς φιλέρωτος / Ζηνοφίλας ψαύει τοῦ λαλιοῦ στόματος · / ὄλβιον · εἴθ᾽ ὑπ᾽ἐμοῖς νῦν χείλεσι χείλεα θεῖσα / ἀπνευστὶ ψυχὰν τὰν ἐν ἐμοὶ προπίοι, 12, 208, 1-4 (Strat.) εὐτυχές, οὐ φθονέω,βιβλίδιον·ἦ ῥά σ᾽ἀναγνούς / παῖς τις ἀναθλίβει πρὸς τὰ γένεια τιθείς / ἢ τρυφεροῖς σφίγξει περὶ χείλεσιν ἢ κατὰ μηρῶν / εἰλήσει δροσερῶν, ὦ μακαριστότατον, Ouid. *Her.* 18,15 ff. *protinus haec scribens "felix i littera" dixi* / *"iam tibi formosam porriget illa manum.* / *Forsitan admotis etiam tangere labellis,* / *rumpere dum niueo uincula dente uolet"*[64]. On the very theme of the μακαρισμός of the bed cf. Prop.2, 15, 1 f. *o me felicem! o nox mihi candida! et o tu* / *lectule deliciis facte beate meis*[65] and Martial. 10,38,7 *felix lectulus.*

Therefore I believe that in the missing part after l. 107 of c.61 there must have been the τόπος of the μακαρισμός of the bed (like in Ticidas' epithalamium), all the more so as, in this case, the motif would be followed (in the strophe celebrating Manlius' erotic *gaudia*) by another analogous and traditional motif: the praises of love bliss, for which cf. Theocr. 12,34 ὄλβιος ὅστις παισὶ φιλήματα κεῖνα διαιτᾷ, Bion. 12(9), 1 ὄλβιοι ⟨οἱ⟩ φιλέοντες

---

63. G. LEJEUNE DIRICHLET, *De ueterum macarismis,* cit., 35: "Apparet sensisse ueteres in talibus macarismis ominandi quandam facultatem. Hac igitur formula pronuntiata commodum aliquod euenturum putabant."

64. Cf. G. LEJEUNE DIRICHLET, *De ueterum macarismis,* cit., 42.

65. In Propertius, perhaps, one could also compare 2,6,23 *felix Admeti coniunx et lectus Vlixis,* where, anyway, *lectus Vlixis,* according to Enk *ad loc.,* means *coniugium Vlixis* and designates Penelope.

ἐπὴν ἴσον ἀντεράωνται and other instances cited by Dirichlet.[66]

Whatever the subject of the strophe, however, it is sure that it followed Hellenistic patterns and schemes: as a matter of fact, the invocation to the bed is of Hellenistic origin, often in connection with the one to the *amorum conscia* oil-lamp[67]: indeed, the invocation to the bed recurs in Philodemus (*Anth. Pal.* 5,4,5 f.) σὺ δ', ὦ φιλεράστρια κοίτη, / ἤδη τῆς Παφίης ἴσθι τὰ λειπόμενα and in the above mentioned Ticidas' fragment (*Frg.* 1 Morel); the Hellenistic technique was promptly accepted by Propertius[68] and afterwards resumed by Apul. *Met.* 1,6 *"iam iam grabattule"*, inquam, *"animo meo carissime, ... conscius et arbiter"*. As for the frequent invocations to the oil-lamp see e.g. Philodemus' epigram, combining the two motifs, and also *Anth. Pal.* 5,5,1 f. (Statil. Flacc.); 7,1 (Asclepiad.); 8,1 (Meleag.). Abel[69] thinks it possible that the motif already existed in Sappho; but this is a mere inference, because the only proof he brings is the presence of the invocation to the bed in Ticidas and Catullus; in my view, it is highly unlikely that this technique might be pre-Hellenistic.

Candido pede lecti (l. 108) raises another problem: *candidus* is commonly interpreted as meaning "ivory-like"[70] and, considering the phrase complete as it is, the adjective is referred to the bed's foot: due to the lacuna of the text, it would be advisable to be more cautious, because on the grounds of ll. 9-10 (where *niueo ... pede*, attributed to Hymen, clearly connotes a peculiarity of the bride) one could imagine that also *candido pede* is related to Junia.

Refinement of images and expressions is present in the strophe that describes the quantity and intensity of the groom's erotic *gaudia*: notice the triple anaphora of *quae*,[71] interrupted and

66. G. LEJEUNE DIRICHLET, *De ueterum macarismis*, cit., 42.

67. Cf. J. SVENNUNG, *Cat. Bilderspr.*, cit., 107.

68. Cf. the above-cited case of 2,15,1; on the mentioning of the bed in Greek and Latin love songs cf. the examples quoted by B. LIER, *Ad topica carminum amatoriorum symbolae*, Stettin 1914, 45-46.

69. W. ABEL, *Die Anredeformen bei den römischen Elegikern*, Diss. Berlin 1930, 16.

70. Cf. R. ELLIS, *A Commentary on Catullus*, cit., 224, W. KROLL, *Cat.*, cit., 115 and C.J. FORDYCE, *Catullus*, cit., 247.

71. On this type of anaphora cf. the instances reported and analyzed by ÉVRARD-GILLIS, *La récurrence lexicale dans l'oeuvre de Catulle*, cit., 206.

varied by *quanta*, and the presence of the etymological figure *gaudia* ... *gaudeat*: further archaic and classic evidences of *gaudium gaudere* are Ter. *Andr.* 964 *hunc scio mea solide solum gauisurum gaudia* and Cael. *ap.* Cic. *Fam.* 8,2,1 *ut suum gaudium gauderemus.* On the basis of these indications, commentators suppose that this phrase belongs to *sermo communis*[72]: but Heinz Haffter, in his fundamental study of archaic poetic language, warns us against labelling *gaudia gaudere* as a formula of popular language, and underlines that "Umgangssprache" (Caelius' epistle to Cicero) and elevated poetry (Catullus' c. 61) "jede für ihren individuellen Zweck, von einem gleichen stilistischen Mittel Anwendung machen können"[73]; in the case in question, then, the *figura etymologica* is employed to eighten the stylistic level of the context.

As concerns lexicon, the use of *erus* is remarkable: it often recurs in archaic language (Plautus and Terentius), but practically disappears in classic prose.[74] For Catullus *erus* represented a refined synonym of *dominus*, endowed with a flavour of obsolescence and specifically appropriate for the invocation to the personified bed: Heusch had pointed out that "*erus* ist besonders der Herr vom Diener aus gesehen, enthält also oft ein gefühlsbetontes, subjektives Moment im Gegensatz zu dem objektiven Begriff *dominus*, der auch ausserdem den Besitzer von Sachen kennzeichnet. So findet sich *erus* oft in Anreden auch von Göttern und Göttinnen, zu denen der Mensch das Gefühl der Dienerschaft und Untergebenheit ausdrücken will. Handelt er sich aber doch um den Besitzer von Sachen, so sind diese meist personifiziert, so dass ein Gefühlsmoment hier in analoger Weise,

210-211. As for the case of anaphora of ll. 110-111, the parallelism is proved by the fact that the two terms *nox*/*dies* represent an antinomy; R. JAKOBSON, *Le parallélisme grammatical et ses aspects russes*, in: *Questions de poétique*, Paris 1973, 252 rightly observes on this point: "le rapprochement de mots antonymes est un procédé marquant du parallélisme". For the change *quae* ... *quanta* cf. Plaut. *Aul.* 808, Hor. *Sat.* 1,5,43 and E. TESTORELLI, *Analisi stilistica della satira 1,5 di Orazio*, Lugano 1977, 109.

72. Also for RONCONI, *Studi catulliani*, cit., 20 the formula *gaudia gaudere* is "prettamente *umgangssprachlich*".

73. H. HAFFTER, *Untersuchungen zur altlateinischen Dichtersprache*, Berlin 1934, 15.

74. The only certain evidences are in *Rhet. Herenn.* 4,63; Cic. *Off.* 2,24; *Rep.* 1,64; Varr. *L.L.* 10,12.

wie wenn es sich um Diener und Herren handelt, mitschwingt".[75]

With regard to the dative after the verb *uenire*, it is not a case of dative of direction, as someone asserts: as a matter of fact, such a use is never to be found before Virgil: Catullus still follows the archaic practice, according to which the dative case in connection with *uenio* is a dative of interest.[76] Finally, we must take into consideration the "iunctura" *uaga nocte*, recalling the Θοὴ νύξ of Hom. *Il.* 10,394 or the description of the chariot of the night in Enn. *Scaen.* 112 f. V.[2] *(nox) quae caua caeli / signitenentibus conficis bigis*, resumed by Verg. *Aen.* 5,721 *nox atra polum bigis subiecta tenebat*, 8,407 *medio iam noctis abactae / curriculo.*[77]

75. H. HEUSCH, *Das Archaische i. d. Sprache Catulls*, cit., 42.
76. Cf. E. LÖFSTEDT, *Syntactica*, I[2], Lund 1942, 182.
77. Cf. C.J. FORDYCE, *Catullus*, cit., 247.

CHAPTER V

THE DEDUCTIO AND THE FESCENNINA IOCATIO

The bride leaves her old home and the poet-coryphaeus, seeing that she is coming nearer, invites the *pueri* to raise the torches and the maidens[1] to repeat the ritual refrain in Hymen's honour. Catullus' love for colour elements is remarkable here as well as in other cases: the detail of the bride's progression that impresses his imagination is the *flammeum*, and he underlines it by saying: *flammeum uideo uenire* (l. 115). Now the *deductio* can start and the *fescennina iocatio* can be given free play.

The *deductio* is divided into two parts: ll. 114-148, containing the *fescennina iocatio*, whose words accompany the phases of the ceremony till the arrival to the groom's house, and ll. 149-183, where the next stages up to the *collocatio* are described. The *fescennina iocatio* itself can be divided into two parts: the longer one presents the jesting about the groom and, above all, about his *concubinus*, now neglected by him (ll. 124-143); the other one consists in one strophe only (ll. 144-148), in which the bride is invited to satisfy her husband's erotic desires, *ni petitum aliunde eat*. Lines 114-123 announce the *deductio* and at the same time introduce, by means of the mentioning of the *concubinus*, the fescennine jokes.

> tollite, ⟨o⟩ pueri, faces:
> flammeum uideo uenire.   115
> ite concinite in modum
> "Hymen o Hymenaee io,
>   Hymen o Hymenaee".   (125)

---

1. Compare what has been said with regard to ll. 36-45.

ne diu taceat procax
Fescennina iocatio,   120
nec nuces pueris neget
desertum domini audiens
concubinus amorem.   (130)

As regards the description of the waiting before the bride's door,
I have already pointed out that the probable source of inspiration
is Callimachus (the waiting for Apollo's epiphany in hymn 2)[2];
possibly, the image of the sudden coming out of the bride is
derived from Callimachus too: it may have been suggested to
Catullus by Athena's epiphany, often invoked (cf. l. 33, 43, 55)
and waited for a long time, in Callimachus' hymn 5: cf. ll. 137-139
ἔρχετ' Ἀθαναία νῦν ἀτρεκές . ἀλλὰ δέχεσθε / τὰν θεὸν, ὦ
κῶραι, τὦργον ὅσαις μέλεται, / σὺν τ'εὐαγορίᾳ σὺν τ'εὔγμασι
σὺν τ'ὀλολυγαῖς. But it is only a starting point, for the description of the phases of the deductio, with the fescennina iocatio,
the concubinus, the praetextatus and the pronubae, reproduces
customs of the Roman world.

Typically Roman is the motif upon which Catullus dwells most,
the fescennina iocatio,[3] although not all the critics share this view:
according to Gow "the obscene jokes ... were no doubt as regular
a feature of Greek marriage ritual as of Roman".[4] He cites Hesiod
and Aristophanes: but at ll. 281 ff. of the Scutum it is only said:
ἔνθεν δ'αὖθ'ἑτέρωθε νέοι κώμαζον ὑπ'αὐλοῦ, / τοί γε μὲν αὖ
παίζοντες ὑπ'ὀρχηθμῷ καὶ ἀοιδῇ / ... πρόσθ'ἔκιον: there is
no mentioning, then, of obscene jokes concerning the bride and
groom; it is equally impossible to put on the same level of the
Roman fescennina iocatio the spicy words exchanged by Trigeus
with the chorus in the finale of Aristophanes' Peace (l. 1333 ff.).

2. The mimetic description of the god's epiphany, matching the technique
employed by Catullus, is now acutely pointed out by F. WILLIAMS, Callimachus Hymn to Apollo, cit., 15.
3. Cf. WISSOWA in "R.E.P.W." VI 2 (1909) 2222 f.; even though the
question of its origins has not found a definite answer, the most probable
hypothesis is that it derives from Fescennium, a Faliscan town in the south
of Etruria: cf. Seru. ad Verg. Aen. 7,695, Paul. ap. Fest. 76,6 L., Porph. ad
Hor. Epist. 2,1,145. Cf. also F. LEO, Geschichte der römischen Literatur,
Berlin 1913, 17 and E. FRAENKEL in "Gnomon" 32 (1962) 257.
4. A.S.F. GOW, Theocritus, II, Cambridge 1950, 351.

On the other hand, when comparing Catullus with Theocritus we see the different ways of dealing with the motif in Greece and Rome: how unlike the jesting of the *fescennina iocatio* in c. 61 is from the benevolent reproaches to the groom (Menelaus) in Theocritus 18,9-15, where the "pointe" is reached by the insinuation that he is sleepy because he has drunk too much wine! The main difference between the Greek and the Roman habits seems to be the fact that in Greek wedding songs the obscene jokes never concern past life – like those referred to Manlius in c. 61 – but they appear limited to the future erotic intercourse of the couple,[5] or, like in Sapph. 111 L.-P., to the praises of the exceptional manliness of the groom, when he is on the point of joining the bride in the thalamus. One could even suppose that the very absence of such a custom in Greece and, consequently, the absence of this theme in literary epithalamia (or sometimes, perhaps, its presence in the form of malitious allusions, like in Sappho and in Theocritus), led Catullus to moderate the tones of his fescennine, where there is no trace of the obscene words uttered in the real ceremony: Catullus' target is practically the *concubinus*, whereas he does not exaggerate the ironic badinage to the groom and ignores that to the bride almost completely. Therefore, we can agree with Gordon Williams' conclusion that "no choir would have sung the jokes in a Grecising hymn at a real wedding, and so Catullus has accommodated the obscenities to their present artistic setting, contenting himself with the relatively mild joke about a disappointed *concubinus*. This is not to be taken seriously: it is a mere *iocatio*".[6] This attitude of Catullus is another proof that this wedding song is not meant for a practical purpose (i.e., accompanying the various stages of the real ceremony), but it is a literary creation.

A fundamental feature that distinguishes the Greek *deductio* from the Roman one, and that demonstrates that Catullus describes Roman habits, is represented by the structure of the wedding procession[7]: in Greece the *deductio* took place after the

5. Like in Theocr. 18,54 ff.: furthermore, in Theocritus this is the stage of the epithalamium proper.
6. G. WILLIAMS in "Journ. Rom. Stud." 48 (1958) 16.
7. Cf. DAREMBERG-SAGLIO III 1651, J. HECKENBACH in "R.E.P.W." VIII 2 (1913) 2130.

wedding banquet (compare the setting of Catullus' c. 62); the procession was headed by the προηγητής,[8] who preceded the coach in which the bride and groom sat with the παράνυμφος: the latter, also called πάροχος or νυμφευτής,[9] was one of the groom's friends and took the couple to the husband's house. After the coach there were the νυμφεύτρια – whose task was to escort the bride[10] – and the bride's parents: her mother carried the δᾷδες νυμφικαί, the wedding torches testifying the legitimacy of the marriage.[11] The παῖδες προπέμποντες followed, singing hymns in Hymen's honour, and the couple's relatives and friends.

There are evident reasons, then, to exclude the hypothesis of Greek influences on Catullus' description of the phases of the *deductio*: the chief difference consists in this, that while Catullus, conforming to the Roman ritual, makes Manlius wait for Junia inside the house, in Greece the groom participated in the *deductio*, unless he was getting married for the second time: in that case a friend, called νυμφαγωγός,[12] took his place in the *deductio*; in Greece, moreover, the coach was used only very rarely.[13]

Another typically Roman motif is that of *nuces dare*, to which there are allusions in ll. 121, 123, 128 and 133. The detail of the groom throwing the nuts to the *pueri* (cf. Paul. *ap.* Fest. 172 L.

8. Cf. Hyper. 1,5 Kenyon ἀνάγκη γάρ ... πρῶτον μὲν ὀρεωκόμον καὶ προηγητὴν ἀκολουθεῖν τῷ ζεύγει, ὃ ἦγεν τὴν γυναῖκα, ἔπειτα δὲ παῖδας τοὺς προπέμποντας αὐτὴν ἀκολουθεῖν καὶ Διώξιππον, Hesych. s.v. προηγητής· ὁ προηγούμενος τοῦ ζεύγους ... καὶ ὁ χειραγωγὸς τοῦ τυφλοῦ.
9. Cf. Poll. 3,40 ὁ δὲ καλούμενος παράνυμφος νυμφευτὴς ὀνομάζεται καὶ πάροχος.
10. Cf. Poll. 3,41 ἡ δὲ διοικουμένη τὰ περὶ τὸν γάμον γυνὴ νυμφεύτρια.
11. Cf. Schol. Eur. *Phoen.* 344, Schol. Eur. *Troad.* 315 and E. SAMTER, *Geburt, Hochzeit und Tod*, Leipzig 1912, 72.
12. Cf. Hesych. s.v. νυμφαγωγός · ὁ μετερχόμενος ἑτέρῳ νύμφην καὶ ἄγων ἐκ τοῦ πατρὸς οἰκίας, ᾧ πρότερον γεγαμηκότι οὐκ ἔξεστι μετελθεῖν · διὸ ἀποστέλλουσι τῶν φίλων τινάς . Διαφέρει γὰρ ὁ νυμφαγωγὸς τοῦ παρόχου · καλεῖται γὰρ πάροχος τῶν φίλων τις ὁ ἐπὶ τῷ ὀχήματι ἅμα τῇ νύμφῃ καὶ τῷ νυμφίῳ ὀχούμενος, οἷον παράνυμφος, Poll. 3,41 ὁ δ' ἄγων τὴν νύμφην ἐκ τῆς τοῦ πατρὸς οἰκίας νυμφαγωγός, ὁπότε μὴ ὁ νυμφίος μετίοι · οὐ νενόμιστο δὲ μετιέναι τοὺς δευτερογαμοῦντας.
13. Cf. Poll. 3,40 ἐπὶ ζεύγους γὰρ τὰς νύμφας ὡς τὸ πολὺ μετῄεσαν · εἰ δὲ πεζῇ ἀφίκοιτο ἡ νύμφη, χαμαίπους ἐλέγετο.

nuces flagitantur nuptis et iaciuntur pueris, Seru. *ad* Verg. *Buc.*
8,30 *ut rapientibus pueris fiat strepitus*) belonged to a traditional
aspect of wedding ceremonies, according to what is attested in
Verg. *Buc.* 8,30 *sparge marite nuces* and Plin. *Nat. Hist.* 15,86
nuces iuglandes ... nuptialium Fescenninorum comites. On the
origin of this custom many unlikely hypotheses have been handed
down from ancient times[14]; Festus asserts that it was simply done
to wish the couple well.[15] Servius, in his commentary on *Buc.* 8,
30, provides a series of fanciful explanations: 1. in Varro's opinion,
the throwing of the nuts was required to celebrate the wedding
Iouis omine, because nuts *in tutela sunt Iouis, unde et iuglandes
uocantur, quasi Iouis glandes*; 2. the noise of the nuts was necessary to drown the moaning of the bride *uirginitatem deponen-
tis*; 3. the noise of the nuts caused a *tripudium solistimum,*
representing the best auspice *ad rem ordiendam*[16]; 4. the noise of
the nuts and the din of the *pueri* helped *ne quid noua nupta
audiat aduersum, quo dies nuptiarum dirimatur*; 5. nuts produce
an aphrodisiac effect. Servius' own hypothesis, on the contrary,
is particularly interesting as regards Catullus' text; he maintains
that, by throwing the nuts, the paramours meant the abandon-
ment of childish games: *nam meritorii pueri, id est catamiti,
quibus licenter utebantur antiqui, recedentes a turpi seruitio nuces
spargebant, id est ludum pueritiae, ut significarent se puerilia
cuncta iam spernere.* This is the same theory as the one suggested
by Catullus; since it is the only case, besides Catullus, in which
the *concubinus*, and not the husband, throws the nuts – as it is
unanimously attested by tradition and seems more logical – it is
highly likely that Servius' hypothesis depends on Catullus' use of
it in c. 61. The most reliable explanation of the meaning of this
habit is that the groom's act symbolizes his giving up the games
pertaining to childhood: it is indeed well known that nuts were

14. I cite them for Catullus implicitly gives his own explanation of the
habit.

15. Paul. *ap.* Fest. 172 L. *nuces flagitantur nuptis et iaciuntur pueris,
ut nouae nuptae intranti domum noui mariti secundum fiat auspicium.*

16. This explanation is criticized by Pliny, who provides his own improbable one (*Nat. Hist.* 15,86), according to which the double covering of
nuts symbolizes a solid union: cf. J. ANDRÉ, *Pline l'Ancien. Histoire
naturelle, Livre XV*, Paris 1960, 107.

commonly used in children games[17] and that the phrase *nuces ponere (relinquere)* meant the end of childhood.[18]

This is a further proof of the fact that Catullus does not follow the real ceremony strictly, but he varies it at will: not only does he refer the act to the *concubinus* instead of the husband, but he also anticipates the moment when it happens: in the proper wedding, in fact, the throwing of the nuts could not take place during the *deductio*, because the groom did not participate in it; it occurred at the end of the *deductio*, when the wedding procession arrived at the husband's house. By attributing the act to the *concubinus*, Catullus, apart from changing an actual element again, in accordance with a frequent practice in the poem, shifts the reader's attention to the *concubinus*, hinting, in this way, that he and not the bride and groom will be the main target of the jokes of the *fescennina iocatio*.

Who does the poet-coryphaeus refer to at l. 114? For Gordon Williams, the *pueri* are the bride's companions and this would therefore be a new element in the Roman ritual, "for the bride was closely accompanied by three boys, two of them supporting her and one carrying a torch of whitethorn".[19] He repeats Riese's hypothesis, according to whom "der Dichter sieht ... die Braut endlich aus dem Hause erschienen und fordert die *pueri (prae-textati)* auf, die Fackeln ... zu ergreifen, und die Menge, während der *domum deductio* echt römische Lieder zu singen".[20] In Roman ceremonies, unlike the Greek habits above mentioned, the bride was accompanied by three *pueri patrimi et matrimi*,[21] two of them supporting her, while only one carried the torch of whitethorn, lit at the hearth of the bride's house.[22] At l. 114,

17. Cf. Hor. *Sat.* 2,3,171; Suet. *Aug.* 83 and see M. MANSON in "Mél. Éc. Fr. Rome" 90 (1978) 260.

18. Cf. Martial. 14,185,2 *ne nucibus positis "arma uirumque" legas*, Pers. 1,10 *nucibus facimus quaecumque relictis*.

19. G. WILLIAMS, *Tradition and Originality*, cit., 200.

20. A. RIESE, *Die Gedichte des Catullus*, cit., 121.

21. Cf. Fest. 282,22-25 L. *patrimi et matrimi pueri praetextati tres nubentem deducunt; unus, qui facem praefert ex spina alba, quia noctu nubebant; duo, qui tenent nubentem*.

22. Cf. Varr. *ap.* Non. 112,23-25 M. *cum a noua nupta ignis in face adferretur e foco eius sumptus, cum fax a spina alba esset et eam puer ingenuus anteferret*.

90

howcver, Catullus invites some *pueri*, and not only one, to lift the torches: this implies that the explanation is to be found somewhere else: it would surely not be surprising that Catullus, modifying again the ritual of the ceremony, introduces several torch-bearer *pueri praetextati*; but the previous mentioning of the sparkling torches (ll. 77-78; 93-94) make it more probable that Catullus' words refer to the παῖδες προπέμποντες: now that the fescennine takes the place of the hymenaeus it would be impossible for the chorus of maidens to sing the licentious songs related to the bridal pair; it is at this point that Catullus introduces – as Wilamowitz believed[23] – the chorus of torch-bearer *pueri*, singing the fescennine and alterning it with the refrain in Hymen's honour, as well as lighting with their torches the people participating in the wedding procession.

Which is the exact form of the refrain sung by the *pueri* in Hymen's honour? The problem is not easy to solve: codices read, at the beginning of the last glyconic of the strophe and of the following pherecratic, *io*, corrected by the vulgate into *o*; recent editors,[24] and some famous scholars with them,[25] accept *io* and consider it monosyllabic, *i* being a consonant. Martial 11,2,5 *clamant ecce mei "io Saturnalia" uersus* is usually cited as a case analogous with the one in question and supporting this solution; but there the prosody of the word is "fortasse ... ĭŏ potius quam jō, id quod etiam Leo apud Plautum statuit".[26] And certainly the indication in Terentianus Maurus (*De syllabis* 529 ff. = *Gramm.* VI 341 K.) that *io* is a disyllable must be of some significance: ἰῶτα *quis si praelocetur, tres uidemus uocales, / e quibus constare supra syllabam negauimus. / sic* ἰού ἰού *tragoedus Graius et ceryx donat, / sic io matres Latinae, sic Iulum dicimus; / quia duas edat necesse est syllabas, cum praedita est, / quas uidemus separatas esse uocales duas.* If we take into account, besides

23. U. v. WILAMOWITZ-MOELLENDORFF, *Hell. Dicht.*, cit., II 284: "Hier erst hören wir, dass die Fackeln von einem Knabenchor geschwungen werden, dem auch die Feszenninen zufallen".

24. Ellis, Kroll and – though with some hesitation – Fordyce.

25. It is sufficient to cite H.A.J. MUNRO, *Criticisms and Elucidations of Catullus*, Cambridge 1878, 135 ff., P. MAAS in "Philol." 66 (1907) 529 n. 8 and G.B. PIGHI in "Humanitas" 2 (1948/9) 47.

26. W. HERAEUS in his edition of Martial (Leipzig 1925, p. XLVII); cf. also E. FRAENKEL in "Gnomon" 34 (1962) 255.

Catullus, all the other instances for which it is possible to verify the prosody of *io*, in Plaut. *Pseud.* 702 f. and Apriss. *ap.* Varr. *L.L.* 6,68, we find *ĭŏ* for the *correptio iambica*, whereas Ouid. *Met.* 5,6 is respectful of the original prosody,[27] but admits the hiatus (*bis "io Arethusa, io Arethusa" uocauit*). It seems wiser, then, to accept the text of the vulgate, as Lachmann and Lucian Müller[28] do; anyway, this too is liable to serious objections: in the first place, I have observed already, with regard to l. 4, that there are no evidences, in the literary tradition of the hymenaeus, of *o Hymen* at the beginning of the invocation; and, above all, the synapheia would be destroyed, if we accept *o*, because we would have to admit either a hiatus or a *syllaba anceps* in more than a case: cf. l. 116 *modum* / *o*, 136 *abstine* / *o*, 146 *eat* /*o*, 151 *seruiat* / *o*, 156 *aduenit* / *o*, 161 *forem* / *o*, 166 *tibi* / *o*, 171 *magis* / *o*, 176 *uiri* / *o*, 181 *puellulam* / *o*. In order to avoid this difficulty, Riese[29] proposes to change the refrain into *Hymen o Hymenaee, io,* / *Hymen o Hymenaee*; the final syllable of the third glyconic of the strophe, then, would not be *anceps*, but long because of its position, neither would it originate a hiatus, for Catullus – in Riese's view, on the basis of an unknown theory – always regards the *H* of *Hymen* as a normal consonant: he mentions examples of an analogous use of it made by Catullus in 62,4 *dicetŭr hymenaeus*, 64,20 *despexĭt hymenaeos*, 66,11 *auctŭs hymenaeo* and Virgil in *Aen.* 10,720 *profugŭs hymenaeos*. I accept Riese's solution, but with no enthusiasm, since it is not devoid of obscure points itself: the technique used by Catullus in poems 62, 64, 66 and by Virgil in his Aeneid (14 times before *hymenaeus*) which was dealt with by Eduard Norden[30] to a great extent, is of Greek origins and was employed at the end of the hexameter. Is it possible that Catullus makes use of it also in the glyconic and the pherecratic?

27. On *io* deriving from ἰώ cf. WALDE-HOFMANN s.v.

28. L. MÜLLER, *De re metrica poetarum Latinorum praeter Plautum et Terentium libri septem*, Leipzig 1894[2], 369: "Formula usus certa, Catullus ponit hoc: *o Hymen Hymenaee io,* / *o Hymen Hymenaee*, ubi mira quadam peruicacia membranae habent *io Hymen*. Sed enim *i* in hac uocula, ut et Graecorum monstrat exemplum, semper uocalis."

29. A. RIESE, *Die Gedichte des Catullus*, cit., 112.

30. E. NORDEN, *Aen.*, cit., 438.

Now that the *deductio* has started with its picturesque procession, Catullus' language begins to become more colourful and
livelier: it is an anticipation of the use of the *sermo communis*
in the *fescennina iocatio* proper. *Procax*[31] is an adjective present
in comedies and mostly in prose; it is seldom employed with
reference to abstract nouns: besides Catullus, there is an instance
of it in Sall. *Cat.* 26,5 *sermone uti ... procaci*, in the description
of Sempronia, to whom *cariora semper omnia quam decus et
pudicitia fuit*; it is remarkable that Seneca use a similar adjective
(*dicax*) to define the fescennine: cf. *Med.* 113 *festa dicax fundat
conuicia fescenninus.* Furthermore, we must consider the use of
iocatio to define fescennine jesting: for *Thes.* VII 2,282,33 ff. this
is the only mentioning of the word in poetry; it recurs in *Rhet.
Herenn.* 3,23.25, in Cic. *Att.* 2,8,1, *Fam.* 9,16,7 and, at the end
of the fifth century, in Pomerius 3,6,4 (= LIX 482 B Migne). Anyway, abstract nouns ending in *-tio* represented a class "particularly
productive ... in the *sermo plebeius*"[32]; they were generally
avoided in poetry and in literary prose; in Catullus they are only
to be found in poems in various metres.[33]

Audio with the meaning of *intellego* (l. 122 *audiens*) is frequent
in comedies and in prose: cf. *Thes.* II 1287,34 ff.; Ferrero, on the
contrary, interprets *audiens* in the literal sense and, of course,
changes the value of the expression and the function of the jokes
referred to the *concubinus*: according to him, the paramour too
is far away; he will only get to know about the wedding indirectly
desertum domini audiens ... amorem; this dual being far away of
the two main characters of the fescennine song introduces – in
Ferrero's view – an atmosphere of moderation and a shade of
conventionality, only just hinted at, in the popular boorishness
of the jesting, resounding in the refrain *da nuces pueris.*[34] But
the presence of the *concubinus* during the *deductio* is required
by the *fescennina iocatio*.

---

31. Cf. A. KIESSLING - R. HEINZE, *Q. Horatius Flaccus. Oden und
Epoden*, Berlin 1960[10], 167: "Die *procacitas*, von *lasciuia* wesentlich ver-
schieden, richtet sich stets gegen einen anderen."
32. D.O. ROSS, *Style and Tradition*, cit., 111 f.
33. Cf. D.O. ROSS, *Style and Tradition*, cit., 112.
34. L. FERRERO, *Interpretazione di Catullo*, cit., 304.

Desertum domini audiens (l. 122 f.) is, in Kroll's opinion[35] "etwas gezwungen ausgedrückt" instead of the usual *dominus amorem (concubini) deseruit*; the structure will then be imitated by the author of the *Epistula Sapphica*, l. 155 *Sappho desertos cantat amores*. Finally, at l. 123 there is the first indication of *concubinus*, derived from *concubina* (normally employed from Plautus on), which reappears, after c. 61, in *Bell. Hisp.* 33,4 and in the prose of the first century A.D.; the only evidences in poetry, apart from Catullus, are in Martial. 6,22,1; 12,49,4, where, however, *concubinus* is synonymous with *adulter*.[36]

*

The *pueri* begin to sing the *fescennina iocatio*, the arrows of which are directed towards the *concubinus* and the groom. Two strophes of the fescennine are referred to the *concubinus*, two to the groom; but the *concubinus* is the target of the spiciest jokes: it is high time for him to give up the amusements of childhood and throw the nuts to the boys! He has enjoyed these childish games too much; now *lubet seruire Talasio*. In the next strophe the contempt of the *concubinus* for the *uilicae* is maliciously underlined and his destiny is foretold: the refined young man used to prefer the love-affairs offered by the town rather than the embraces with *uilicae*; but he will soon have what he deserves! The *cinerarius* will see to the cutting of his long hair. The mentioning of the *cinerarius* is not without an ironic meaning: the cutting of his hair is not entrusted to the *tonsor*, but exactly to the person who, in fact, should have looked after the *concubinus'* curls! The *cinerarius'* job was actually to warm the tongs used to curl the hair of matrons and, presumably, of *pueri delicati*.[37] The section dedicated to the *concubinus* ends with a new invitation

35. W. KROLL, *Cat.*, cit., 116.
36. Cf. *Thes.* IV 99,46 ff.
37. Cf. Varr. *L.L.* 5,129 *calamistrum, quod his calefactis in cinere capillus ornatur. Qui ea ministrabat, a cinere cinerarius est appellatus*, Pseudacr. *ad* Hor. *Sat.* 1,2,98 *cinerarii ... ab officio calamistrum i.e. ueruum in cinere calafaciendorum, quibus matronae capillos crispabant*. The "pointe" of Catullus' verse has been missed by F. MARX, *C. Lucilii carminum reliquiae*, II, Leipzig 1905, 95 ff., who asserts, in relation to Lucilius' *Frg.* 249: "Eundem esse cinerarium atque tonsorem ... Catullus docet."

to throw the nuts, expressed in words full of ironic compassion.
In the two strophes addressing the husband, after a hint at his
feeble enthusiasm on leaving his paramours and an invitation to
give up this habit, it is stressed that, after all, these pleasures were
lawful when he was single, but they would no longer be so when
he becomes a husband (*scimus haec tibi quae licent / sola cognita,
sed marito / ista non eadem licent*). With this facetious form of
praeterition, Catullus passes over the husband's past life and does
not undermine his dignity, which is in fact elevated by the grave
and concise tone of the warning[38]; but Catullus seems to be some-
how delighted to point out Manlius' qualities as a lover that made
the *nouus maritus* famous during his single life. In the strophes
dedicated to the husband the auspicious refrain in honour of the
god Hymen reappears.

> da nuces pueris, iners
> concubine! satis diu   125
> lusisti nucibus: lubet
> iam seruire Talasio.
> > concubine, nuces da.   (135)
>
> sordebant tibi uilicae,
> concubine, hodie atque heri: 130
> nunc tuum cinerarius
> tondet os. miser a miser
> > concubine, nuces da.   (140)
>
> diceris male te a tuis
> unguentate glabris marite   135
> abstinere, sed abstine.
> Hymen o Hymenaee io,
> > ⟨Hymen o Hymenaee.⟩   (145)
>
> scimus haec tibi quae licent
> sola[39] cognita, sed marito   140

---

38. L. FERRERO, *Interpretazione di Catullo*, cit., 305.
39. O. SKUTSCH's opinion in "Bull. Inst. Class. Stud. London" 16
(1969) 40 seems remarkable to me: "What we must look for is not 'you
know only what is permitted' (*fescennina iocatio* indeed!), but 'you are
familiar with what is permitted to a single man (*consuetudo glabrorum*), but
to a married man the same thing is not permitted'." He suggests that *sola*

ista non eadem licent.
Hymen o Hymenaee io,
Hymen o Hymenaee. (150)

It is pointless to keep on stating the Roman spirit of the fescennine, since I have underlined it previously; the ample part
occupied by the motif in c. 61 shows how attached Catullus was
to a peculiarly Roman archaic tradition; anyhow, the mere
mentioning of the technical expression *fescennina iocatio* proved
to the reader that Catullus, in this section of the poem, did not
reproduce Greek customs, but Roman ones.[40] On the same level
one should put the mentioning of *Talasius*, initially *uox nuptialis*
of the archaic ceremony,[41] later designating the Roman god of
marriage; the origins of the invocation to *Talasius*, become ritual
during the *deductio*, are uncertain[42]; but it is important to notice
that Catullus inserts the theme in the appropriate part of the
poem, where his connection with the Roman tradition of wedding
ceremonies is stronger than ever. A proof of this is the insistence
on the motif of the throwing of the nuts, which does belong to
the Roman tradition.

Although the Roman theme of this part of the poem is unquestionably Roman, Catullus does not − or maybe does not want
to − succeed in freeing himself completely from the literary traditions of Greek origins in this case either: even the fescennine
presents some scattered elements that Catullus may have derived
from Greek sources. A motif belonging to the tradition of the
epithalamium, and particularly emphasized by Catullus, is that
the married state necessarily implies the giving up all illicit affairs:
there is a reference to this in the rhetoricians' theory on *genus*;
Pseudo-Dionysius (VI 1, p. 263,9 ff. Usener-Radermacher) asserts

should be corrected into *soli* (Achilles Statius); but the difficulty is that no
instances exist of *solus* in the sense of *caelebs*. Compare then M. LENCHAN-
TIN DE GUBERNATIS, *Il libro di Catullo*, Torino 1966, 115: "La morale
romana era in proposito di manica larga e purché n,on si toccassero le
matronae honestae e i *liberi*, lasciava correre: cfr. Hor. *Sat.* 1,2."
    40. Cf. A.L. WHEELER, *Catullus and the Tradition*, cit., 197.
    41. Cf. Liu. 1,9,12.
    42. Cf. for the various theories C.J. FORDYCE, *Catullus*, cit., 248, R.M.
OGILVIE, *A Commentary on Livy. Books 1-5*, Oxford 1965, 69 and
R. SCHMIDT, *De Hymenaeo et Talassio*, Diss. Kiel 1886.

ὁ γὰρ γάμος εὐθὺς καὶ σωφροσύνης δόξαν περιτίθησι τοῖς ἀνθρώποις, καὶ οἱ τοιοῦτοι δοκοῦσιν τῆς μὲν ἀτάκτου μίξεως ἀπηλλάχθαι, πρὸς δὲ μίαν ἀφορᾶν μόνην τὴν ἑαυτοῦ ἕκαστος γυναῖκα. Soon after this, Pseudo-Dionysius explains the reason why Catullus insists on this motif, included in the fescennine, which could therefore be the least suitable part for such moral precepts: ἐκ δὲ τούτου καὶ ἐντιμοτέρους ἀνάγκη γίγνεσθαι τοὺς ἀνθρώπους καὶ πιστοτέρους δοκεῖν καὶ εὐνουστέρους περὶ τὰς αὐτῶν πατρίδας ἐν παντὶ διὰ τὸ ὥσπερ ὅμηρα δεδωκέναι ταῖς πατρίσι τοὺς ἑαυτῶν παῖδας, δι᾽οὓς ἀναγκαῖον καὶ μᾶλλον εἰς τὰς συμβουλίας παραλαμβάνεσθαι. Catullus implies this idea, without expressing it, both because its importance and dignity prevent its presence in connection with the fescennine jests and because he has already mentioned it in the image of the children that will defend their home-country (l. 71 ff.), apropos of the eulogy of sacred lawful marriages. The motif of marriage regarded as the renouncing of all illicit love affairs represents thus a τόπος of Greek origin, to which anyway Catullus seeks to lend a new vivacity by introducing it into the typically Roman section of the poem (i.e. the fescennine) and also by mentioning people present at the actual ceremony and the Roman habit of the throwing of the nuts.

There is no reason to believe that the reference to the *concubinus* is a literary τόπος; in all probability Catullus alludes to a real person, but in this case too he fuses real experience and literary tradition: Eduard Fraenkel[43] rightly attracts our attention to the fact that the hint at the cutting of the hair, joined with the poet's words of mock and ironic pity, echoes an analogous motif present in Anacreon *Frg.* 71 Gentili: καὶ κ[όμη]ς, ἥ τοι κατ᾽ἁβρόν / ἐσκία[ζ]εν αὐχένα. / νῦν δὲ δὴ σὺ μὲν στολοκρός, / ἡ δ᾽ἐς αὐχμηρὰς πεσοῦσα / χεῖρας ἀθρόη μέλαιναν / ἐς κόνιν κατερρύη / τλημόν[ω]ς τομῇ σιδήρου / περιπεσοῦσ᾽ . ἐγὼ δ᾽ἄσῃσι / τείρομαι . τί γάρ τις ἔρξῃ / μηδ᾽ὑπὲρ Θρήκης τυχών;[44]. Catullus finds a compromise solution and mixes Greek and Roman customs in the description of the husband's tasks during the

43. E. FRAENKEL in "Gnomon" 34 (1962) 259.
44. Cf. B. GENTILI, *Anacreonte*, Roma 1958, 52: "De pulchra agitur promissaque coma pueri eximia uenustate ... misere recisa; quo facinore subtiliter arguteque dolorem poeta dissimulat."

various phases of the ceremony: I have underlined already that in Greece the groom takes part in every phase of the wedding celebration, so also in the *deductio*, while in Rome he waits for the bride in the house where they will live together; Catullus follows the Roman tradition – it will be evident later on in the poem – and still in the fescennine he addresses Manlius as if he were participating in the *deductio*, according to the customs of Greece.[45]

Despite the presence of traditional elements of Greek epithalamia, however, one can surely assume that this is the most profoundly Roman part of the poem. Leonardo Ferrero has rightly pointed out the function of the fescennine and its position in the structure of the poem: not only does the fescennine occupy the central part of the poem, but, since it accompanies the bride's passage from her old to her new house, it also underlines a change in poetic perspective and the passage to the most humane and concrete aspect of the ritual drama. As the bride leaves her old home so the groom is invited to give up his past way of living.[46] The presence of this deep meaning too can justify Catullus' use of gentle and not too realistic tones in the *fescennina iocatio*.

The language here is the greatest change in comparison with the other parts of the poem, just because Catullus wants to emphasize the difference between the fescennine and the other sections by means of a style that could not be the same as he uses in the hymn. Most of the stylistic patterns present in the *fescennina iocatio* belong to the *sermo communis*. The "*iunctura*" *satis diu* pertains to comedies and prose; apart from the instances in Plautus and Terentius, the one in Catullus seems to be the only example to be found in poetry.[47] *Sordeo* (l. 129) + dative is typical of familiar language: it is proper to the "Umgangssprache"[48] to employ verbs indicating a bad smell or dirt to express a mild idea in a pregnant way (in this case *sordere* is synonymous with *displicere*); as concerns *sordeo* + dative, it is proved by the

45. Cf. A. RIESE, *Die Gedichte des Catullus*, cit., 124.
46. L. FERRERO, *Interpretazione di Catullo*, cit., 303.
47. *Thes.* V 1,1558,35 ff. attests its presence in Plaut. *Capt.* 792; Ter. *Eun.* 1085; Cic. *Cluent.* 202; *Marc.* 25.27; *Phil.* 13,10; *De orat.* 2,290; *Brut.* 324; *Bell. Alex.* 14,5; Liu. 9,36,10; Cels. 3,27,2; Sen. *Marc.* 24,1; *Epist.* 51, 13; 121,1; Quintil. *Decl. min.* 306, p. 203,28 Ritter; Papir. *Dig.* 48,16,18.
48. Cf. J.B. HOFMANN, *Lateinische Umgangssprache*, cit., 154.201.

presence of the same structure in Verg. *Buc.* 2,44 *et faciet quoniam sordent tibi munera nostra,*[49] Liu. 4,25,11 *adeo se suis etiam sordere nec a plebe minus quam a patribus contemni,*[50] Martial. 9,70,9 *non nostri* (scil. *mores*) *faciunt, tibi quod tua tempora sordent,* Stat. *Sil.* 1,3,98 *cur oculis sordet uicina uoluptas* and also Curt. Ruf.10,2,23; 10,8.[51] This verb, however, belongs to comedies also in its absolute sense: cf. Plaut. *Poen.* 315.1179; *Rud.* 222; *Truc.* 379.381; Horace only employs it in his *Epistulae* (1,11,4; 18,18), in contexts influenced by colloquial style.

As for *hodie atque heri* (l. 130), Kroll[52] follows Otto[53] and recalls πρώην τε καὶ χϑές attested in Herodot. 2,53; but it is unlikely that Catullus found inspiration in Greek sources; although the phrase *hodie atque heri* is present only here, such expressions recur in the language of comedies: cf. Plaut. *Most.* 953 *hodie atque heri, Rud.* 128 *aut hodie aut heri, Stich.* 152 *heri aut hodie.* A proof of the belonging of these "iuncturae" to familiar language is given by the fact that thus "certis positis infinitam quandam temporis diuturnitatem indicant"[54]; Ehlers in *Thes.* VII 2849,63 cites this reference in Catullus as one of the passages in which the simple *hodie* has the meaning of *usque ad hunc diem* (like *hodie atque heri* here); among the instances mentioned by him there is the significant case of Plaut. *Amph.* 177 f. *hodie qui fuerim liber, eum nunc / potuit pater seruitutis.*

With respect to *cinerarius* (l. 131), Hoppe in *Thes.* III 1061, 75 ff. thinks that this is the only evidence of the term to be found in poetry.[55] The verb *tondeo* is seldom used, with reference to people, in poetry, where in fact the normal *iunctura* is *tondere*

49. Lines 43-44 of the second Bucolic present various elements of prosaic language: cf. the commentary by J. PERRET, *Les Bucoliques*, Paris 1961, 31.
50. It is a context where *principes plebis* are dealt with; R.M. OGILVIE, *A Commentary on Livy*, cit., 575, observes with regard to this that it is "a good touch for plebeians to use coarse and plebeian language."
51. Cf. J. SVENNUNG, *Cat. Bilderspr.*, cit., 128.
52. W. KROLL, *Cat.*, cit., 116.
53. A. OTTO, *Die Sprichwörter und sprichwörtliche Redensarten der Römer*, Leipzig 1890, 164 s.v. *hodie.*
54. J. VAHLEN, *Opusc.*, II 219.
55. If we accept Marx's correction, *cinerarius* is attested also in Lucil. 249 f. M. *zonatim circum impluuium cinerarius … cludebat.*

capillum (Ouid. *Met.* 8,151) or *tondere comam* (Ouid. *Met.* 1,147; *Her.* 11,116).

The emphatic gemination *miser a miser* itself does not represent an element suitable for characterizing the style: it can pertain both to affectionate everyday language and to dignified poetry, for his particularly expressive nature[56]; as regards Catullus, Ronconi has underlined efficaciously that the gemination – like the anaphora in general – is not a distinctive feature of his style and can have a different explanation and appraisal each time, but it can and must always be a reason to appreciate his style, if one tries to see deeply into it to find out in what way and to what extent and for what purpose the poet employs it. Most commonly only the context tells us to which sphere of language this stylistic device is to be attributed each time.[57] The very formula *miser a miser* can help us to understand the accuracy of this view: in the case in question, the tone and character of the context show that Catullus uses it as an expression of affectionate and colloquial language; in this occasion too Ferrero proves that he has gathered the sense of Catullus' attitude by saying that the emphatic repetition of *miser a miser / concubine* echoes the burlesque parody of a pitiful expression.[58]

The use of *male* (l. 134) meaning *uix*, in connection with verbs, belongs to the comedy and to prose: *Thes.* VIII 243,21 ff. cites Plaut. *Curc.* 169, *Epid.* 607, *Pseud.* 208, *Trin.* 1048; it is remarkable that Cicero, besides *Catil.* 3,22 employs it in a Verrina (2,3,277) and in some epistles (*Att.* 5,20,5; *Fam.* 15,4,10). In poetry this device is frequent only from Ovid on; in the period after Catullus and before him there are only two instances in

---

56. Cf. J.B. HOFMANN - A. SZANTYR, *Lat. Syntax u. Stilistik*, 809 f.; J.B. HOFMANN, *Lateinische Umgangssprache*, cit., 58.

57. A. RONCONI, *Studi catulliani*, cit., 42.

58. L. FERRERO, *Interpretazione di Catullo*, cit., 304. The expression ἆ δειλέ (δείλαιε) is frequent in Greek poetry: cf. Theocr. *Epigr.* 6,1 and A.S.F. GOW, *Theocritus*, II, Cambridge 1965, 532, who quotes Hom. *Il.* 11,441.452; *Od.* 11,618; 18,389; *Anth. Pal.* 7,466. As for the repetition *miser a miser*, Mrs. ÉVRARD-GILLIS, *La récurrence lexicale dans l'oeuvre de Catulle*, cit., 113 underlines that it has the same value as a superlative, here and in 58,1-2; 62,60-61; 63,61; 64,26-27; 64,143-144. 403-404; 67,1; 91,2; 107,4-5. Cf. also what I have written in "Riv. Filol. Istr. Class." 106 (1978) 49 and n. 6.

Virgil (*Georg.* 1,360.448) and two in Horace, in his Satires and Epistles (*Sat.* 2,6,87; *Epist.* 1,20,15). *Vnguentatus* and *glaber* (l. 135) are favourite terms of comedies, although *glaber*, used as a noun, was the official way of designating a *puer delicatus*.[59] On *se abstinere a glabris* cf. maybe Lucil. 781 M. *utrum anno an horno te abstinueris a uiro.*[60] As for *haec ... quae licent* (l. 139) Fordyce observes that, if it is not rare to find a pronoun as the subject of *licet*, it is very rare, before the "silver" age, that this pronoun should be in the plural form.[61]

The same results are obtained when one shifts the analysis from the lexicon to the structure of the strophe: ll. 124-128 present the chiasmus of the first and last line (*da nuces ... nuces da*) and frequent repetitions (*nuces ... nucibus ... nuces; concubine ... concubine*). In the next strophe, apart from the gemination *miser a miser* and the usual repetition of the vocative *concubine*, the sequence of three adverbs of time (*hodie, heri, nunc*) is relevant at ll. 130-131. At ll. 134-136 the pleonasm *te a tuis* occurs, as well as the polyptoton with epanalepsis *abstinere sed abstine* at l. 136[62]; also in this circumstance, like in that of the gemination, Catullus certainly employs this device for its vividly suggestive character. Notice the repetition *haec ... quae licent ... ista non eadem licent* at ll. 139 ff.[63] Finally, it is worth considering the difference between the lively and aggressive tone of the

59. Cf. *Thes.* VI 2, 1998,39 ff.; 1999,11 ff.

60. The text of the fragment is controversial: *te abstinueris* is Scaliger's conjectural reading – not accepted, however, either by Marx or by Krenkel – instead of *te abstuleris* present in Nonius' codices.

61. C.J. FORDYCE, *Catullus*, cit., 249.

62. Cf. A. RONCONI, *Studi catulliani*, cit., 78.

63. An analogous play on words is in Cic. *Cael.* 48 *quando denique fuit ut quod licet non liceret?.* Cf. C.J. FORDYCE, *Catullus*, cit., 249. The repetition of the verb in a different form (*abstinere ... abstine*) is included by Mrs. ÉVRARD-GILLIS, *La récurrence lexicale dans l'oeuvre de Catulle*, cit., 50 among the examples in which a variation of the morphological characteristics of the term is privileged due to the repetition itself. Mrs. Évrard-Gillis observes that all these instances are verbs (4,14-5; 8,11-12; 21,1-3; 37,7-9; 45,20) and explains this circumstance by saying that "le verbe recevant différentes marques grammaticales, celles de voix, de mode, de temps, de nombre, de personne, une variation portant sur l'une de ces catégories est fortement ressentie, car elle se détache sur la coïncidence de plusieurs autres éléments."

refrain in the fescennine (*concubine, nuces da*) and the one in the hymn (*quis huic deo compararier ausit?*) or the one in the exhortation to Junia (*prodeas, noua nupta*).

All these reasons lead us to refuse Wheeler's conclusion definitely: according to him, even in the fescennine Catullus uses a refined and elevated language to violate the stylistic dignity of the poem.[64]

*

After addressing the *concubinus* and the groom, the fescennine jokes should be referred to the bride[65]; but when we consider the tone of ll. 144-146 we must admit that it is a mild and malicious warning how to behave in her married life, rather than an obscene motif: the wife's duty is to meet her husband's wishes, so he will not try to satisfy them elsewhere.[66]

> nupta, tu quoque quae tuus
> uir petet, caue ne neges,   145
> ni petitum aliunde eat.
> Hymen o Hymenaee io,
> Hymen o Hymenaee.   (155)

How is this attitude of Catullus' towards the bride to be explained? Does it spring from his respect for Junia or does it follow a

64. A.L. WHEELER, *Catullus and the Tradition*, cit., 198: "The intrusion of vulgar words would have violated the rather dignified tone and style of the poem. Thus in that part of the ceremony (the procession) in which the Greeks, according to the extant evidence, employed a song, Catullus substitutes the native element of the Fescennine verses, but in so doing he elevates this Roman element, 'epithalamizes' it, so to speak."

65. Cf. Varr. *Sat. Frg.* 10 Buecheler *pueri obscenis uerbis nouae nuptulae aures returant.*

66. I am not convinced of this chaste interpretation any longer. I think that P. PARRONI is right in "Riv. Fil. Istr. Class." 101 (1973) 490, when he asserts that here the poet implicitly advises the bride not to deny her husband *quod pueri dare solent*, because otherwise — one would assume on the basis of his past preferences — he might be tempted to resume his old customs; but now that he is married this would be unbecoming (ll. 140-141 *sed marito / ista non eadem licent*). This correct view is shared by F. DELLA CORTE, *Catullo. Le poesie*, cit., 294. Of course this changes my opinion that there are no stinging remarks towards the bride in the *fescennina iocatio.*

definite tradition? I believe that an answer to these questions may now be given, on the grounds of Gordon Williams' research,[67] who has proved that such instructions were not customary in Greece and therefore Catullus' sources must be Roman. The fundamental point of his demonstration is the analysis of the undoubtedly Roman (for its tone and themes) part of *Casina*, in which words of advice of a peculiar kind are addressed to the bride:[68] ll. 815-821 *sensim super attolle limen pedes, mea noua nupta. / Sospes iter incipe hoc, ut uiro tuo / semper sis superstes, / tuaque ut potior pollentia sit, uincasque uirum uictrixque sies, / tua uox superet tuumque imperium; uir te uestiat, tu uirum despolies. / Noctuque et diu ut uiro subdola sis, / opsecro, memento.* Paradoxically the affinity between Plautus' and Catullus' admonitions lies in this, that the warnings referred to Calinus – disguised as the bride – are the very opposite of those given to Junia.

According to the manuscripts, in Plautus it is the woman-slave Pardalisca who utters these instructions; but, it is well known, codices have no authority as for the attribution of cues.[69] On the contrary, it is preferable to agree with Williams on attributing ll. 815-821 to the matron Cleostrata, present on the stage herself, who would then fulfill the task of the *pronuba* in Roman wedding ceremonies. In Roman ceremonies, before the bride passed from her father's *potestas in manus* of her husband (cf. l. 56 *tu fero iuueni in manus*), the *pronuba* gave her a series of solemn admonishments that can be summarized in the invitation to be *morigera*. Williams' theory is indeed based on various passages in which there is always this adjective or the periphrasis (*uiro*) *morem gerere.*[70]

On carefully examining the meaning of ll. 144-146 of c. 61, we realize that the advice referred to Junia is after all that of being

67. G. WILLIAMS in "Journ. Rom. Stud." 48 (1958) 16-22.

68. In the burlesque ceremony of *Casina* in fact it is the slave Chalinus, disguised as a bride to make fun of old Lysidamus and the slave Olympio.

69. On this subject compare the fundamental studies of J. ANDRIEU, *Étude critique sur les sigles de personnages et des rubriques de scène dans les anciennes éditions de Térence*, Paris 1940; ID., *Le dialogue antique*, Paris 1954.

70. Cf. Naeu. *Com.* 90-91 R.³, Plaut. *Amph.* 839, *Cist.* 173 ff., *Men.* 787 f., *Most.* 188 f., 224-226, Lucr. 4,1278 ff. and also Ter. *Andr.* 282 ff.

morigera, i.e. *morem Manlio gerere*. By introducing a new change in the description of the phases of the ceremony, Catullus takes the place of the *pronuba* and includes and concentrates in the *fescennina iocatio* the admonitions she used to give to the bride; at the same time he strives to make these instructions match the atmosphere of the fescennine, by means of the cunning expression *ni petitum aliunde eat*.[71] In this way Catullus also establishes a logical connection with the immediately subsequent section of the poem; the tone of the fescennine is mitigated by the warnings to the bride and therefore, from the instructions how to behave towards her husband, Catullus can go on without any irksome hiatus to depict a quick sketch of connubial life – from the exact moment when she enters the groom's house till she reaches old age – in ll. 149-156.

It seems that Catullus tries to emphasize the difference between ll. 144-146 and the previous part of the fescennine from the stylistic point of view: otherwise one could not explain the presence of the archaic form *ni*, originally a mere negative particle, here used with an idea of purpose. Such a use is to be found also in Lucr. 3,286.734, Prop. 2,7,3 and in Virgil it is attested by Servius as for *Aen.* 3,686 and by Rufinianus (*Rhet. Lat. Min.* p. 56,7 Halm) as for *Aen.* 6,353.[72] I do not share Fordyce's opinion, then, for whom the use of *ni* "may be due to desire to avoid having two *ne*-clauses depending on the same verb".[73]

*

The second part of the *deductio* is divided into two distinct stages: ll. 149-163 describe the arrival of the procession in front

71. With regard to c. 61 it has been rightly pointed out by G. WILLIAMS in "Journ. Rom. Stud." 48 (1962) 22 that "when he came to the *Fescennina iocatio*, Catullus avoided impropriety and instead alluded to the instructions given to the bride by the *pronuba* to be dutiful to her husband in all things, and he jokingly adds the reason *ni petitum aliunde eat* to introduce something of the raillery that belonged to the occasion and connect the remark to what had already been said to her husband."

72. Cf. J.B. HOFMANN - A. SZANTYR, *Lat. Syntax u. Stilistik*, 535; E. NORDEN, *Aen.*, cit., 232 f.; H. HEUSCH, *Das Archaische i. d. Sprache Catulls*, cit., 126 ff.

73. C.J. FORDYCE, *Catullus*, cit., 249.

of the groom's house and the invitation to the bride to cross the threshold: the scene is therefore still laid outside. In ll. 164-183, on the other hand, Catullus describes the phases taking place inside the house: first the groom's attitude (ll. 164-173) and then the bride's arrival in the bedchamber and the *collocatio* (ll. 174-183).

Once the fescennine is over, Catullus imagines that the procession has reached the groom's house: he points it out to Junia and outlines swiftly the course of her future existence as a wife, from her going into the new home to the twilight of her life. The brief story of the events related to Junia presents a *klimax* analogous – though in a different tone – with the one concerning the groom, whose passage from the unrestrained life as a single man to the serious life as a husband has been dealt with in the fescennine song. The connection with the *fescennina iocatio* is represented, besides this analogy of the groom's past and future events to the bride's similar ones, also by the fact that in the strophe of the fescennine dedicated to Junia Catullus has described the first stage of her new life, that is, the concession of the first gift of love that will bind the husband and prevent him from searching other amusements in his youth:[74] in ll. 149-151 there is a hint at Junia's future condition as a rich and happy matron and housewife, and at old age that will make her head tremble (ll. 154-156). The last strophe instead provides a link with the following part through the invitation to cross the threshold *omine cum bono*.

> en tibi domus ut potens
> et beata uiri tui,   150
> quae tibi sine seruiat
> (Hymen o Hymenaee io,
>   Hymen o Hymenaee)   (160)
>
> usque dum tremulum mouens
> cana tempus anilitas   155
> omnia omnibus[75] annuit.
> Hymen o Hymenaee io,
>   Hymen o Hymenaee.   (165)

74. L. FERRERO, *Interpretazione di Catullo*, cit., 305.

75. On *omnia omnibus* cf. J. ÉVRARD-GILLIS, *La récurrence lexicale dans l'oeuvre de Catulle*, cit., 28.92.

transfer omine cum bono
limen aureolos pedes   160
rasilemque subi forem.
Hymen o Hymenaee io,
Hymen o Hymenaee.   (170)

Also in this section of the *deductio* tone and motifs are purely
Roman: I do not know on what basis Mangelsdorff can assert that
the theme of the praises of the groom's home (l. 149 f.) "geht
wahrscheinlich auf Sappho zurück"[76]; such hazardous hypotheses
have contributed to create the image of Sappho as Catullus'
supreme source of inspiration in c. 61. In fact, the idea expressed
in ll. 149-151 is typically Roman, for it exalts the power and
wealth of the household with a sense of pride, and not only does
it mention its *domina*, served by everybody, but also kindly asks
the *domina* to accept everybody's service (*quae tibi sine seruiat*).
If parallels had to be looked for, one could suppose, at the most,
that Catullus took inspiration from Theocritus to convey a
peculiarly Roman view: compare, as a matter of fact, the words
referred to Helen by the chorus of maidens in Theocritus' epithalamium (18,38): ὦ καλά, ὦ χαρίεσσα κόρα, τὺ μὲν οἰκέτις
ἤδη.

The custom described at ll. 159-161 is Roman: the bride's care
in going into her new house for the first time is never cited in
relation to the Greek ritual of marriage.[77] In Rome the *pueri
praetextati* helped the bride, or even lifted her when crossing the
threshold, lest she should stumble. An instance of the first habit
is in Plautus,[78] in the above-quoted passage from *Casina*, in which,
of course, the *pueri praetextati* are replaced with quite different
companions: cf. the advice given to the mock-bride (l. 815 f.):
*sensim super attolle limen pedes, mea noua nupta. / Sospes iter
incipe hoc.* The second habit is mentioned by Plut. *Quaest. Rom.*

76. E.A. MANGELSDORFF, *Lyr. Hochzeitsged.*, cit., 40.
77. Cf. G. WILLIAMS in "Journ. Rom. Stud." 48 (1958) 16.
78. Cf. G. WILLIAMS in "Journ. Rom. Stud." 48 (1958) 17: "The
Roman motif of the bride instructed to cross the threshold with care is
immediately apparent in the opening words. The hand of Plautus is
evident, however, not only in this Romanization but also in the fact that he
attaches the instruction to an inappropriate point. For here the bride is
merely leaving her old home, not crossing the threshold into the new."

29 τὴν γαμουμένην οὐκ ἐῶσιν αὐτὴν ὑπερβῆναι τὸν οὐδὸν τῆς οἰκίας, ἀλλ᾽ ὑπεραίρουσιν οἱ προπέμποντες. Many hypotheses have been handed down from the past as for the value of this act: in somebody's opinion, the bride was lifted, because the *pedis offensio* would mean bad luck on the wedding day itself, whereas according to others it would symbolize the *raptio* of archaic origin.[80] Further unlikely hypotheses are added by Varr. *ap.* Seru. *ad* Verg. *Buc.* 8,29 *quas etiam ideo limen ait non tangere, ne a sacrilegio incoharent, si depositurae uirginitatem calcent rem Vestae, id est numini castissimo, consecratam* and by Isid. *Orig.* 9,17,12 *moris ... erat antiquitus ut nubentes puellae simul uenirent ad limen mariti et postes, antequam ingrederentur, ornarent laneis uittis et oleo unguerent ... quae ideo uetabantur limen calcare, quod illic ianuae et coeant et separentur.* Saying *transfer omine cum bono* (l. 159) Catullus follows the first view, no doubt the most plausible one, for great importance was attached to the *pedis offensio*, especially at the beginning of a new occupation. On the *pedis offensio* cf. also Cic. *Diuin.* 2,84 *pedis offensio nobis... obseruanda est* and Tib. 1,3,19 f. *o quotiens ingressus iter mihi tristia dixi / offensum in porta signa dedisse pedem!*.

On the other hand, an Hellenistic influence is evident in the technique of interrupting a sentence with the refrain and continuing it soon afterwards: the same device is attested in Theocr. 2,103 ff. ἐγὼ δέ νιν ὡς ἐνόησα / ἄρτι θύρας ὑπὲρ οὐδὸν ἀμειβόμενον ποδὶ κούφῳ / (φράζεό μευ τὸν ἔρωθ᾽ ὅθεν ἵκετο, πότνια Σελάνα) / πᾶσα μὲν ἐψύχθην χιόνος πλέον κτλ.

But in ll. 149-163 it is the analysis of the style that presents the most interesting aspect: a sharp difference is indeed noticeable between the strophe underlining the solidity and wealth of the household and those describing Junia's old age and her entering the groom's house. The search for a elevated stylistic tone in ll. 149-151 can be detected a) in the anticipation of the subject after *en tibi*, a rare technique which contributes to stress the most

79. According to other sources it was the *pronuba* who lifted the bride: cf. E. SAMTER, *Geburt, Hochzeit und Tod*, cit., 134-146.
80. On this problem cf. K. MEISTER, *Die Hausschwelle in Sprache und Religion der Römer*, Sitzungsber. Heidelb. Akad. Wiss., Philol.-Hist. Klasse, 1924/5, 3. Abh.

relevant motif[81]; b) in the use of two adjectives, *potens* and *beatus*, that highlight the characteristics of the groom's *domus*; c) in the alliteration *sine seruiat*: it is significant that *sino* is a verb of sacral language, the use of which is discussed by Eduard Norden.[82]

In the next two strophes, on the contrary, affectionate and familiar language prevails, justified by both the hint at Junia's old age and the tenderness with which the poet describes her going into her husband's house: for *usque dum* cf. Plaut. *Asin.* 328 and Cat. *Agr.* 22,2[83]; *tremulus*, said *de senibus*, is a proverbial adjective, while the noun with which it is made agree (*tempus*) is rarely employed in the singular form as synonymous with *caput*.[84] *Anilitas* is Catullus' coinage, invented by analogy to nouns like *puerilitas, iuuenilitas* and *uirilitas*; it is a rather unlucky innovation, since *anilitas* will only recur in Isid. *Orig.* 11,2,28 *sicut a sene senectus, ita ab anu anilitas nominata est*; in Catullus the abstract noun *anilitas* is even made the subject of the sentence. The double accusative in connection with *transfero* (l. 159) is only to be found in *Bell. Alex.* 60,5 *Marcellus castra Baetim transfert*. Typical of affectionate language is *aureolus*, used not in the sense of *aureus* or *auratus*, but in that of *pulcher, egregius*; there are evidences of *aureolus* in comedies and in Lucilius, and it reappears in later authors.[85] The singular *foris* is frequent in comedies and in prose.[86]

I would not say that the description of the arrival in front of the groom's house is a successful part from the artistic point of view: above all in ll. 154-156 some effort is noticeable, on Catullus' part, to express an idea which was difficult to include

---

81. Cf. *Thes.* V 2, 547,17; *en tibi*, on the other hand, belongs to collo-quial style: cf. J.B. HOFMANN - A. SZANTYR, *Lat. Syntax u. Stilistik*, 93; but the ethical dative is used at the beginning with the intention of attracting Junia's attention by means of an expression of familiar language.

82. E. NORDEN, *Aus altrömischen Priesterbüchern*, cit., 130 ff.

83. Cf. J.B. HOFMANN - A. SZANTYR, *Lat. Syntax'u. Stilistik*, 615.

84. Cf. F. NEUE -C. WAGENER, *Formenlehre der lateinischen Sprache*, I³, Leipzig 1902, 669.

85. Cf. *Thes.* II 1488,53 ff.

86. Cf. C.J. FORDYCE, *Catullus*, cit., 250 e *Thes.* VI 1057,59 ff.; on *rasilis*, ξεστός, rather unconvincing remarks are made by K. LATTE in "Glotta" 32 (1952/53) 35 f.

in a wedding song; moreover, in order to introduce the eulogy of the noble family, while showing the new house to Junia, Catullus leaves out the description of the door, wreathed with flowers, as the custom of wedding ceremonies required, which would have accorded with his preference for the pictorial element. It seems to me that this is the most laboured strophe, alongside the too affected one on *Torquatus paruolus* at the end of the poem. Ferrero shares my opinion and thinks that it is one of the less successful points, where some Baroque mannerism of imagery, although stemming from a spontaneous sense of humour, forces both the expression and the structure with an artifice.[87]

*

Drawing a parallel with the previous strophe, Catullus puts an imperative at the beginning of ll. 164-168. It is a new invitation for the bride — whom Catullus follows ideally, now that Junia has crossed the threshold of the house — to turn her eyes to her husband: he is lying *Tyrio in toro* and, without concealing his desire, he is stretching full of passion towards Junia. On the intensity of the groom's passion Catullus insists at ll. 169-171, asserting that, even though the fire that makes the couple burn with desire is the same, Manlius' own one inflames him more deeply.

Penite magis (l. 171) has been debated by Otto Skutsch,[88] who suggests that *penite* should be changed into *perit en*; but in my view the expression may be accepted in a context in which Catullus, through hyperbolical imagery (cf. *totus immineat tibi* at l. 116), wants to point out Manlius' love wish; furthermore, saying that he burns with passion more deeply than his wife adds a touch of reserve and modesty to Junia, who cannot certainly be depicted as so desirous a woman as her manly husband.

87. L. FERRERO, *Interpretazione di Catullo*, cit., 298.
88. O. SKUTSCH in "Bull. Inst. Class. Stud. London" 16 (1969) 40: "No commentator explains how the statement that the groom is tortured no less than the bride by the flame 'deep inside', can be followed by 'but more deeply inside him' or 'but more so, deep inside him'." Against the correction made by O. Skutsch cf. now M. CITRONI in "Stud. Ital. Filol. Class." 51 (1979) 27.

The traditional interpretation (*penite magis* = "more covertly") has been resumed by Della Corte[89] for whom Catullus does not want to emphasize the different intensity of the passion, but he tries to explain that the man, in spite of his loving with the same intensity, has more self-control because his flame is more internal; he recalls Ps. Tib. 3,11,17 *optat idem iuuenis quod nos, sed tectius optat.* Nevertheless Citroni[90] has confirmed lately that in love contrasts usually each lover says that he (or she) loves more than the other one, so as to make the partner happy: telling Junia that Manlius' love is greater than hers is a complimentary remark: it implies that the woman is in a condition of superiority since she is the source of inspiration of the stronger feeling. Citroni rightly cites c. 45, where Acme answers (ll. 15-16) to Septimius' oath of love: *multo mihi maior acriorque / ignis mollibus ardet in medullis*; cf. also Theocr. 17,38-40.

> aspice intus[91] ut accubans
> uir tuus Tyrio in toro　　　　　　　　　165
> totus immineat tibi.
> Hymen o Hymenaee io,
> 　　Hymen o Hymenaee.　　　　　　　(175)
>
> illi non minus ac tibi
> pectore uritur intimo　　　　　　　　　170
> flamma, sed penite magis.
> Hymen o Hymenaee io,
> 　　Hymen o Hymenaee.　　　　　　　(180)

We have underlined already that the groom's absence during the *deductio* means that Catullus follows the Roman habit, in this

89. F. DELLA CORTE, *Catullo. Le poesie*, cit., 294.
90. M. CITRONI in "Stud. Ital. Filol. Class." 51 (1979) 26.
91. It is possible perhaps to keep *unus* as the manuscripts read: with regard to this, J. GRANAROLO observes (*L'oeuvre de Catulle*, cit., 340 n. 1): "peu importe qu'il s'agisse ou non d'une *cena nuptialis* (...), et que l'époux puisse ou non se trouver seul dans l'*atrium*! Le mot *unus* n'est pas synonime de *solus*. Comme l'a bien vu Ellis, le marié est *unus* tant qu'il n'a pas été rejoint par celle qui complétera le couple." F. DELLA CORTE, *Catullo. Le poesie*, cit., 103 accepting *unus* but conferring it the meaning of *solus*, translates: "guarda come, rimasto solo, tuo marito, disteso sul letto di porpora, tutto verso di te si protenda". Bardon too, in his Teubner edition, accepts *unus*.

circumstance in evident contrast with the Greek one: he imagines therefore that once the banquet at the bride's house is over at nightfall, Manlius has preceded the procession and waited for its arrival in the house. Now that the picturesque wedding procession, lighted by torches, has arrived in front of the groom's house, accompanied by the fescennine song and by the praises of Hymen; now that the bride has crossed the threshold with great care not to stumble, Catullus can show her Manlius, waiting for her, full of desire *accubans Tyrio in toro*.

Which *torus* does Catullus allude to and what is Manlius' condition? Riese and Ellis, on the basis of the normal meaning of *accubo*, maintain that Manlius is lying on a triclinium, surrounded by his friends, after banqueting; consequently the *cena nuptialis* would have taken place in the groom's house and the bride would have been excluded from it. Riese mentions[92] c. 62, where the situation is however thoroughly different from c. 61; if Catullus had really imagined Manlius giving a banquet, most likely he would have expressed the motif clearly and would have hinted at the presence of glad and joyful friends. In Rome it was possible that exceptionally the banquet might take place in the groom's house: but in that case the bride was there, at his side, during the *cena nuptialis*.[93] The only proof of some significance that could support Riese and Ellis' hypothesis is the linguistic one, i.e. the meaning of *accubo*; but true as it is that *accubo* is used *epulandi causa* in most circumstances, there are passages in which it is employed *quiescendi causa*, as a sheer opposite of *sto*.[94] No evidence then exists of a hint on Catullus' part at a banquet at the groom's house; nor should his silence be surprising on such a noteworthy detail of the ceremony: if Catullus does not mention the wedding banquet, it is due to the fact that it happened before the *deductio*, and it is from the *deductio* on — therefore the most picturesque stage of the ceremony — that he describes, even though with the greatest freedom, some particulars of the wedding.

92. A. RIESE, *Die Gedichte des Catullus*, cit., 126.
93. Cf. Cass. Dio 48,44,3; Iuuen. 2,120; Tac. *Ann.* 11,27 and L. FRIED-LÄNDER, *Darstellung aus der Sittengeschichte Roms*, I[9], Leipzig 1919, 275.
94. Cf. *Thes.* I,339,61 ff.
95. G. FRIEDRICH, *Catulli Veronensis liber*, cit., 275.

Further theories have been put forward to explain the meaning of the strophe: Friedrich's one[95] is utterly improbable, according to which the groom, after reaching his house before the procession, being worn out because of the feast, would have lain down on a *lectus*, and there he would be now (definitely not in a physical condition such as to justify his passional fits!). Fordyce's interpretation too seems banal to me: he imagines Manlius as lying weary on any bed, "as his modern counterpart would sit on a chair"[96]; what a wonderful and attractive sight for the bride, on her arrival home! A mixture of various interpretations is in Lafaye[97]: "Non pas sur le lit nuptial, mais sur un sofa dressé dans l'*atrium* devant une table servie; c'est là que l'époux, accueillant l'épouse, va l'admettre à la communauté du feu et de l'eau".

Pasquali's hypothesis[98] in fact seems more convincing to me; for him *torus* is the *lectus genialis*, put in the hall of the house; against this view Fordyce objects that the *lectus genialis* had become, in the classic age, a purely symbolical thing: anyway, we have already noticed that Catullus, in his free exposition of the wedding ceremony, revives obsolete customs, apart from modifying some details, on the other hand, the assumption itself that the *lectus genialis* was a symbolical object is in favour of this interpretation.[99] In this context surely it cannot be the nuptial bed, mentioned by Catullus later on (cf. l. 176 ff.); but it cannot

96. C.J. FORDYCE, *Catullus*, cit., 250 f.
97. G. LAFAYE, *Catulle. Poésies*, Paris 1923, 61. The same explanation is provided by M. LENCHANTIN DE GUBERNATIS, *Il libro di Catullo*, cit., 116.
98. G. PASQUALI in "St. Ital. Filol. Class." N.S. 1 (1920) 3 ff.
99. G. PASQUALI in "St. Ital. Filol. Class." N.S. 1 (1920) 4 asserts on this: "Al tempo di Catullo il letto geniale nell'atrio era ridotto a un simbolo, ma a un simbolo indispensabile a persone bennate. Per Orazio l'ammogliato è colui al quale *lectus genialis in aulast* (*Epist.* 1,1,87). Di una donna che si era rimaritata col marito della figlia divorziata, dice Cicerone (*pro Cluent.* 14): *lectum illum genialem, quem biennio ante filiae suae nubenti strauerat, in eadem domo sibi ornari et sterni expulsa atque exturbata filia iubet*; e riassume subito dopo in due parole quello che ha esposto sin qui pateticamente: *nubit generi socrus*. Per Festo (83,11 L.) il letto geniale è quello *qui nuptiis sternitur in honore genii*, dove le parole ultime mostrano di per sé sole che quello era ormai un mobile di parata. Ma appunto nei riti nuziali esso aveva ancora parte cospicua, quando forse già da secoli le persone agiate celebravano la prima notte non nell'atrio, ma in una stanza nuziale a parte".

either be any bed in the house; in this solemn stage of the ceremony (the bride's entrance into what will be her new home till
her old age!) something worthy of the importance of the moment
and of the nobility of the groom's birth is required: after Catullus
has praised the *potens et beata* groom's household, in the words
referred to Junia (ll. 149-151), and has invited her to go in, could
any particular be more appropriate than the *lectus genialis*, placed
in the hall as a symbol of the prestige of the family name? The
lectus genialis is the first object of the new house, so emphatically
depicted to Junia, that must attract her attention, and Manlius,
laying on the *lectus genialis*, asserts – to say it in Ferrero's
words[100] – his right and shows himself to be the master of the
household. *Intus* alludes to the atrium[101] and for Catullus' con-
temporaries it must have been clear that a *torus* placed in the hall
could be nothing but the *lectus genialis*.

All this makes us understand that in this case too Catullus has
shortened one of the phases of the ceremony, for in the *atrium*
the husband received his wife and offered her water and fire
symbolizing the union of life and worship: cf. Paul. *ap*. Fest. 3 L.
*aqua et igni tam interdici solet damnatis quam accipiunt nuptae
uidelicet quia hae duae res humanam uitam maxime continent*[102];
in contrast with it, Catullus is not interested in these details of
the ceremony taking place in the *atrium*, but his imagination is
struck by the ancient and purple[103] *lectus genialis* in the hall.

The image of the bride and groom aflame with passion, on the
contrary, is conventional; it pertains to the well-known motif of
Eros penetrating as deep as the lovers' bones, of which there is an
instance already in Archil. *Frg*. 104 D. = 203 Tarditi δύστηνος
ἔγκειμαι πόθῳ / ἄψυχος, χαλεπῇσι θεῶν ὀδύνῃσιν ἕκητι/

---

100. L. FERRERO, *Interpretazione di Catullo*, cit., 297.
101. G. PASQUALI in "St. Ital. Filol. Class." N.S. 1 (1920) 4 rightly
criticizes some archaeologists, who show an inclination to put the *lectus
genialis* not in the *atrium*, but in the *tablinum*. All Roman literary sources
clearly refer to the *atrium*.
102. Cf. further instances of the habit in DAREMBERG-SAGLIO III
1656 n. 21.
103. On the purple colour of the *lectus genialis* (Catullus has *Tyrio in
toro*) cf. E. SAMTER, *Geburt, Hochzeit und Tod*, cit., 186 ff.; on the
contrary the use of the *lectus genialis* was ignored in Greece: cf. G.
PASQUALI in "St. Ital. Filol. Class." N.S. 1 (1920) 6.

πεπαρμένος δι'όστέων. In Catullus cf. 35,15 *ignes interiorem edunt medullam* and 64,92 f. *cuncto concepit corpore flammam* / *funditus atque imis exarsit tota medullis.*[104] Catullus' *uariatio* of the motif in c. 61 consists in the distinction between the intensities of Junia's and Manlius' love passion, the latter rising *penite magis*; it is an innovation caused by the special atmosphere of the wedding song, in which the respect for the bride's *pudicitia* is evident even in the fescennine. The conventional image of the *cupidus maritus* is resumed in 64,374 *dedatur cupido iam dudum nupta marito.*

From the stylistic point of view, the same livelier and fluent tone of the previous strophes is continued: besides the hyperbolical images (l. 166 *totus immineat tibi,* l. 170 f. *pectore uritur intimo* / *flamma*), the use of *aspice ut* is significant: the imperative of *aspicio,* rare in prose, is frequent in comedies and in poetry, from Catullus onwards[105]; Catullus echoes Plaut. *Most.* 855 *quin tu illam aspice ut placide accubat. Accubo* (l. 164) is a verb of comedies and prose,[106] in spite of its presence in Verg. *Georg.* 3,333 *sicubi ... sacra nemus accubet umbra, Aen.* 6,605 f. (where, anyhow, it is justifiable owing to the context) *furiarum maxima iuxta /accubat* and in Hor. *Carm.* 4,12,18 *qui (cadus) nunc ... accubat horreis.* On *accubare in toro* and similar phrases cf. Plaut. *Bacch.* 938. As concerns *immineat tibi* (l. 166), Ehlers in *Thes.* VII 1,67 ff. observes that *imminere,* used "erotice, i.q. procacem esse", is to be found in Catullus as well as in Arnob. *Nat.* 3,25 *iam feruentes ... atque imminentes mariti.*

With regard to *non minus ac tibi* (l. 169), we must remember that *ac (atque)* after comparatives occurs in comedies, in Catullus and in Lucretius, whereas it is avoided in Cicero's prose; in Augustan poetry, apart from Verg. *Aen.* 3,561, *ac* is frequently used after comparatives in Horace, but only in his Epodes and Satires.[107] Finally the adverb *penite* (l. 171) is an ἅπαξ derived

104. On this motif cf. A.S.F. GOW, *Theocritus,* cit., II 67 and R.G.M. NISBET - M. HUBBARD, *A Commentary on Horace,* cit., 174.
105. Cf. *Thes.* II 830,57.
106. Cf. *Thes.* I 339,20 f.
107. Cf. *Thes.* II 1084,38 ff.; J.B. HOFMANN - A. SZANTYR, *Lat. Syntax u. Stilistik,* 478; W. KROLL, *Cat.,* cit., 119. H. HEUSCH, *Das Archaische i. d. Sprache Catulls,* cit., 119 f., does not convince when he talks about archaism "ohne Konnex mit der gesprochene Sprache".

from the archaic *penitus*, an adjective sprung itself from the original adverb[108] and employed by Plautus.[109]

Once the bride has gone into her new home, the *praetextatus* has fulfilled his task and Catullus urges him to let go of Junia's arm: now it is time for the bride to approach the marriage-bed. All this is expressed by means of the usual imperatives (or exhortatory subjunctives) typical of the poet-coryphaeus, who directs the various stages of the ceremony. After the instructions given to the *praetextatus* and the bride, the *bonae feminae* are invited to prepare the girl for the wedding night,[110] while the refrain in Hymen's honour rings out for the last time, the following strophes are indeed the section of transition from the hymenaeus to the epithalamium proper. Lines 174-183 bring the *deduction* to an end, and it finishes in the same tone of tenderness towards the bride in which it has started.

mitte brachiolum teres,	
praetextate, puellulae:	175
iam cubile adeat uiri.	
Hymen o Hymenaee io,	
Hymen o Hymenaee.	(185)
⟨uos⟩ bonae senibus uiris	
cognitae bene feminae	180
collocate puellulam.	
Hymen o Hymenaee io,	
Hymen o Hymenaee.	(190)

Wheeler includes the mentioning of the *praetextatus* among the motifs that are "either exclusively or predominantly Roman".[111] Nevertheless it is to be explained why Catullus addresses only one *praetextatus*, whereas according to the Roman tradition of wedding ceremonies, the *pueri* accompanying and supporting the bride during the *deductio* were two and a third one carried the

---

108. Cf. J.B. HOFMANN - A. SZANTYR, *Lat. Syntax u. Stilistik*, 173.

109. Cf. *Asin.* 41 *ex penitis faucibus*, *Pers.* 541 *ex Arabia penitissima*, *Cist.* 63 *pectore penitissimo* and C.J. FORDYCE, *Catullus*, cit., 251.

110. There is an incredible carelessness in G. LAFAYE, *Catulle et ses modèles*, cit., 71: he asserts that Junia "est conduite à table (*sic!*) par des matrones d'âge mûr".

111. A.L. WHEELER, *Catullus and the Tradition*, cit., 196.

torch of whitethorn.[112] I am not convinced by Fordyce,[113] who states that the invitation is referred to each of the two *praetextati* at the same time and therefore the singular is appropriate[114] or by Kroll,[115] who posits that there was only one *praetextatus* in Catullus' times. Actually Catullus has changed again the traditional customs of the Roman ceremony, as for both its chief characters and its course. His innovation is partly an attempt to make to Roman habit similar to the Greek one: in reducing the two *praetextati* to one he may have been influenced by the Greek tradition that attached an important rôle to the παράνυμφος in the development of the ceremony.[116] As for Catullus' alteration of the course of events in the ceremony, it lies in this, that the function of the *praetextati* in Roman weddings ended on the bride's entering her husband's house; from then on the *pronuba* appeared, the most important character in the wedding ceremony after the bridal couple, and whose task was νυμφαγωγεῖν: in Catullus, however, it is the *praetextatus* - παράνυμφος who accompanies the bride to the thalamus.

Catullus hints at the main function of the *pronuba* in ll. 179-181, where he urges the *bonae feminae*, defined *bene cognitae senibus uiris*, to see to the *collocatio*: it may be a cunning way, on Catullus' part, to allude to the indispensable condition for a *pronuba*, i.e. that of being *uniuira*, which is after all the greatest praise of a Roman matron: cf. Varr. *ap.* Seru. *ad* Verg. *Aen.* 4,166 *Varro pronubam dici quae ante nupsit et quae uni tantum nupta est*, Fest. 282 L. *pronubae adhibentur nuptiis, quae semel nupserunt.*[117]

112. Cf. the above-quoted Fest. 282 L. *patrimi et matrimi pueri praetextati tres nubentem deducunt, unus qui facem praefert ex spina alba ... duo qui tenent nubentem.*

113. C.J. FORDYCE, *Catullus*, cit., 251.

114. G. WILLIAMS, *Tradition and Originality*, cit., 200, seems to follow the same interpretation: he writes that "the boys who have accompanied her (again Roman, not Greek) are told to leave her and she is to approach the marriage bed".

115. W. KROLL, *Cat.*, cit., 119.

116. Cf. what has been said on the παράνυμφος with regard to ll. 114 ff.; in Rome one or more *paranymphi* appear in the wedding ceremonies only later on: cf. Augustin. *Ciu. Dei* 14,18 and G. HERZOG-HAUSER in "R.E.P.W." XVIII 4 (1949) 1294.

117. Cf. also G. HERZOG-HAUSER in "R.E.P.W." XVIII 4 (1949) 1294

But the activity of the *pronuba* started as early as the beginning of the ceremony: on the morning of the same day, after the auspices had turned out propitious, she accompanied the bride in front of the groom and performed the *dextrarum iunctio*, putting the wife's right hand in the husband's and exhorting the bride solemnly to be *morigera*.[118] At the end of the *deductio*, when the wedding procession had reached the groom's house, the *pronuba* had not only the duty of receiving the bride at her arrival and taking her in the thalamus,[119] but also that of praying and sacrificing to the gods in the *atrium* to wish the couple a happy union. Moreover the *pronuba* supervised other accessory rituals, mentioned by the sources with scantiness of details[120]: the most famous is the offering of *tres asses*, the first to the husband, the second to the Lares, the third to the altar of the nearest cross-roads, for which cf. Varr. *ap.* Non. 531,8 M. *nubentes ueteri lege Romana asses III ad maritum uenientes solere peruehere atque unum, quem in manu tenerent, tamquam emendi causa marito dare; alium, quem in pede haberent, in foco Larium familiarium ponere; tertium ⟨quem⟩ in sacciperione condidissent, compito uicinali solere reseruare.*[121]

In Catullus, also in this case, it would be useless to look for precision of antiquated particulars: nowhere else is there any mentioning of more *pronubae*, nor does Mangelsdorff[122] succeed in explaining it when he quotes Ter. *Eun.* 593 *iit, lauit, rediit, deinde eam in lectulo locarunt*, where the setting is different and *ancillae* in a general sense are dealt with. Furthermore Catullus, in contrast with the usual procedure of the poem, gives no

and, on the value of the term *uniuira*, G. WILLIAMS in "Journ. Rom. Stud." 48 (1958) 23 ff.

118. Cf. DAREMBERG-SAGLIO III 1655 and n. 20, E. PERNICE in GERCKE-NORDEN, *Einleit. i. d. Altertumswiss.*, cit., II³, 57, G. WILLIAMS in "Journ. Rom. Stud." 48 (1958) 21.

119. Statius too discusses this task of the *pronuba*, describing Venus the *pronuba* in his epithalamium (*Sil.* 1,2,11 ff.): *ipsa manu nuptam genetrix Aeneia duxit / lumina demissam et dulci probitate rubentem, / ipsa toros et sacra parat.*

120. Cf. DAREMBERG-SAGLIO III 1656.

121. On this custom cf. DAREMBERG-SAGLIO III 1656 and J. HECKENBACH in "R.E.P.W." VIII 2 (1913) 2133, who anyhow mentions only one *as*.

122. E.A. MANGELSDORFF, *Lyr. Hochzeitsged.*, cit., 42.

advices to the *bonae feminae* in relation to the *collocatio*, unlike the anonimous author of the *epithalamium Laurentii* (*Poet. Lat. Min.* III 42,69 ff. Baehrens), who uses a great wealth of details: *teque etiam paucis moneamus, pronuba, uerbis.* / *Cum fuerit uentum ad thalamos primumque cubile,* / *sit tibi cura uigens innoxia reddere membra* / *uirginis, ut totum quod possit laedere demas:* / *nullum sit capiti quo crinis comitur aurum,* / *nec collo maneant nisi quae sunt leuia fila,* / *anulus et digitis tollatur mollibus asper,* / *ac niueos auro propera spoliare lacertos,* / *ne, faciant dum ludum atque oscula dulcia iactant* / *exercentque toris Veneris luctamen anhelum,* / *puncta per amplexus foedentur membra mariti* / *atque inuita uiri maculet quae diligit ora.*

The most relevant point, however, is that Catullus limits the presence and activity of the *pronuba* to the phases of the *deductio*, thus leaving out all the particulars of the ceremony that happened in the atrium and assigning to the *praetextatus* - παράνυμφος the task of accompanying the bride to the thalamus. The actions of the *pronuba* at the beginning of the ceremony in fact could not be included in c. 61, since the first stage represented in it is the *deductio*; but I have already pointed out, with regard to ll. 144 ff., that Catullus transfers an important function usually attributed to the *pronuba* (i.e. warning the bride to be *morigera*, while the *dextrarum iunctio* took place) into the fescennine: he has then considered it necessary to mention the instructions given during the *dextrarum iunctio* and, as they were prior to the *deductio*, he has inserted them into the fescennine, consequently stressing the bride's erotic duties in a cunning tone.

The image of the bride is the focus of attention in the two strophes that describe her approaching the thalamus and the *collocatio*: it is understandable, therefore, that affectionate language prevails in them. It has been rightly observed[123] that when Catullus speaks about Junia he employs delicacy of tone and of imagery. An evident proof of this technique is the use of diminutives in describing Junia: *puellula* recurs four times altogether in Catullus and three times in c. 61; two of these instances belong exactly to this context (ll. 175-181), which starts with the image of the *brachiolum teres* of the bride and

---

123. Cf. A. RONCONI, *Studi catulliani*, cit., 122 ff.

ends with the diminutive *puellulam*. Truly *puellula* was frequently used in Catullus' times and was losing its original characteristics by then; but we must not forget that, rather than stating how rare this diminutive was, it is remarkable to see whether and to what extent a special shade of affection is required and justified by the passage.[124] In this case it is necessary both because Junia is mentioned and because it is now time for the bride to offer her virginity to her husband, having left in tears her mother and her old home.

The affectionate tone becomes evident if one takes into consideration the presence of the diminutive *brachiolum*, which occurs with the same meaning, and under the influence of Catullus, only in *Carm. Lat. Epigr.* 950,1 f. Buecheler *o utinam liceat collo complexa tenere / braciola et teneris oscula ferre labellis*; in late Latin *brachiolum* is often used by Vegetius, in *Mulomedicina Chironis* and by Pelagonius, but in order to designate a muscle of the horse's leg[125]; so probably it is Catullus' creation, on which some influence may have been exerted by *manciola*, as Cichorius believes[126]; this term was employed by Levius — a poet that was unquestionably imitated by Catullus several times[127] — and in a similar context (*Frg.* 9 Morel *manciolis tenellis*).

A malicious "double entendre" on the other hand is referred to the *bonae feminae*, that is, the use of the verb *cognoscere* with an erotic meaning. In this sense it is to be found in Turpil. *Com.* 42 R.³ *mulier meretrix, quae me quaesti causa cognouit sui,* Ouid. *Her.* 6,133 *turpiter illa uirum cognouit adultera uirgo,* Colum. 6,37,9 *nisi prius ea (femina) marem cognouerit,* Tac. *Hist.* 4,44 *Octauius Pontiam stupro cognitam et nuptias suas abnuentem interfecerat* and in late Latin authors.[128]

124. A. RONCONI, *Studi catulliani*, cit., 123.

125. Cf. *Thes.* II 2156,34 ff.; as for *teres* cf. R.G.M. NISBET - M. HUBBARD, *A Commentary on Horace: Odes. Book 2*, cit., 75.

126. C. CICHORIUS in "Rhein. Mus." 73 (1920) 124 ff. criticizes W. MEYER-LÜBKE who in "Rhein. Mus." 72 (1917/18) 153 ff. takes *manciola* and *brachiolum* into consideration, regarding the latter diminutive as the original form.

127. Cf. M. SCHANZ - K. HOSIUS, *Geschichte der römischen Literatur,* I⁴, München 1927, 269.

128. Cf. *Thes.* III 1503,83 ff.; analogous is the use of γιγνώσκειν for which LIDDELL-SCOTT-JONES quotes Menand. *Frg.* 382,5 Körte, Heracl.

It might seem surprising that Catullus uses a cunning expression with relation to the *pronuba*, who was a fundamental character in the religious ceremony; but in doing so he prepares the atmosphere for the epithalamium proper. Anyway, the dignity of the function of the *pronuba* is emphasized by the use of the technical verb *collocare*: in the chaotic article of *Thesaurus* Catullus' line is listed among the passages attesting the official phrase *in matrimonium collocare* i.e. *in matrimonium dare*.[129] Catullus' choice of the verb may have been determined, then, by the influence of the formula *in matrimonium collocare*, employed by Catullus in the solemn moment when the marriage contract is to be consecrated through the physical union of the bride and groom. But the use of *colloco* sc. *in thalamo* too seems to belong to the official terminology of the wedding: cf. the words of the groom Olympio in Plaut. *Cas.* 881 ff. *ut intro hanc nouam nuptam deduxi, recta uia in conclaue abduxi. / ... Con lo co, fulcio, mollio, blandior*, Ouid. *Met.* 2,525 f. *cur non et pulsa ducit Iunone meoque / collocat in thalamo socerumque Lycaona sumit?*, Pallad. *Hist. Mon.* 1,2 *nouis nuptis in lectulo collocatis* and above all Donatus' comment on Ter. *Eun.* 593: *uide an aliquid desit a legitimis nuptiis; nam et ipsum uerbum "collocarunt" proprium est et ascribitur pronubis.*

*

Now that Junia is waiting in the wedding-chamber, where the *bonae feminae* have prepared her to meet her husband, Catullus urges Manlius to reach his wife: he imagines thus that during the *phases* of the *collocatio* Manlius has been waiting in the hall where the poet has depicted him as he stretched full of passion towards the bride on her arrival home. However, in wedding ceremonies the presence of the husband in the hall was necessary both because the bride, going into the new house, pronounced the formula *ubi tu Gaius ego Gaia*,[130] and because he had to present her with

Pol. 64, Septuag. *Ge.* 4,1, *Euang. Matt.* 1,25 and Plut. *Galb.* 9. On *cognitae* cf. now the useful remarks made by R. HEINE in "Anz. Altertumswiss." 29 (1976) 204.

129. *Thes.* III 1644,46 ff.

130. Cf. Plut. *Quaest. Rom.* 30 and DAREMBERG-SAGLIO III 1656;

water and fire, the symbols of the community of love and worship. It is worth noticing that the invitation of Manlius repeats the same words employed to urge Junia to come out of her house, in the previous stage of the *deductio*: cf. ll. 192-193 *sed abit dies: perge, ne remorare* and *sed moraris, abit dies* (l. 91), *sed abit dies* (l. 105; 112): it is Manlius' turn, now, to be waited for.

Once again the eulogy of the bride's beauty is expressed in ll. 184-193, followed by the eulogy of the groom's handsomeness, an equally traditional motif but not included in the poem yet. The two strophes are strictly connected by the logical sequence of ideas: the first begins with the invitation to Manlius to reach the bride and then developes the theme of the praise of Junia's beauty, from which the eulogy of Manlius' *pulchritudo* derives; this is present in the second strophe, ending with a new exhortation to harry up and not to hesitate. The repetition of the same verb (*perge, ne remorare. / Non diu remoratus es*) creates at the same time a link between this strophe and the next one.

According to some critics,[131] the epithalamium proper starts at l. 184: but it is uncorrect to regard it as a song before the thalamus right now, since it supposes the presence of both the bride and the groom; in this circumstance, in fact, Manlius is still imagined as being in the hall, waiting for the invitation to approach Junia in the bed-chamber. Only from l. 204 on – when Catullus addresses the couple and exhorts them to enjoy the pleasures of love – will the poem show the typical tones of the epithalamium proper.

> iam licet uenias, marite:
> uxor in thalamo tibi est,[132]   185
> ore floridulo nitens,

J. CARCOPINO, *La vie quotidienne à Rome à l'apogée de l'Empire*, Paris 1939, 101 ff., does not share this view, but he often uses his imagination to complete the sources as regards wedding ceremonies.

131. W. KROLL, *Cat.*, cit., 120, E.A. MANGELSDORFF, *Lyr. Hochzeitsged.*, cit., 42.

132. The best manuscripts read *est tibi*; the transposition is necessary to avoid the hiatus and is to be found as early as the codex *Paris. Lat.* 7989, before it was suggested by Bentley; Mynors, in his apparatus, ignores the presence of this correction in a manuscript; cf. also M. HAUPT, *Opusc.*, I 18 f.

alba parthenice uelut
luteumue papauer. (195)
at, marite, ita me iuuent
caelites, nihilo minus 190
pulcer es, neque te Venus
neglegit. sed abit dies:
perge, ne remorare. (200)

The giving up of the description of exclusively Roman customs
marks the return to a traditional literary themes originated in
Greek poetry: the description of the bride's complexion indeed
follows a pattern peculiar to Hellenistic literature, which has a
preference for the τόπος of the contrast of colours on women's
faces.[133] The motif had a literary dignity, as it occurred in Callimachus' Hymn 5, with reference to Athena: l. 27 ff. τὸ δ᾽ ἔρευϑος
ἀνέδραμε, πρώιον οἴαν / ἢ ῥόδον ἢ σίβδας κόκκος ἔχει χροϊάν.
As a latter example cf. Ps. Bion. Epithal. Achill. et Deidam. 17 ff.
ἐφαίνετο δ᾽ἠΰτε κώρα · / καὶ γὰρ ἴσον τήναις θηλύνετο καὶ τόσον
ἄνθος / χιονέαις πόρφυρε παρηίσι, Aristaenet. Ep. 1,1 ἐκείνη
γάρ ... λευκαὶ μὲν ἐπιμὶξ καὶ ὑπέρυθροι παρειαὶ καὶ ταύτῃ τὸ
φαιδρὸν ἐκμιμοῦνται τῶν ῥόδων, Achill. Tat. 1,4,3 λευκὴ
παρειά, τὸ λευκὸν ἐς μέσον ἐφοινίσσετο καὶ ἐμιμεῖτο πορφύραν,
οἵαν εἰς τὸν ἐλέφαντα Λυδία βάπτει γυνή, Mus. Her. et Leand. 58
ἄκρα δὲ χιονέης φοινίσσετο κύκλα παρειῆς / ὡς ῥόδον ἐκ
καλύκων διδυμόχροον. In Rome the τόπος appears in Ennius'
Annales (352 V.[2] et simul erubuit ceu lacte et purpura mixta)
and after being used by Catullus it will be very dear to the
Augustan poets: cf. Prop. 2,3,10-12 lilia sint domina non magis
alba mea / ut Maeotica nix minio si certet Hibero / utque rosae
puro lacte natant folia, Lygd. 4,31-34 ut iuueni primum uirgo
deducta marito / inficitur teneras ore rubente genas, / et cum
contexunt amarantis alba puellae / lilia et autumno candida mala
rubent, Verg. Aen. 12,67 ff. Indum sanguineo ueluti uiolauerit
ostro / si quis ebur, aut mixta rubent ubi lilia multa / alba rosa:
talis uirgo dabat ore colores, Ouid. Am. 3,3,5 ff. candida can-
dorem roseo suffusa rubore / ante finit: niueo lucet in ore rubor,
Met. 3,423 in niueo mixtum candore rubore. It is significant that
even the author of the Epithalamium Laurentii (Poet. Lat. Min.

---

133. Cf. J. SVENNUNG, Cat. Bilderspr., cit., 75.

III 42,33-35 Baehrens employed it: *puro formosa colore / lilia ceu lucent rutilis commixta rosetis, / sic rubor et candor pingunt tibi, florida, uultus.* The presence of this motif in the epithalamium of Pseudo-Bion, in Catullus c. 61 and in the *Epithalamium Laurentii* leads us to think that it had become conventional for wedding songs.

The motif of the eulogy of the husband's handsomeness too belonged to the τόποι of epithalamia: in this case I do not share Ferrero's view, for whom it is a sudden recollection, detached from the natural flowing of imagination.[134] In reality, Catullus knew perfectly well that in a wedding song, besides the eulogy of the bride's beauty, the praises of the groom's handsomeness were necessary: therefore he preferred to insert them in this section of the poem, in which Manlius plays a relevant rôle and his being a dominus is emphasized.[135]

The fact that this is a τόπος is proved by the rhetoricians' theory of the ἐπιθαλάμιος λόγος: cf. Menand. *Rhet. Gr.* III 404,5 ff. κάλλος δὲ παρ'ἀμφοῖν κατὰ ἀντεξέτασιν, πάντως οὐχ ἡ μὲν φυτῶν καλλίστῳ ἐλαίᾳ, ὁ δὲ φοίνικι παραπλήσιος; καὶ ὅτι ὁ μὲν ῥόδῳ προσέοικεν, ἡ δὲ μήλῳ . διαγράψεις δὲ καὶ τὸν νεανίαν οἷος ἰδεῖν, οἷος ὀφθῆναι, ὡς χαρίεις καὶ εὐπρόσωπος, ὡς ἰούλοις κατάκομος ὡς ἄρτι ἡβάσκων, Ps. Dion. Hal. VI 1, p. 270 Usener-Radermacher εἶτα μεταβήσῃ ἐπὶ τὰ πρόσωπα τῶν συνιόντων εἰς τὸν γάμον, ὁποῖοί τινες οὗτοι . ἐν ᾧ περὶ γένους ἐρεῖς αὐτῶν καὶ τροφῆς, καὶ περὶ κάλλους σωμάτων καὶ ἡλικίας. Moreover the τόπος recurs in Sappho's epithalamia, both in a fragment containing the traditional motif of the

134. L. FERRERO, *Interpretazione di Catullo*, cit., 312.

135. It is not exact to assert that "der Dichter fingiert, dass der Bräutigam erst jetzt erscheint und er von seiner Schönheit betroffen ist" (W. KROLL, *Cat.*, cit., 120); if Kroll's statement refers to Manlius' first appearance, we must remember that he has already been mentioned, when Junia was entering the house (ll. 164 ff.); if, on the other hand, Kroll hints at Manlius' approaching the marriage-bed, then *perge ne remorare* at l. 193 and the analogy with Junia's situation and Catullus' exhortations to her before the *deductio* imply that the groom has not left the *atrium* yet.

136. I follow Lobel and Page, who join this line, quoted by Choricius, p. 16 Förster (*Ind. lect. Vratisl.* Breslau 1891), with the previous ones, mentioned by Hephaest. *Ench.* 15,26 p. 55 Consbruch ὄλβιε γάμβρε, σοὶ μὲν δὴ γάμος ὡς ἄραο ἐκτετέλεστ', ἔχῃς δὲ πάρθενον κτλ.; Choricius, however, believes that Sappho referred the compliment to the bride.

εἰκάζειν (115 L.-P. τίῳ σ᾽, ὦ φίλε γάμβρε, κάλως ἐικάσδω; /
ὄρπακι βραδίνῳ σε μάλιστ᾽ἐικάσδω) and in the mentioning
of Aphrodite's gifts, lavished on the groom more than any other
mortal being, in *Frg.* 112,5 L.-P. τετίμακ᾽ἔξοχά σ᾽ Ἀφροδίτα;
this τόπος is resumed in the form of a parody by Lucian. *Conu.*
41 νυμφίε, καὶ σὺ δὲ χαῖρε, κρατερῶν κράτιστε ἐφήβων, /
κρέσσων Νιρῆος καὶ Θέτιδος παϊδός. It should also be considered that the eulogy of the bride's beauty and the groom's
physical vigour was recommended by Menander, apart from the
ἐπιθαλάμιος λόγος, in the κατευναστικὸς λόγος too: *Rhet. Gr.*
III,405,19 ff. οἱ μὲν οὖν ποιηταὶ διὰ τοῦ παρορμᾶν ἐπὶ τὸν
θάλαμον καὶ προτρέπειν προάγουσι τὰ κατευναστικὰ ποιήματα ...·
ἔστι γὰρ ὁ κατευναστικὸς προτροπὴ πρὸς τὴν συμπλοκήν ...·
ἐροῦμεν δὲ ἐγκώμιον τῆς νύμφης διὰ βραχέων, οὐ τὸ ἀπὸ τῆς
σωφροσύνης οὐδὲ ἀπὸ φρονήσεως οὐδὲ τῶν λοιπῶν ἀρετῶν τῆς
ψυχῆς, ἀλλὰ τὸ ἀπὸ τῆς ὥρας καὶ τοῦ κάλλους . τοῦτο γὰρ
οἰκεῖον καὶ πρόσφορον μόνον, τοῦ νεανίσκου τὴν ἀλκὴν καὶ τὴν
ῥώμην παραινοῦντες μὴ καταισχῦναι ταῦτα τοσούτων μαρτύρων
γενησομένων τῇ ὑστεραίᾳ τῆς τελετῆς.

The κατευναστικὸς λόγος refers to the epithalamium proper,
that is, to the last part of the ceremony, in which before the bed-
chamber's door the couple was wished a happy future life and offspring and was invited to enjoy the pleasures of love. Menander
advises that the eulogy should be expressed in a few words (διὰ
βραχέων); Catullus keeps to the recommended *breuitas*, especially
in the part concerning the husband; and so also in c. 61 we have
reached the phase of transition to the epithalamium in the strict
sense.

The simile with the *alba parthenice* too seems to be of Hellenistic origin: I agree with Ronconi[137] who posits that the parallel
was not normally used, but it was connected with learned
proverbial expressions; comparisons between one's loved woman
and flowers are frequent in love songs, especially in Greece, and it
is highly likely that Catullus derives this motif from a Greek
pattern: the term itself, in addition, seems to prove it for its in-
disputable Greek origin and because it does not recur in any other
author.

The lively language, rich in tones peculiar to familiar style —

137. A. RONCONI, *Studi catulliani*, cit., 150.

already pointed out in relation to the previous strophe – appears also in ll. 184-188. A diminutive is employed, as usual, with reference with Junia, in this case to define her face: it is *floridulus*, only attested in Catullus and not different, as for meaning, from *florens* or *floridus*.[138] By choosing the diminutive, however, Catullus adds an intimate tone to the adjective, thus showing an attitude of tenderness towards the person described by the adjective; excluded the sense of 'fairly flourishing' – Ronconi observes – an idea of tenderness remains, a sense of intentional caressing: otherwise the poet would have simply used *florido ore* and not a form that here is consciously affectionate.[139] *Nitens*, said *de formosis*,[140] occurs also in Catull. 2,5 *desiderio meo nitenti*; its use is analogous with *nitidus* in Plaut. *Mil.* 1003 *nimis nitida femina*. In the following line there is the typically neoteric technique (resumed then by the poets of the Augustan age) of inverting a conjunction (*uelut*).

In the next strophe the dignified *caelites*[141] is introduced in a context of familiar tone. For Riese "*me iuuerint caelites* ist erhabener Stil, wie *ita me diui iuuerint* 66,18"[142]: but such formulae are rather superstitious expressions proper to the religion of the common people, employed to avert the gods' wrath[143]; indeed it is significant that formulae to call upon the gods beginning with *at ita* + a personal pronoun belong to the vivid language of comedies: cf. Plaut. *Mil.* 501 *at ita me di deaeque omnes ament, Poen.* 1258 *at me ita me dei seruent* and J. Wackernagel, *Kl. Schr.*, I 78[144]; generally speaking, prayers introduced by *ita* pertain to

138. Cf. *Thes.* VI 295,11. On *licet* cf. E. MAASS in "Herm." 31 (1896) 406 f.

139. A. RONCONI, *Studi catulliani*, cit., 102.

140. Cf. *niteo* in Forcellini's lexicon, and A. GRIFFITHS in "Quad. Urb. Cult. Class." 14 (1972) 16 on the use of *niteo* here and of the compound form at l. 21, to designate the bride's splendour.

141. Cf. what has been observed with regard to l. 49.

142. A. RIESE, *Die Gedichte des Catullus*, cit., 128.

143. Cf. K. ZIEGLER, *De precationum apud Graecos formis quaestiones selectae*, Breslau 1905, 35 f.

144. As concerns the position of the pronoun, Catullus confirms what has been said on this by J. WACKERNAGEL, *Kl. Schr.*, I 78: "Von besondrer Bedeutung ist aber, dass, wenn an der Spitze des Satzes ein *ita, itaque, ut, utinam, hercle, qui, at* steht, darauf nicht etwa zuerst *di* oder der Göttername und dann erst das Pronomen folgt, sondern in diesem Fall das Pronomen

the *detritae precationes*[145] of everyday language, frequently present in comedies.[146] Furthermore it is worth noticing that presumably *ita* was not endowed with a particularly poetic character; it is well known, for instance, that the Augustan poets felt a strong aversion to this particle.[147]

Catullus makes use of a litotes at ll. 191-192 (*neque te neglegit* instead of *et te diligit*); from the stylistic point of view the litotes — as well as other devices such as the anaphora or the alliteration — can have a double function: it can be employed both as a sheer poetic device (Virgil) and as a feature of colloquial language (which is demonstrated by its frequent presence in comedies).[148] Analogous remarks can be made about the imperative depending on *ne* (l. 193 *ne remorare*): Fordyce merely asserts that it is an archaism[149]; but in Hofmann-Szantyr's words this use "gehört in erster Linie der Volkssprache an".[150] After the numerous instances of it in Plautus and Terentius, anyway, further evidences can only be found in Catullus (here, in 62,59 and 67,18) and then in the Augustan poets. Therefore *ne* + present imperative may have been used in poetry, from the first century B.C. onwards, for its archaic nature (Virgil, Tibullus) as well as for its belonging to the "Umgangssprache" of the comedy, like in this case — I suppose — in which not a solemn style, but a lively and familiar tone is required. As for the other two references in Catullus, Heusch reaches the same conclusion, when he underlines that the context of 62,59 ff. "durch den rein assozierenden Gedankenverlauf der einfachen Umgangssprache bestimmt wird" and that the dialogue with the door (67,18) "trägt sogar unverkannbare Züge der naiven Kindersprache".[151]

*

dem nominalen Subjekt vorangeht."

145. G. APPEL, *De Romanorum precationibus*, cit., 177.

146. Cf. the various examples quoted by G. APPEL, *De Romanorum precationibus*, cit. 178 f.

147. Cf. B. AXELSON, *Unp. Wört.*, cit., 121 f., D.O. ROSS, *Style and Tradition*, cit., 73.

148. Cf. J. WACKERNAGEL, *Vorlesungen über Syntax*, II², Basel 1957, 297-299, J.B. HOFMANN - A. SZANTYR, *Lat. Syntax u. Stilistik*, 777 f.

149. C.J. FORDYCE, *Catullus*, cit., 252.

150. J.B. HOFMANN - A. SZANTYR, *Lat. Syntax u. Stilistik*, 340.

151. H. HEUSCH, *Das Archaische i. d. Sprache Catulls*, cit., 155.

Resuming the last idea expressed in the previous strophe (*perge ne remorare.* / *Non diu remoratus es*), with a technique common in the finale of the poem, Catullus makes it clear that Manlius' delay has been short[152]: the groom rushes at the call of the poet, who wishes him the favour of *bona Venus* and justifies this wish by saying that his desire is right and that he shows a lawful love. The love at which Catullus hints, while the groom is on the point of reaching the bride in the thalamus, is, of course, the satisfaction of the senses: by means of a hyperbole he asserts that the couple's erotic *ludi* will be more numerous than the grains of sand in the African desert and the stars twinkling in the sky.

non diu remoratus es:
iam uenis. bona te Venus   195
iuuerit, quoniam palam
quod cupis cupis et bonum
   non abscondis amorem.   (205)

ille pulueris Africi
siderumque micantium   200
subducat numerum prius,
qui uestri numerare uolt
   multa milia ludi.   (210)

The erotic pleasures of connubial love have already been exalted as lawful in the ὕμνος κλητικός, where Catullus put them in connection with the δύναμις of the god Hymen (ll. 61-64), reminding us that no *bona Venus* could be present without the existence of the marriage tie. The link between this part of the poem (which represents the transition to the epithalamium in the literal sense) and the solemn section of the ὕμνος κλητικός is reinforced by the echoes present in ll. 195-198 of formulae employed in ll. 44-45 to emphasize the value of connubial love: cf. *bonum amorem* (ll. 197-198) and *boni amoris* (ll. 44-45); *bona Venus* (l. 195) and *bonae Veneris* (l. 44).

152. Catullus uses the same verb at the end of a strophe and at the beginning of the next one in order to emphasize the passage of time: Mrs. ÉVRARD-GILLIS, in *La récurrence lexicale dans l'oeuvre de Catulle*, cit., 52 has pointed out that the change from *remorare* (indicating that the action is to be performed) to *remoratus es* (showing that the action has been performed), necessarily implies the idea of time between the two lines.

But Catullus simply repeats such expressions, since the tone of the contexts where they occur is quite different: actually in ll. 193-198 the emphatic and solemn tone characterizing the same formulae in the ὕμνος κλητικός is detectable only to some extent: in the hymn the value and meaning of the marriage union had to be exalted, as it had not been settled yet; now, on the contrary, this phase is over and Catullus is ready to introduce the motif of the *multa milia ludi*, of the erotic joys necessary to connubial love.

As Ferrero observes, the tone and the parenesis in ll. 194-198 are extremely straightforward. The poet's encouragement to Manlius is open and clear, since his desire now is open and clear (*palam ... amorem*). At last, passion is let gone free, after the restraints of the groom's anxiety and the delay of the ritual.[153]

After creating this atmosphere, Catullus can go on without any contrast to exhorte the bride and groom to enjoy the erotic *ludi*. The style of ll. 194-198 swings from tones of sacral language, in the wishes to the groom, to familiar accents, in the description of his love desire: at l. 195, as a matter of fact, *bonus* is the conventional epithet of the divinity, as it has been noticed with regard to l. 44; equally conventional in the language of prayers is the use of *iuuo* (l. 196) to indicate the favourable intervention of the gods.[154] The expression *quod cupis cupis* (l. 197), however, belongs to a different stylistic field: it is a paronomastic repetition, peculiar to spoken language, consisting in the use of the same verb both in the main and in the subordinate clause; Ronconi[155] discusses this technique and cites some examples to be found in Plautus, which are significant to understand the stylistic level of such formulae that even become ways of saying: cf. *Most.* 329 *si cades non cades quin cadam tecum, Cist.* 211 *ubi sum, ibi non sum, ubi non sum, ibi est animus, Trin.* 853 *ille qui me conduxit, ubi conduxit, adduxit domum*; Petronius will employ the same device (43,1 *itaque creuit, quidquid creuit, tamquam fauus*). In Catullus, in addition to this instance, compare 48,2 f. *si quis me sinat usque basiare, / usque ad milia basiem trecenta,* 87,1 f. *nulla*

153. L. FERRERO, *Interpretazione di Catullo*, cit., 312.
154. Cf. *Thes.* VII 2,745,79 ff.
155. A. RONCONI, *Studi catulliani*, cit., 60; cf. also J.B. HOFMANN - A. SZANTYR, *Lat. Syntax u. Stilistik*, 709.

potest mulier tantum se dicere amatam | uere, quantum a me Lesbia amata mea est, 98,1 f. *in te, si in quemquam, dici pote, putide Victi, | id quod uerbosis dicitur et fatuis*; in all these passages the style is definitely narrative. In the case in question Catullus uses the device not only for its tone, appropriate to the intimate character of the context, but also in order to avoid an obscene way of expressing a not too decent idea.[156]

The style is certainly more familiar and fluent in the subsequent strophe, in which Catullus introduces, with hyperbolical expressions, the image of love's *ludi*. Apart from the proverbial nature of the words, consider the phrase *multa milia*, that occurs several times in Catullus[157]: stress has been laid by Ronconi[158] on its colloquial character and he has proved that it is a formula of alliteration typical of familiar style. We cannot disregard the use of the genitive collective singular *ludi* and the erotic sense of the noun: *ludus* and *ludere* imply an erotic meaning on the model of παίζειν and συμπαίζειν: cf. Xen. *Conu.* 9,2 μετὰ δὲ τοῦθ᾽ ἥξει Διόνυσος ὑποπεπωκὼς παρὰ θεοῖς καὶ εἴσεισι πρὸς αὐτὴν (scil. Ἀριάδνην), ἔπειτα παιξοῦνται πρὸς ἀλλήλους, Theocr. 11,77 πολλαὶ συμπαίσδεν με κόραι τὴν νύκτα κέλονται. In Rome this meaning appears in the language of comedies[159] and it is frequent in Catullus and in the elegiac poets.[160]

In this stylistic context the two hyperbolical images employed by Catullus find a proper place: they belong to the range of proverbs and, despite their famous antecedents, they keep a popular-like character typical of such expressions. The first hyperbole pertains to the impossibility of ἄμμον μετρεῖν, which occurs, in contexts quite different from this, as early as Hom. *Il.* 2,800 f. λίην γὰρ φύλλοισιν ἐοικότες ἢ ψαμάθοισιν | ἔρχονται πεδίοιο μαχησόμενοι προτὶ ἄστυ, 9,385 f. οὐδ᾽εἴ μοι τόσα δοίη ὅσα ψάμαθός τε κόνις τε κτλ.: consider, besides Pythia's words

156. Cf. W. KROLL, *Cat.*, cit., 120. I do not agree with Mrs. ÉVRARD-GILLIS, *La récurrence lexicale dans l'oeuvre de Catulle*, cit., 33-34, who includes this among the cases of repetition "ressentie comme une nécessité, n'ayant pas d'autre effet que la clarté et résultant de l'indifférence de l'écrivain à une sélection poussée du vocabulaire".
157. Cf. also 5,10; 16,12; 66,78.
158. A. RONCONI, *Studi catulliani*, cit., 25.
159. Cf. e.g. Ter. *Eun.* 586.
160. Cf. R. PICHON, *Index uerborum amatoriorum*, Paris 1902, 192.

in Herod. 1,47,3 οἶδα δ'ἐγὼ ψάμμου τ'ἀριθμὸν καὶ μέτρα θαλάσσης, also Pind. *Pyth.* 9,46 ff. ὅσσα τε χθὼν ἠρινὰ φύλλ᾽ ἀναπέμπει, χὠπόσαι / ἐν θαλάσσᾳ καὶ ποταμοῖς ψάμαθοι / κύμασιν ῥιπαῖς τ'ἀνέμων κλονέονται, / ... εὖ καθορᾷς, *Olymp.* 2,98 ἐπεὶ ψάμμος ἀριθμὸν περιπέφευγεν. There are examples of this proverbial image in Hellenistic poetry too: cf. Callim. *Hym.* 3,252 f. ἐπὶ δὲ στρατὸν ἱππημολγῶν / ἤγαγε Κιμμερίων ψαμάθῳ ἴσον, *Anth. Pal.* 12,145,3 f. (adesp.) ἴσον ἐπὶ ψαφαρὴν ἀντλεῖν ἅλα κἀπὸ Λιβύσσης / ψάμμου ἀριθμητὴν ἀρτιάσαι ψεκάδα. In Rome the theme does not seem to be used before Catullus[161]; afterwards it recurs in Virgil,[162] in Horace[163] and after in Ovid.[164]

The second proverbial image reproduces the motif of the impossibility of ἀστέρας μετρεῖν, this too attested in Homer (*Il.* 8,554 ff. πυρὰ δέ σφισι καίετο πολλά . / ὡς δ'ὅτ'ἐν οὐρανῷ ἄστρα φαεινὴν ἀμφὶ σελήνην / φαίνετ'ἀριπρεπέα, ὅτε τ'ἔπλετο νήνεμος αἰθήρ), and much appreciated later on by the Alexandrians: cf. e.g. Callim. *Hym.* 4,175 f. νιφάδεσσιν ἐοικότες ἢ ἰσάριθμοι / τείρεσιν, ἡνίκα πλεῖστα κατ'ἠέρα βουκολέονται, Herond. 1,32 f. γυναῖκες, ὁκόσους οὐ μὰ τὴν Ἅιδεω Κούρην / ἀστέρας ἐνεγκεῖν οὐρανὸς κεκαύχηται. In Rome the hyperbolical parallel with the number of the stars appears as early as Plaut. *Poen.* 431 ff. *quantum Acheruntest mortuorum* ... / *neque quantum aquaist in mari* ... / *neque nubes omnes quantumst* ... / *neque stellae in caelo*; after Catullus it will be frequent in Ovid.[165]

161. Cf. A. OTTO, *Sprichwörter*, cit., 8.
162. Verg. *Georg.* 2,105 f. *quem qui scire uelit, Libyci uelit aequoris idem / dicere quam multae Zephyro turbentur harenae.*
163. Hor. *Carm.* 1,21,1 *numero ... carentis harenae*; cf. R.G.M. NISBET - M. HUBBARD, *A Commentary on Horace*, cit., 321.
164. Cf. e.g. *Met.* 11,614 f. *somnia uana iacent totidem, quot messis aristas / silua gerit frondes, eiectas litus harenas, Ars* 1,253 f. *quid tibi femineos coetus uenatibus aptos / enumerem? numero cedet harena meo.* A. OTTO, *Sprichwörter*, cit., 8 quotes also Claudian. *In Eutr.* 1,32 f. *si pelagi fluctus, Lybicae si discis harenas, / Eutropii numerabis eros.*
165. Cf. e.g. *Ars* 1,59 *quot caelum stellas, tot habet tua Roma puellas, Trist.* 1,5,47 *tot mala sum passus, quot in aethere sidera lucent* and A. OTTO, *Sprichwörter*, cit., 321 f. On the motif of innumerability cf. now M. CITRONI in "Stud. Ital. Filol. Class." 51 (1979) 44-45. The examples of the *adynaton* "counting the grains of sand" are collected by E. DUTOIT,

In Catullus the two themes are employed together here and in 7,3 ff. *quam magnus numerus Libyssae harenae / lasarpiciferis iacet Cyrenis / ... aut quam sidera multa, cum tacet nox, / furtiuos hominum uident amores*; Svennung[166] thinks that Catullus' source is Theocritus, who similarly combines the two motifs in some of his verses: 30,25 ff. ὅττις δοκίμοι τὸν δολομάχανον / νικάσην Ἔρον, οὖτος δοκίμοι τοῖς ὑπὲρ ἀμμέων / εὔρην βραϊδίως ἄστερας ὁππόσσακιν ἔννεα. Svennung's hypothesis is possible, though uncertain, since the union of the two themes was in all probability normal and commonly regarded as proverbial by then: it is indeed attested in Plat. *Euthyd.* 294 B ἦ καὶ τὰ τοιαῦτα, τοὺς ἀστέρας ὁπόσοι εἰσὶ καὶ τὴν ἄμμον; cf. also *Paroem. Gr.* II 4 Leutsch.

Le thème de l'adynaton dans la poésie antique, Paris 1936, 10-12. 44-45. 66. 75. 103 (Catullus' instance). 172; cf. also L. ROBERT in *L'épigramme grecque*. Entr. sur l'Ant. Class. XIV, Vandoeuvres-Genève 1968, 266.
166. J. SVENNUNG, *Cat. Bilderspr.*, cit., 85.

CHAPTER VI

THE EPITHALAMIUM

Now that the bride and the groom are left by themselves in the thalamus, Catullus dedicates the last part of the poem to the advices and wishes traditional in the final stage of the ceremony. It is the part of the epithalamium proper,[1] beginning with the invitation to enjoy the pleasures of love, although this invitation is strictly related to the exhortation to procreate; with typically Roman pride Catullus asserts that being childless does not become such an ancient and noble family. This invitation represents a point of transition: Catullus then wishes the couple a *Torquatus paruolus* and imagines him while, smiling, he stretches his arms towards his father; the future baby must take after his father, in order to bear witness to his mother's modesty, like in the famous case of Telemachus and Penelope.

As regards the technique of organizing the various sections together, it is mainly in the epithalamium that Catullus strives to create a strong connection between the strophes, which all express ideas in logical sequence and not distinct themes: the invitation to give birth to children to propagate the illustrious family (ll. 204-208) obviously leads to the wish for a *Torquatus paruolus*

---

1. Many explanations – more or less fantastic ones – have been handed down from the ancient past in relation to the song before the closed door of the bed-chamber: for the scholiast of Theocritus' epithalamium, this song was necessary to drown the bride's moaning while she was losing her virginity: ᾄδουσι δὲ τὸν ἐπιθαλάμιον αἱ παρθένοι πρὸ τοῦ θαλάμου, ἵνα τῆς παρθένου βιαζομένης ὑπὸ τοῦ ἀνδρὸς ἡ φωνὴ μὴ ἐξακούηται, λανθάνῃ δὲ κρυπτομένη διὰ τῆς τῶν παρθένων φωνῆς. According to others, on the contrary, songs and noises in front of the thalamus (cf. Hesych. s.v. κτυπία · ὁ ἐπιθαλάμιος κτύπος, s.v. κτυπιῶν · τῶν ἐπικρουμάτων τοῦ θαλάμου, ἃ ἐπικτυποῦσιν ἔξωθεν, ὅταν συγκατακλίνηται τῷ νυμφίῳ ἡ γημαμένη) had the purpose of putting evil spirits to flight.

133

(ll. 209-213). In the last two strophes of the epithalamium it is the repetition of a noun that causes the logical link: in this way *dulce rideat ad patrem semihiante labello* (l. 212 f.) resounds in *sit suo similis patri* (l. 214) and the expression *pudicitiam suae matris indicet ore* (l. 217 f.) is continued by *talis illius a bona matre* (l. 219).

In the structure of the poem Catullus developes the epithalamium in the literal sense only to a certain extent; it is limited to the *allocutio sponsalis*, which in practice simply expresses the two motifs of the joys of love and the wish for offspring. The shortness of this part is explained by the fact that Catullus has already dealt with the principal themes of the epithalamium — like the eulogy of the bridal pair[2] — in the previous sections of the poem.

ludite ut lubet et breui	
liberos date. non decet	205
tam uetus sine liberis	
nomen esse, sed indidem	
semper ingenerari.	(215)
Torquatus uolo paruolus	
matris e gremio suae	210
porrigens teneras manus	
dulce rideat ad patrem	
semihiante labello.	(220)
sit suo similis patri	
Manlio et facile omnibus	215
noscitetur ab insciis[3]	
et pudicitiam suae	
matris indicet ore.	(225)

2. Cf. A. RIESE, *Die Gedichte des Catullus*, cit., 42 f.

3. I accept Dawes' transposition, which keeps the synapheia and seems more advisable than the banal *obuiis* suggested by Pleitner; on the other hand, both Mynors and Fordyce maintain the *collocatio uerborum* of the manuscripts, whereas M. HAUPT, *Opusc.*, I 20 does not reach any conclusion and merely asserts that (...). However, it must be added that, even though Fordyce accepts the metrical anomaly in the text (compelled as he is to print Mynor's own reading), then he rejects it in his comment (p. 253), as it is pointed out by D.F.S. THOMSON in "Phoenix" 28 (1974) 266. G. LIEBERG in "Gnom." 47 (1975) 356 (cf. also "Latinitas" 22 [1974]

talis illius a bona
matre laus genus approbet,   220
qualis unica ab optima
matre Telemacho manet
fama Penelopeo.   (230)

Catullus' epithalamium reproduces traditional schemes of Greek origins: the rhetoricians, as we have already noticed in relation to the τόπος of the husband's handsomeness (l. 189 ff.), mention the epithalamium proper in their discussions on the κατευναστικὸς λόγος, whose rules were expounded by Menander[4] and which was defined by him a προτροπὴ πρὸς τὴν συμπλοκήν: it is exactly in the κατευναστικὸς λόγος that τόποι employed by Catullus in the epithalamium proper appear, such as wishing the couple children who take after their parents.

In this case too Catullus follows the Greek literary tradition, but he does not repeat the Greek customs concerning wedding ceremonies: as a matter of fact, in the final phase of the Greek ceremony the θυρωρός was introduced, one of the husband's friends whose function was to close the door of the thalamus[5]; against him the people present uttered their jokes, as far as we can deduce from a Sapphic fragment (110 L.-P.): θυρώρῳ πόδες ἐπτορόγυιοι, / τὰ δὲ σάμβαλα πεμπεβόηα, / πίσσυγγοι δὲ δέκ᾿ἐξεπόναισαν.[6] On the contrary, there is no mention-

220), on the contrary, relies firmly on the manuscripts (here and at l. 185). The same problem has been dealt with by M.L. WEST, *Textual Criticism and Editorial Technique*, Stuttgart 1973, 137-138, who admits the difficulty in avoiding the synapheia; however, for him "Dawes' transposition is not very felicitous: *inscieis* is better in the predicative position, the desired emphasis being *ab omnibus, etiam inscieis*, not *ab inscieis, et quidem omnibus*"; consequently, as "no convincing solution seems yet to have been found, and as the scope for emendation appears so limited it may be that having stated the anomaly we should with due reserve accept it". On the synapheia cf. now L.E. ROSSI, *La sinafia*, in "Studi in onore di A. Ardizzoni", II, Roma 1978, 791-821.

4. Menand. *Rhet. Gr.* III 405 Spengel.

5. Cf. Hesych. s.v. θυρωρός ὁ παράνυμφος ὁ τὴν θύραν τοῦ θαλάμου κλείων, Poll. 3,42 καλεῖται δέ τις τῶν τοῦ νυμφίου φίλων καὶ θυρωρὸς ὃς ταῖς θύραις ἐφεστηκὼς εἴργει τὰς γυναῖκας τῇ νύμφῃ βοώσῃ βοηθεῖν.

6. Cf. also Demetr. *De elocut.* 167, p. 37 Radermacher ἄλλως δὲ σκώπτει (ἡ Σαπφώ) τὸν ἄγροικον νυμφίον καὶ τὸν θυρωρὸν τὸν ἐν τοῖς γάμοις εὐτελέστατα καὶ ἐν πεζοῖς ὀνόμασι μᾶλλον ἢ ἐν ποιητικοῖς.

ing of the ϑυρωρός in Catullus and in the last strophe it will be specified that the maidens themselves close the door of the bed-chamber.

Another difference consists in this: in the Greek literary tradition a chorus of maidens or *pueri* was appointed to sing the epithalamium proper,[7] whereas in Catullus the chori are quiet in the final stage of the ceremony and it is the poet who undertakes the task of expressing the ritual wishes to the bride and groom.

First of all, there is the invitation to *ludere ut lubet* (l. 204), regarded by the rhetoricians as a fundamental element of the epithalamium: cf. e.g. Menand. *Rhet. Gr.* III 407,20 Spengel εἶτα εὐχὴν ἐπάξεις αἰτῶν παρὰ τῶν κρειττόνων αὐτοῖς εὐμένειάν τε καὶ ὁμόνοιαν, συμπλοκῆς ἑστίαν, κρᾶσιν ψυχῶν, ὥσπερ καὶ τῶν σωμάτων: in fact it is sufficient to remember that for Menander the κατευναστικὸς λόγος is a προτροπὴ πρὸς τὴν συμπλοκήν, as it has been pointed out above. In Theocritus the exhortation to *ludere* is expressed, in the finale of the epithalamium, through a more realistic imagery then in Catullus and it is connected with facetious allusions: 18,54 ff. εὕδετ' ἐς ἀλλάλων στέρνον φιλότατα πνέοντες / καὶ πόθον . ἐγρέσθαι δὲ πρὸς ἀῶ μὴ 'πιλάθησθε. / νεύμεθα κάμμες ἐς ὄρθρον, ἐπεί κα πρᾶτος ἀοιδός / ἐξ εὐνᾶς κελαδήσῃ ἀνασχὼν εὔτριχα δειράν.[8] Catullus, on the other hand, in the epithalamium in the strict sense, reduces the invitation to consummate the marriage to the discreet formula *ludite ut lubet.*[9] It is significant that, also in this circumstance, his technique accords with the principles that will be fixed by the rhetoricians: Menander (*Rhet. Gr.* III 406,4 ff. Spengel) actually states that in the κατευναστικὸς λόγος undignified or foul words should be carefully avoided: φυλακτέον δ' ἐν τούτῳ, μή τι τῶν αἰσχρῶν μηδὲ τῶν εὐτελῶν ἢ φαύλων λέγειν δόξωμεν, καθιέντες εἰς τὸ αἰσχρὰ λέγειν καὶ μακρά, παρ' ὅσα ἔνδοξά ἐστι δικαίως, ἃ σεμνότητα φέρει καὶ ἔστιν εὐχαρῆ.

---

7. Cf. e.g. the case of Theocritus' epithalamium.
8. Cf. E.A. MANGELSDORFF, *Lyr. Hochzeitsged.*, cit., 20.
9. On the interpretation of *ludere* here and at line 225 cf. R. MUTH in "Serta Philol. Aenip." 1972, 68-69.

The exhortation to procreate is obviously traditional in epithalamia, for children are necessary to propagate one's descent and good family name; in the rhetoricians' theory cf. e.g. Ps. Dion. Hal. VI 1, p. 264 Usener-Radermacher ἐπειδὰν δὲ ἱκανῶς περὶ τούτων διέλθῃς, εὐχῇ χρηστέον ἀγαθῶν μὲν αἴτησιν ἐχούσῃ περὶ τὸν γάμον καὶ τὰς παιδοποιίας, ἀποτροπὴν δὲ τῶν κακῶν. As for literary epithalamia compare also Theocr. 18,51 f. Λατὼ μὲν δοίη, Λατὼ κουροτρόφος, ὕμμιν / εὐτεκνίαν and Stat. Sil. 1,2,266 f. heia age praeclaros Latio properate nepotes, / qui leges, qui castra legant, qui carmina ludant. In Catullus and Statius, as well as in Theocritus, the motif recurs at the end of the poem, and anyway the rhetoricians confirm that that was its usual place in the structure of wedding songs.[10] Moreover, in Catullus and Statius it is mentioned explicitly that the bride and groom must have children in a short time (breui in Catullus, properate in Statius): the same idea appears in Ps. Dion. Hal. VI 1, p. 271 Usener-Radermacher ἐπὶ τέλει δὲ καὶ εὐχῇ χρῆσθαι, ὅπως ὅ τι τάχιστα παῖδες γένοιντο, ὡς καὶ τούτων ἐπιδεῖν γάμους καὶ ᾆσαι τὸν ὑμέναιον καὶ ὑπόθεσιν ἔχειν αὖθις τοιούτων λόγων.

By tightly joining the motif of connubial love with that of procreation, Catullus wanted to attach a deep meaning to his verses: thus he underlines that love passion in married life does not exist for its own sake, but it is subordinate to a higher purpose. With his usual fineness Ferrero observes that once again the individual element is inserted into the main branch of society, which is any human being's duty to continue (ludite ... liberos date!): from the individual to the connubial society, from the latter to another new individual, to more complex relations, to a widening of their circle that creates another situation, another complex unity.[11]

In ll. 209-213 the allocutio sponsalis takes the shape of a request for the birth of a Torquatus paruolus, even though Catullus does not address any particular divinity directly, but he expresses his wish in generic terms by using the verb uolo. This motif, too, belongs to the traditional patterns of the epithalamium; the form of prayer is indeed recommended by the

10. A.L. WHEELER in "Amer. Journ. Phil." 51 (1930) 215.
11. L. FERRERO, Interpretazione di Catullo, cit., 286.

rhetoricians at the end of the λόγος ἐπιθαλάμιος[12]: apart from the above-cited passages by Menander (*Rhet. Gr.* III 407,20 ff. Spengel) and Pseudo-Dionysus (Ps. Dion. Hal. VI 1, p. 264. 271 Usener-Radermacher), cf. Himer. *Or.* 9,21 Colonna στὰς δὲ παρ᾽αὐτὸν τὸν θάλαμον Τύχη καὶ Ἔρωτι καὶ Γενεθλίοις προσεύξομαι . τῷ μὲν τοξεύειν εἰς τέλος, τῇ δὲ διδόναι βίον, τοῖς δὲ παίδων γνησίων γένεσιν, ἵνα τῷ γαμηλίῳ κρατῆρι ποτὲ καὶ τὴν γενέθλιον σπονδὴν συνάψωμεν, Choric. *Or.* 2, p. 24 Förster καταβήσομαι τοίνυν θεοῖς προσευξάμενος γαμηλίοις φῦναί τε παῖδας ὑμῖν καὶ τραφῆναι καὶ πρὸς ἥβην ἐλθεῖν καὶ πρὸς ἄνδρα ἐκβῆναι καὶ τοιαύτας εὐτυχῆσαι γυναῖκας.

I doubt whether, with regard to the affected description of the child smiling[13] and stretching towards his father, we can share Ferrero's appraisal, according to which this is Catullus at his best, who efficaciously evokes a picture of family life by means of a felicitous detail; for Ferrero the tone and atmosphere, due to their grace and delicacy, remind us of the happy and naïve idyll between Acme and Septimius.[14] However, it seems more relevant to understand what is the meaning of the strophe in the structure of the poem and, as concerns this, Castorina grasps its value perfectly when he underlines that in ll. 209-213 there is the sense of the family peculiar to the Romans.[15]

The child, fruit of Manlius' and Junia's love, will necessarily take after his father so that everybody looking at him will easily understand that he is his son; in this way *paruolus Torquatus* will bear witness to his mother's modesty. Catullus resumes here the very ancient τόπος of children looking like their parents, which

12. Cf. E.A. MANGELSDORFF, *Lyr. Hochzeitsged.*, cit., 20.

13. Verg. *Buc.* 4,61 *incipe parue puer risu cognoscere matrem* is usually cited as being parallel to the motif of the child's smile in front of his parents; but commentators should mention at least that E. NORDEN, *Die Geburt des Kindes*, Leipzig 1924, 61 ff. suggests a different − and plausible, in my view − interpretation of the context in Virgil.

14. L. FERRERO, *Interpretazione di Catullo*, cit., 302. Too much attention has been paid to the family picture by M. MANSON in "Mél. Ec. Fr. Rome" 90 (1978) 260-263: he sees a novelty in it (the description of a "restreinte, moderne" family) and a mirror of sensitivity towards children, that he regards as typical in Rome after Sulla's time.

15. E. CASTORINA, *Questioni neoteriche*, cit., 92.

is to be found for the first time in Hes. *Erga* 235 τίκτουσιν δὲ γυναῖκες ἐοικότα τέκνα γονεῦσιν[16]; cf. then Aeschin. 3,111 ἐπεύχεται αὐτοῖς μήτε γῆν καρποὺς φέρειν, μήτε γυναῖκας τέκνα τίκτειν γονεῦσιν ἐοικότα ἀλλὰ τέρατα, Ps. Phoc. 178 D. οὐ γὰρ τίκτει παῖδας ὁμοίους μοιχικὰ λέκτρα, Theocr. 17,43 f. ἀστόργου δὲ γυναικὸς ἐπ᾽ἀλλοτρίῳ νόος αἰεί, / ῥηίδιοι δὲ γοναί, τέκνα δ᾽οὐ ποτεοικότα πατρί, Oppian. *Hal.* 1,644 f. αὐτίκα παῖδες / ἐκ γενετῆς ἀνέχουσιν ἐοικότες οἷσι τοκεῦσι. In Rome the theme occurs in Chremes' words to Sostrata in Ter. *Heaut.* 1018 ff. *quo magis credundum siet / id quod est consimilis moribus; / conuinces facile ex te natum; nam tui similis est probe, / nam illi nihil uiti est relictum quin sit et itidem tibi; / tum praeterea talem nisi tu nulla pareret filium* and reappears in Hor. *Carm.* 4,5, 23 *laudantur simili prole puerperae*, Ouid. *Trist.* 4,5,31 f. *similisque tibi sit natus et illum / moribus agnoscat quilibet esse tuum*, Martial. 6,27,3 f. *est tibi, quae patria signatur imagine uultus, / testis maternae nata pudicitiae.*

The fact that the motif was traditional in epithalamia is proved by the numerous hints at it made by the rhetoricians, who in their precepts on the ἐπιθαλάμιος λόγος and the κατευναστικὸς λόγος advise that it should be employed. They merely mention a resemblance between children and parents: cf. e.g. Menand. *Rhet. Gr.* III 404,27 f. Spengel τέξετε παῖδας ὑμῖν τε ὁμοίους καὶ ἐν ἀρετῇ λαμπρούς, 407,8 Spengel ἵνα δημιουργήσητε παῖδας ὁμοίους μὲν σοί, ὁμοίους δὲ ἐκείνῃ, 407,23 f. Spengel ἵνα οἱ παῖδες ἀμφοτέροις ὅμοιοι γένωνται. Catullus in ll. 214-218 follows the trend of those who wish or highlight the resemblance with the father, which is indispensable to demonstrate that the child is legitimate. In contrast with Catullus are Theocritus and Statius, in their epithalamia: in the epithalamium dedicated to Helen the wish is that her children may take after their mother (18,21 ἦ μέγα κά τι τέκοιτ᾽, εἰ ματέρι τίκτοι ὁμοῖον), but the variation of the theme is justified by Helen's extraordinary beauty; Statius tries to fuse the two aspects, but he asserts that a son should look more like his mother than like his father (*Sil.* 1,2,271 ff. *cumque*

16. On the motif cf. A. RZACH, *Hesiodi Carmina*, Leipzig 1902, 169; A.S.F. GOW, *Theocritus*, cit., II 334; J. WACKERNAGEL, *Kl. Schr.*, I 491 n. 1.

tuos tacito natura recessu / formarit uultus, multum de patre decoris, / plus de matre feras).

In the λόγος ἐπιθαλάμιος the rhetoricians advise that mythical comparisons should be employed to expund an idea; this instruction was surely based upon the observation of the traditional practice of poets[17]: in Catullus, however, such a technique (which will be developed in Statius' epithalamium even too much) is used only sporadically, in the parallels Manlius/Paris and Junia/Venus in the ὕμνος κλητικός (ll. 16-19) and in the one between Penelope Telemachus and Junia - Torquatus jun. (ll. 219-222). There are no further instances of the same comparison in wedding songs; nevertheless, Wheeler seems to be quite right when he supposes[18] that it must be frequent in the genre of the epithalamium. In addition, we must remember that the eulogy of Penelope's *pudicitia* was a traditional motif: cf. e.g. Prop. 2,6,23; 9,3; 3,12,38; 13,24; 4,5,7.[19]

This section of the poem, then, seems to be constructed — more than the previous ones — on a series of τόποι; but one realizes easily that Catullus' participation in the event is complete and it appears both in his wish for children and in the psychological remark about little Torquatus' smile and the eulogy of his mother's modesty; the τόποι have become in Catullus purely decorative and accessory elements that amplify and enrich the original poetic intuition.[20]

*

Of course the style is refined in lines that express so dignified and solemn ideas; it is also obvious that, in the strophe containing

17. It is significant that on such comparisons ironical remarks have been made by Lucian. *Conu.* 41 ἡ οἴη πότ᾽ ἄρ᾽ ἦγε Ἀρισταινέτου ἐν μεγάροις / δῖα Κλεανθὶς ἄνασσ᾽ ἐτρέφετ᾽ ἐνδυκέως, / προὔχουσα πασάων ἀλλάων παρθενικάων, / κρέσσων τῆς Κυθέρης ἠδ᾽ αὖ τῆς Σελήνης. / Νυμφίε, καὶ σὺ δὲ χαῖρε, κρατερῶν κράτιστε ἐφήβων, / κρέσσων Νιρῆος καὶ Θέτιδος παΐδός. / Ἄμμες δ᾽ αὖθ᾽ ὑμῖν τούτον θαλαμήϊον ὕμνον / ξυνὸν ἐπ᾽ ἀμφοτέροις πολλάκις ἀσόμεθα.

18. A.L. WHEELER, *Catullus and the Tradition*, cit., 195.

19. Cf. M. ROTHSTEIN, *Sextus Propertius. Elegien*, I², Berlin 1920, 249.

20. L. FERRERO, *Interpretazione di Catullo*, cit., 302.

the description of the smile of *paruolus Torquatus*, intimate and familiar tones take the place of gravity. As an evidence of the first motif, consider that the "iunctura" *dare liberos* (l. 205) probably reproduces an ancient formula.[21] At ll. 205-206 Catullus employs the sententious and emphatic expression *non decet tam uetus sine liberis nomen esse.* The adverb *indidem* (l. 207), frequent in archaic language (Plautus, Pacuvius, Cato), was regarded perhaps as an archaism in Catullus' times; it is indeed relevant that before Livy it only occurs in Cic. *Rosc. Amer.* 74,[22] in Corn. Nep. *Epam.* 5,9 and in Varro's *De lingua latina*[23] and that, afterwards, Apuleius and Gellius will have a preference for it. Notice the refinement of the use made of *ingenerare* (l. 208) – a verb attested from Cicero on, and maybe used in the sense of *generando renouare* only by Catullus[24] –, the alliteration *sit suo similis* (l. 214) and the insistence on the word *mater* at ll. 218-222. The frequentative verb *noscito* too is employed for its flavour of ancientness: it is often to be found in Plautus (cf. *Cist.* 682; *Epid.* 537; *Men.* 961. 1064; *Mil.* 521; *Trin.* 863), it occurs only in Catullus and then from Livy on[25]; the use of *inscius* as a noun is refined too, for which *Thes.* VII 1,1845,52 ff. cites Cic. *Acad.* 2,22 and some examples from late Latinity. The search for symmetry in ll. 219-223 is remarkable: *talis ... a bona/matre ... qualis ... ab optima/ matre*; the simile with *talis ... qualis* belongs to the category defined of Homeric kind, "mit epischer Breite ausgesponnen",[26] by Svennung. It is evident that emphasis is laid on the formula *laus genus approbet* (l. 220), where the verb *approbare* is given the rare meaning of *ostendere*,[27] as well as on the imagery of ll. 221-223. The adjective *Penelopeo* (l. 223) is chosen with the purpose of ending the strophe in a solemn way.[28]

21. Cf. what has been observed with regard to l. 67.
22. Cf. G. LANDGRAF, *Kommentar zu Ciceros Rede Pro Sex. Roscio Amerino*, Leipzig/Berlin 1914[2], 156.
23. Cf. *Thes.* VII 1, 1164, 73 ff.
24. Cf. *Thes.* VII 1, 1519, 31 ff.
25. Cf. Liu. 2,20,8; 23,4; 3,38,9; 6,25,1; 8,32,2; 22,6,3; 26,41,24; Curt. Ruf. 3,11,10; 8,13,24; Quintil. *Inst.* 4,2,124; Plin. *Pan.* 17,1; *Epist.* 6,20, 14; 9,6,2. 23,5; Tac. *Hist.* 12,18.
26. J. SVENNUNG, *Cat. Bilderspr.*, cit., 44.
27. Cf. *Thes.* II 311, 50 ff.
28. Cf. C.J. FORDYCE, *Catullus*, cit., 253; on the origin of *Penelopeus*

In ll. 209-213, on the contrary, the intimate tone stems from the delicacy of imagery, as well as the diminutives *paruolus* (l.209), *labellus* (l. 213[29]) and the "iuncturae" *teneras manus* (l. 211) and *semihiante labello* (l. 213): *semihians*, like all the compound nouns beginning with *semi-*, particularly dear to Catullus,[30] possibly belongs to colloquial language and will never be resumed before Apuleius.[31] On the Graecism *dulce rideat* (which reminds us of the well-known *dulce ridentem* of c. 51,5, translated from the Sapphic γελαίσας ἱμέροεν) compare E. Löfstedt, *Syntactica*, cit., II 420.[32]

*

In the last strophe Catullus urges the maidens to close the thalamus' door[33]: the *ludus* is over and the poem ends with the traditional wish to the bride and groom to *bene uiuere* and practise erotic exercises assiduously. *Claudite ostia uirgines* in the finale re-echoes the *claustra pandite ianuae* of l. 76,[34] underlining in this way, with the technique – of which Catullus was fond – of "Ringkomposition",[35] the terms of the "dramatic" phase of the poem and the unity of this section: as a matter of fact, l. 76 marked the passage from the ὕμνος κλητικός to the description of the *deductio*: by repeating the same formula at the end of the

cf. A.E. HOUSMAN in "Journ. Philol." 33 (1914) 73, on its artistic value D.O. ROSS, *Style and Tradition*, cit., 100.

29. In this respect RONCONI, *Studi catulliani*, cit., 123 observes that "i due diminutivi, che sono d'uso comune, esulano ... da codesta stilizzazione, e ascoltati nel tono di tutta la strofa, suonano come note di squisita delicatezza".

30. Cf. *semimortuus* 50,15, *semilautus* 54,2, *semirasus* 59,5.

31. Cf. J. SVENNUNG, *Cat. Bilderspr.*, cit., 32, D.O. ROSS, *Style and Tradition*, cit., 21 f. and for the prosody of *semihiante* L. MÜLLER, *De re metrica*, cit., 304.

32. On the use of this Graecism cf. also J.B. HOFMANN - A. SZANTYR, *Lat. Syntax u. Stilistik*, 40; on the "iunctura" cf. *Thes.* VI 1, 2196, 55 ff.

33. It is not the door of the house, as G. Friedrich asserts (*Catulli Veronensis liber*, cit., 279).

34. Also for this reason I am more inclined to regard *ianuae* at l. 76 as a vocative, and not a genitive.

35. On the "Ringkomposition" in Catullus cf. E. FRAENKEL, *Kl. Schr.*, II 125 ff., P. FEDELI, *Il carme 30 di Catullo*, in "Studia Florentina Alex. Ronconi sexagenario oblata", Roma 1970, 100.

epithalamium Catullus makes it clear that he regards the ὕμνος as not being part of the real action.[36]

> claudite ostia, uirgines;
> lusimus satis. at boni   225
> coniuges, bene uiuite et
> munere assiduo ualentem
>   exercete iuuentam.   (235)

At l. 224, then, Catullus addresses the *uirgines*, asking them to close the door of the bed-chamber, and his invitation represents another change in the traditional ritual of wedding ceremonies: in Greece, in fact, it was the task of the ϑυρωρός, in Rome probably of the *pronuba*, who had accompanied the bride to the thalamus and prepared her to meet her husband. Catullus' particular, therefore, has no correspondence either in Greek or in Roman ceremonies.

The reason for this variation of an aspect of the ceremony can be understood if one wonders who the maidens are, to whom Catullus refers: according to Mangelsdorff they are the bride's friends, "entsprechend dem griechischen Ritus",[37] whereas for Friedrich the *uirgines* are the women-slaves in the house[38]; in Friedrich's view a reference to the *integrae uirgines* mentioned at l. 36 would be impossible, because he does not believe that they could be present during the *deductio* and the other stages of the ceremony. But the simple fact that both in Greece and in Rome other characters had the duty of closing the thalamus' door should prevent us from looking at all costs for a solution that can accord with the reality of the ceremony.

Most likely Catullus has adapted a motif handed down by literary tradition to his poetic needs: in Greek literary tradition, actually, a chorus of maidens sang the epithalamium[39]; moreover,

---

36. Cf. also L. FERRERO, *Interpretazione di Catullo*, cit., 295.
37. E.A. MANGELSDORFF, *Lyr. Hochzeitsged.*, cit., 43.
38. G. FRIEDRICH, *Catulli Veronensis liber*, cit., 279.
39. Cf. Pind. *Pyth.* 3,30 ff. οὐδὲ παμφώνων ἰαχὰν ὑμεναίων, ἅλικες / οἷα παρθένοι φιλέοισν ἑταῖραι / ἑσπερίαις ὑποκουρί- / ζεσθ᾽ ἀοιδαῖς, Callim. *Frg.* 75,42 Pf. χἠ θεὸς εὐορκεῖτο καὶ ἥλικες αὐτίχ᾽ ἑταίρης / ᾖδον ὑμηναίους οὐκ ἀναβαλλομένους. But for Proclus *ap.* Phot. 321 a 17 Bekker (= V 162,17 Henry) mixed chori of youths and maidens sang the

in Theocritus' epithalamium the maidens sing the whole wedding
song.[40] In c. 61 the maidens are certainly present in the ὕμνος
κλητικός, where, following the poet's invitation, they intone
the songs in Hymen's honour. I have already expressed, with
regard to ll. 36-45, my opinion as for the solution of the doubt
roused by l. 224: I think that, on the model of Theocritus – who
attributes the whole epithalamium to the maidens – in the finale
of his wedding song Catullus addresses the same maidens who have
sung the hymenaeus and have accompanied him during the various
phases of the ceremony, thus connecting the end of the poem to
the beginning also from this angle; in this case *lusimus satis* at
l. 225 is not a *plural maiestatis*, but it is referred to both the poet
and the chorus of *integrae uirgines*.[41]

The greeting to the couple, alongside the wish for a happy
life, constitutes itself a τόπος of wedding songs; the motif is indeed
attested in Sappho's epithalamia, although it is not possible to
infer from the fragments in which part of the Sapphic songs it
appeared: cf. 116 L.-P. χαῖρε, νύμφα, χαῖρε, τίμιε γάμβρε,
πόλλα, 117 L.-P. † χαίροις ἀ νύμφα †, χαιρέτω δ'ὁ γάμβρος.

Aristophanes too, in the hymenaeus of *Peace*, introduces a
humorous wish addressed by the coryphaeus to the bride and
groom (l. 1344 ff.): οἰκήσετε γοῦν καλῶς / οὐ πράγματ'ἔχοντες,
ἀλ-/ λὰ συκολογοῦντες.[42] In Theocritus the wish for happiness
and prosperity is put at the end, like in Catullus, and in all prob-

epithalamium proper: καὶ τὰ ἐπιθαλάμια δὲ τοῖς ἄρτι θαλαμευομένοις
ἅμα οἱ ἠΐθεοι καὶ αἱ παρθένοι ἐπὶ τῶν θαλάμων ᾖδον.

40. Cf. 18,2 f., where is the mentioning of παρθενικαὶ θάλλοντα κόμαις
ὑάκινθον ἔχοισαι, who intone the wedding song before the thalamus.

41. Obviously in this case too, whether *lusimus* reconnects the poet with
the chorus of *uirgines* and so with the beginning of the poem, or (as G. LIE-
BERG asserts in "Gnom." 47 [1975] 357; see also "Latinitas" 22 [1974]
220) it simply refers to the first line of the epithalamium proper (l. 204
ludite ut lubet), not only does the verb *ludere* designate a facetious and
lively song, but it is also necessary "zur Bezeichnung lebensnahen und
eingängigen Dichtens und Singens" (R. MUTH in "Serta Phil. Aenip." 1972,
68). On the *ludus poeticus* cf. above all H. WAGENVOORT, *Studies in
Roman Literature, Culture and Religion*, Leiden 1956, 30-42.

42. According to Dawes, editors usually attributes these lines to Trygaeus,
i.e. to the groom; but, in my opinion, CANTARELLA, *Aristofane. Le com-
medie*, III, Milano 1954, 545 is right in making the coryphaeus pronounce
the wish.

ability that was its fixed place in wedding songs: cf. l. 49 χαίροις ὦ νύμφα, χαίροις εὐπένθερε γαμβρέ, 50 ff. δοίη ... Κύπρις δέ, θεὰ Κύπρις, ἶσον ἔρασθαι / ἀλλάλων . Ζεὺς δέ, Κρονίδας Ζεύς, ἄφθιτον ὄλβον.

In respect to Catullus, not enough attention has been paid to the exact meaning of the exhortation to *bene uiuere*: there is little likelihood that it should be considered a hint at a wealthy existence with no worries,[43] or at the rectitude of life and behaviour,[44] because moralism in Catullus would be out of place in this strophe, ending with the invitation to *ualentem exercere iuuentam munere assiduo*. *Bene uiuite* maybe means *felice, concordes uiuite*, and it is a generic formula for wishing well, implying another τόπος typical of wedding songs, namely the ὁμόνοια[45]: the ὁμόνοια designates both concord of intentions and harmony in sexual life; therefore the presence of the τόπος in this strophe is well appropriate, as here *bene uiuite* is joined with the invitation to enjoy the pleasures of love. Anyhow, it would be surprising not to find in Catullus a theme that the rhetoricians consider very important and advise to employ in epithalamia: cf. for this Ps. Dion. Hal. VI 1, p. 271 Usener-Radermacher ἐπὶ δὲ τοῖς ἐπαίνοις καὶ τοῖς ἐγκωμίοις καὶ προτροπή τις ἔστω τοῖς γαμοῦσιν πρὸς τὸ σπουδάζειν περὶ ἀλλήλους καὶ ὁμονοεῖν ὅ τι μάλιστα ... ὅτι ὁμόνοια πᾶσι μὲν ἀνθρώποις ἡγεῖται τῶν ἀγαθῶν, μάλιστα δὲ τοῖς γεγαμηκόσιν[46], Menand. *Rhet. Gr.* III 407,16 Spengel βίου παντὸς ὁμόνοιαν, Choric. *Or.* 6, p. 40 Förster ἡδὺ μὲν λύρα χορδῶν συμφθεγγομένων ἀλλήλαις, ἡδὺ δὲ ζεῦγος συνωρίδος ὁμονοούσης, ἥδιστον δὲ πάντων γυνὴ ταὐτὰ φρονοῦσα τῷ συνοικοῦντι.

Theocritus hints at the ὁμόνοια in his epithalamium, when he expresses the wish that Venus may allow the couple to ἶσον ἔρασθαι ἀλλάλων (18,51 f.), and Catullus himself underlines its importance apropos of Peleus and Thetis: 64, 334 ff. *nulla domus tales umquam contexit amores, / nullus amor tali coniun-*

---

43. Cf. *Thes.* II 2113, 56 ff.
44. Cf. *Thes.* II 2118, 29 ff.
45. On the motif cf. A.L. WHEELER in "Amer. Journ. Phil." 51 (1930) 214.
46. For this theme Pseudo-Dionys. cites Hom. *Od.* 7,183 f. ἢ ὅτε ὁμοφρονέοντε νοήμασιν οἶκον ἔχητον / ἀνὴρ ἠδὲ γυνή.

145

xit foedere amantes, | qualis adest Thetidi, qualis concordia Peleo.

Catullus ends the poem by inviting the couple to *munere assiduo exercere iuuentam*, which is a spur to give free play to the pleasures of love: on *munus* "in re amatoria" cf. Plaut. *Asin.* 812, Ouid. *Her.* 4,137, *Am.* 1,14,54, *Ars* 2,575, Petron. 87,8, Martial. 9,67,8 and some more recent instances in Thes. VIII 1667,11 ff.; *exercere iuuentam*, in the sense of "adhibere uigorem iuuentutis" and similar,[47] appears here for the first time; this *iunctura* will recur later on in Ouid. *Am.* 1,8,53, Phaedr. *Fab. App.* 10,4, Stat. *Sil.* 1,2,166.[48]

In this way, as Ferrero has rightly observed, in the final part of the poem, Catullus goes back to the same ideas expressed in the ὕμνος, but making his imagination move in the opposite direction: in the ὕμνος κλητικός the passage is from myth to reality, from Hymenaeus, the child of Urania and inhabitant of the Helicon, to Junia and Manlius getting married under favourable auspices, to the mythological sphere again. Here, on the other hand, from *ludite ut lubet*, after the pause of the family picture with little smiling Torquatus, Catullus goes back to the theme of physical love, of *munere assiduo exercete iuuentam*, having touched also on the mythological idealization: *qualis unica ab optima | matre Telemacho manet | fama Penelopeo.*[49]

---

47. Cf. *Thes.* V 2, 1372, 13 ff.

48. *Iuuenta* is a predominantly poetic noun, attested from Cicero (*Carm. Frg.* 11,75 Morel) and Catullus on, which never occurs in prose before Livy: cf. *Thes.* VII 2,740,68 ff.

49. L. FERRERO, *Interpretazione di Catullo*, cit., 313.

CONCLUSION

Eduard Norden's assertion that Catullus presumably tried to make the hymenaeus and the fescennine match each other,[1] must be modified on the basis of the results achieved: it does not grasp, in fact, but a particular facet of a poem originated from the union of far more complex themes.

Nor does Wheeler's theory seem right[2]: he interprets c. 61 as a continuous attempt, on Catullus' part, to adapt a Greek *genus* to Roman conditions; as a matter of fact, such an intention of "romanizing" the wedding song only exists in a special part of it, the one containing the description of the stages of the *deductio*, and even there some elements of evident Greek origins emerge.

No more convincing are those critics who maintain that c. 61 should be regarded allegorically as the symbol of a secret desire of Catullus: this is an interpretation suggested by Ferrero, according to whom in the wedding song Catullus needs to detach himself from his torment, to look at what he considers the complete realization of love, from the outside, in a calm mood, as it happens to somebody else.[3] The same interpretation has been recently resumed by other scholars as well: Salvatore posits that the poem is pervaded with the desire for a blessed, consecrated union. Catullus is extremely sensitive to such an atmosphere, just because it is in contrast with his situation[4]; for Bardon too the epithalamium represents the expression of Catullus' aspiration for marriage.[5]

1. E. NORDEN, *La letteratura romana*, cit., 76.
2. A.L. WHEELER, *Catullus and the Tradition*, cit., 191, 196, 212.
3. L. FERRERO, *Interpretazione di Catullo*, cit., 283.
4. A. SALVATORE, *Studi catulliani*, Napoli 1965, 94.
5. H. BARDON, *Propositions sur Catulle*, cit., 83. The main remark made by G. LIEBERG about my book in his review in 'Gnom." 47 (1975) 357 is that I have not given importance to Catullus' "Sehnsucht nach einer vollständigen Verwirklichung der Liebe in der legitimen Form der Hochzeit",

The genesis of the poem is different, in my opinion: Catullus' task was to sing of the wedding of a couple — probably a noble and educated one[6] — and obviously he starts from a literary experience, upon which any poetic creation was based, for him and for the neoterics, and which chiefly meant following the rules of Alexandrian poetry. If, on the one hand, this literary experience is undoubtedly the origin of the poem, on the other hand Catullus does not consider himself tightly bound to repeat τόποι belonging to the *genus* of wedding songs; he integrates the elements handed

which in his view is present in the poem; he seems to be full of anguish and surprise for this fault. I think that, as there are no certain evidences, it is possible to entertain serious doubt about the truth of an hypothesis that cannot be proved, due to the way it is presented. However, against the strong opinion of Lieberg and of those who agree with him, I prefer to oppose not my words (I have expressed my view on the subject and I am not going to change it at all), but what has been said by M. CITRONI in "Stud. Ital. Filol. Class." 51 (1979) 20, in connection with a general study of the influence exerted by genesis and destination on the formal realization of every poem of Catullus: "anche di questo carme è stata più volte proposta una lettura in chiave lirico-autobiografica (...). Anche qui Catullo carezzereb-be con nostalgico rapimento il suo ideale di un amore ricambiato e duraturo. Ora è vero che questo ideale altre volte lo porta a usare per il suo amore libero espressioni proprie della sfera matrimoniale, ma una stretta identifica-zione del suo ideale erotico con il matrimonio è comunque improbabile. E poi, soprattutto, anche qui il tono brillante e festoso del carme sconsiglia di leggervi profondi contenuti lirici introspettivi".

Fortunately, even in German *milieu*, where such psychological criticism is particularly flourishing in some schools, there is somebody who does not share this view: in reviewing the first edition of my book, R. HEINE in "Anz. Altertumswiss." 29 (1976) 202 is glad that it does not contain "jene weit-gehend spekulative Catullphilologie", which is inclined to establish artificial relations between some lines of c. 61 and lines taken from other poems and, consequently, "c. 61 als Chiffre zu deuten, hinter der Catull seine geheimsten, an der Wirklichkeit scheiternden Sehnsüchte verbirgt".

6. Torquatus' identity has been dealt with by F. DELLA CORTE, *Perso-naggi Catulliani*, cit., 88-94, who has reached the conclusion that he must have been L. Manlius Torquatus, the praetor in 49 B.C., included by Cicero as an interlocutor in books I-II of *De finibus*; in this case he would have been the last heir of a noble family of very ancient republican origins, who was sensitive, however, to the suggestion of Hellenistic philosophy and poetry; this could explain Catullus' acceptance of both the Italic and the Hellenistic tradition; on these themes cf. again F. DELLA CORTE, *Personaggi catulliani*, cit., 95-108.

down by tradition with personal motifs and even employs the former with the greatest freedom.

He has, therefore, started from the hymenaeus to produce something different and more complicated: the hymenaeus itself is dealt with in an independent way and becomes an ample celebration of the god and his δύναμις, by means of the style and technique peculiar to sacred hymns; alongside the ὕμνος and the ἐγκώμιον there are the themes of the parthenius (in the chorus of maidens), of the fescennine (in the description of the *deductio*) and of the epithalamium proper (at the end of the poem); alongside the fusion of τόποι and original motifs there is the lively and brilliant description of the *deductio* and the phases of the ceremony taking place in the groom's house.

The co-existence itself of these elements suffices to point out the fundamental component of Catullus' art, as it proves his faithfulness to the principles of Alexandrinism. An example of the influence of Alexandrian poetry is the great development of the ὕμνος in the wedding song, and not only because it re-echoes formulae of Callimachus' hymns frequently: commentators regard this element as negative and are satisfied to ascertain that the length of the ὕμνος is out of proportion to the general structure of the poem. They could notice at least that in the ὕμνος some fundamental themes occur, like the idea of the family as the basis of the State and the description of the modesty *nouae nuptae*, that will be resumed in the final part of the poem. And they could observe principally that the great development of the ὕμνος is arranged on the model of Alexandrian precepts: it is indeed well-known that Alexandrian poets were not too concerned about the harmony of the various sections of a work and that they introduced many literary genres in a definite *genus*. Therefore, the Alexandrian poet was thoroughly free to expand accessory parts and learned digressions[7]; Catullus, moreover, has been able to fuse this freedom with the need and the search for a unitary character, which he has succeeded in lending to the poem by means of the repetition – above all in the finale – of motifs already expressed in the ὕμνος.

7. On this subject, enlightening remarks have been made by A. LA PENNA, *Virgilio e la crisi del mondo antico*, in *Virgilio. Tutte le opere*, Firenze 1966, XV.

Of Alexandrian origin is also the particular dramatic movement of the poem, in which the poet depicts himself as he directs the various phases of the ceremony: Callimachus' hymns and some of Theocritus' idylls must have exerted a determinant influence as for both this general aspect and other specific themes, like the waiting for the bride to come out (which re-echoes the tone of the waiting for Apollo's epiphany in the second Hymn of Callimachus) or the sudden appearance of the bride (which reminds us of Athena's sudden epiphany in the fifth Hymn of Callimachus). Theocritus' influence must have been decisive with regard to the choice of the chorus of maidens and the ample part given to it.

Alexandrinism is evident especially in the principle of the ποικιλία, which is the basis of the poem: it concerns both style – as we shall see later on – and content and it consists of a mixture of echoes deriving from Sappho, Anacreon, Theocritus and Callimachus: this side of Catullus' neoterism has been underlined efficaciously by Castorina, who observes that it could appear peculiar, due to the heterogeneity of the models, and then concludes by asserting that, after all, also Hellenistic poets imitated 'archaic' poets, such as Archilocus and Sappho. So the neoteric syncretism simply accentuates a phenomenon already present in the Hellenism.[8]

This is an essential aspect to see how illogical the attempts are of those who consider Sappho as the only source for Catullus and want to reconstruct Sappho through Catullus; in contrast with this, I think that Maas' view[9] is right and applicable to Catullus: in his words "in den übrigen Hymenaioi ... wirken nur einzelne Floskeln der Sappho erweislich nach", although the problem of Sappho's influence on Hellenistic wedding songs, and chiefly on Theocritus, remains unsolved.

Finally, there are evident traces of Alexandrinism in the atmosphere of ll. 26-30, with the mentioning of the spring Aganippe and of the Muses' *antrum* near Thespis as well as the constant search for rare myths and erudite details in the hymn (Hymen the son of Urania and *cultor* of the Helicon; *Idalium* as the place of worship of Venus; Paris defined *Phrygius*; myrtle as a term of comparison for the bride and its "iunctura" with the

8. E. CASTORINA, *Questioni neoteriche*, cit., 103.
9. P. MAAS in "R.E.P.W." IX 1 (1914) 132 f.

adjective *Asius*; the mentioning of the nymphs Hamadryads) and in a series of expedients and devices, such as the invocation to the bed, the description of the bride's complexion, the technique (l. 151 ff.) of interrupting a sentence with a refrain and the use itself of refrains.

Besides the Alexandrian component, a determining influence is the one exerted by the literary tradition of the *genus*: the fact that Catullus is bound to the rules of the *genus* is clear – apart from the traditional description of Hymen, *pulchritudine muliebri* – in the numerous τόποι cited by the rhetoricians in their theory of the ἐπιϑαλάμιος and κατευναστικὸς λόγος (the comparison between the bride and a goddess and some natural elements; the eulogy of Hymen as the greatest god; the representation of the groom's mingled feelings of *timor* and *cupiditas*; the exaltation of the δύναμις ϑεοῦ; the eulogy of the bridal pair's beauty; the idea of marriage as the giving up of all unlawful affairs; the invitation to give free play to the joys of love, the exhortation to *bene uiuere* and procreate; the parallel between Junia's and Penelope's *pudicitia*).

Alongside the τόποι of the epithalamium, a wealth of motifs appear, handed down by the Greek literary tradition: among the most famous ones it is worth remembering the metaphor of the *comae* of the torches, the image of sunlight rising from the Ocean and admiring the bride's beauty, the τόπος of children taking after their father to bear witness to the maternal *pudicitia*.

But, La Penna observes, "Catullo col solo nutrimento di dotta poesia ellenistica sarebbe tutt'al più un pascolo per i sottili filologi"[10]; it is remarkable, thus, that even in a poem connected with conventional themes imposed by the literary tradition of the *genus* – a poem, then, in which his "individualità passionale e lirica"[11] could emerge less than ever – Catullus clearly seeks to introduce personal tones and go beyond the sheer emulation of Hellenistic models: he has succeeded in this, not only by means of the particular function of the poet-coryphaeus and some psychological remarks (like the delicate insistence on the bride's tender appearance and the hint at the smile of *paruolus Torquatus*), but also by means of a continuous attempt to change

10. A. LA PENNA in "Maia" 8 (1956) 153.
11. A. LA PENNA in "Maia" 8 (1956) 153.

traditional elements with motifs proper of the Italic *humus* and personal solutions: some proofs of this are the allusion (in the most Alexandrian part of the poem, i.e. the ἐγκώμιον of Hymen) to the *raptio* and the *conuentio in manum*; the mentioning of *amaracus* as one of the flowers of the bride's garland; the picturesque dance of Hymen; the presence of some fundamental principles of Roman ethics (the usefulness of marriage to propagate families and nations; the difference between *legitimi* and *spurii* children; the theory of children as the support of the house) in the exaltation of the δύναμις θεοῦ; the comparison of the bride, on waking up after her first night of love, with a hyacinth and the groom with a vine.

Catullus' originality is apparent mainly in the most Roman part of the poem, that is, the *fescennina iocatio*, and not only in the picturesque description of the wedding procession, but also in some modifications of the ritual and in some very personal innovations: for instance, in the fact that the *concubinus* is the chief target of the jokes, whereas the fescennine directs mild words towards the couple; in the tone of satisfaction when pointing out the qualities of the *nouus maritus* as a lover and praising the groom's *potens et beata* home; in the description of Manlius' attitude in the hall of the new house and in the parallels between Junia's and Manlius' delay; in the idea that the groom's passion is deeper than the bride's and in the hyperbolical imagery employed to describe the erotic intensity of marriage union.

It is unnecessary to underline how style contributes to state Catullus' originality in c. 61: its style is never uniform, but tones change, in the various sections of the poem and even in the same section, as the context may require. In the ὕμνος, besides expressions of sacral language, the principal features of prayers occur: the mentioning of the god's dwelling-place and his origin, the "Relativstil", the "Du-Stil", the ritual invocation with ἀναδίπλωσις, the reason for the calling on the god (*nam ...*), the description of the god's *incessus* and his attitude. But in the ὕμνος itself the stylistic *uariatio* is evident in the series of picturesque details in the representation of the god and the delicate description of the bride, in which familiar language prevails. This dychotomy, in general, is typical of the whole poem, in which elevated style (present above all in the hymn and in the finale) alternates with colloquial style, recurring especially in the fescennine and in the depictions of the bride.

This peculiarity of Catullus' style has been highlighted by La Penna, who has emphasized the fact that in the *carmina docta* themselves, where archaisms with aulic meaning are to be found, there are also, more frequently than elsewhere, stylistic devices connected with everyday language, such as the diminutives[12]; he has rightly deduced Catullus' preference for a mixture of learned and familiar style, in order to obtain a new stylistic effect from the very contrast between them.

For this stylistic attitude Catullus follows, once again, Alexandrian principles, beforehand mainly applied in the epyllion. The Alexandrian ποικιλία is not only a *uariatio* of influences, but also of style; Catullus tried to recreate it in a personal way, by fusing together intimate and delicate expressions and echoes of solemn style.[13] Therefore it is incorrect to regard the *sermo communis* as almost absolutely predominant in c. 61: this poem, in fact, is one of the highest expressions of Catullus' neoterism, and the ideals of neoterism were those — anything but popular — of refinement and elegance, of an art meant for a few adepts, of the equally erudite and refined variation of tones and style. So it is an extremely aristocratic art and not a popular one.[14]

On the other hand, it is also wrong to believe that the *carmina docta* are mere examples of aulic style: generally speaking, I am more and more convinced of the artfulness of the traditional distinction — from the stylistic point of view — between *nugae, carmina docta* and epigrams, which the scholars keep on suggesting, though in different ways. The last attempt is the one made by Ross, who strives to show the stylistic similarity between the poems in various metres and the *carmina docta* and their contrast with the epigrams. Against this opinion Paratore asserts that it is

12. A. LA PENNA in "Maia" 8 (1956) 155.

13. Cf. A. LA PENNA in "Maia" 8 (1956) 156, who points out that Callimachus did not influence the creation of Catullus' style, because one of the essential features of Callimachus' style, the brevity, the attempt at avoiding the superfluous and concentrating the expression, is not much accentuated in Catullus. On the ποικιλία of c. 61 see what has been observed by M. CITRONI in "Stud. Ital. Fil. Class." 51 (1979) 21-29.

14. On these aspects cf. the observations of A. LA PENNA in "Maia" 8 (1956) 152 and of CASTORINA, *Questioni neoteriche*, cit., 80.

a hopeless enterprise to look for sharply different styles, i.e. one used in the *nugae*, one in the *carmina docta*, and one in the epigrams in elegiac distiches: as a matter of fact, in spite of the appearance, the way in which Catullus expresses himself remains constantly homogeneous.[15]

Another definitely misleading opinion is that according to which the poem presents a predominant interest in antique details: in his rightly famous study of everyday life in Rome, Jérôme Carcopino[16] cites c. 61 as the most reliable source of information for his description of wedding ceremonies; and indeed his lively, but scarcely accurate reconstruction of the phases of a Roman wedding proves that he has derived it almost exclusively from the poem on the wedding of Manlius Torquatus and Junia Aurunculeia. Luckily Catullus behaved as a poet, not as an antiquarian, and c. 61 may help at the most to confirm the existence of some Roman customs, not to bear witness to the existence of some others by itself. Surely the poem shows a number of Roman characteristics, even in the description of Hymen, where the themes of the *raptio* and the *conuentio in manum* are underlined, and above all in the details of the *deductio*, with the *fescennina iocatio*, the *concubinus*, the *praetextatus* and the *pronubae*, the motif of *dare nuces*, the mentioning of Thalasius, the attention paid in order to avoid the *pedis offensio*, the hint at the *lectus genialis* and the *collocatio*. Sometimes, however, this does not exclude a medley of Greek and Roman habits in the description of the ceremony and this should alert us not to draw hazardous conclusions concerning the existence of certain customs: this medley regards the groom's function in the *deductio* (he is waiting inside, as Roman habits require, but the poet-coryphaeus addresses him during the *deductio*, as if he partook in it, according to the custom of Greece) and the mentioning of one *praetextatus* – instead of two – to support the bride, on the model of the rôle played by the παράνυμφος in the Greek ritual.

The fact that Catullus did not want to act as an antiquarian is also proved by his resuming peculiarities no longer in use, by his

15. E. PARATORE, *Catullo e gli epigrammisti dell'Antologia*, in *Miscell. di Studi Alessandrini in memoria di A. Rostagni*, Torino 1963, 587.

16. J. CARCOPINO, *La vie quotidienne à Rome à l'apogée de l'Empire*, cit., 101 ff.; 324 n. 16.

modifying some firmly settled habits and leaving out some fundamental stages of the wedding ceremony. The first category is represented by the auspices taken by looking at the birds' flight, an obsolete custom at Catullus' time. The second category can include the mentioning of the bride, and not the groom, in reference to the act of *soluere zonulam*; the throwing of the nuts on the part of the *concubinus*, instead of the groom, and, moreover, during the deductio, the limits set to the task of the *pronuba* (Catullus takes her place in giving the traditional advices to the bride and introduces them into the fescennine; it is the *praetextatus* - παράνυμφος who accompanies the bride to the thalamus, not the *pronuba*; in the *collocatio* various *pronubae* are mentioned, not only one; it is the maidens' duty to close the door of the bedchamber). It is significant, above all, that the epithalamium proper is shortened and kept on a purely literary level.[17]

On the other hand, Catullus has left out all the important phases of the wedding ceremony that preceded the *deductio*; in the poem there is no reference to the bride's childish toys being offered to the gods, to her *tunica regilla*, to the *sex crines* in which her hair was divided; nothing is said about the *dextrarum iunctio* in front of the *pronuba*, the *confarreatio* and the nuptial banquet.

Catullus' description begins with the *deductio*, but even there we find no hint at the musical accompaniment nor at the spindle and distaff, carried in the procession as the symbols of the bride's gifts.[18] When the procession reaches the groom's house, Catullus carefully points out the symbolical value of the bride's going into her new home, without inserting the description of the door and of some noteworthy ritual acts: first of all the custom of rubbing the door jambs with oil and grease and winding wool bands round them; then the formula *ubi tu Gaius ego Gaia*, the *accipi aqua ignique*[19] and the offering of the *tres asses*.

On the reason for the omission of the meaningful details that preceded the *deductio*, nothing can be added to Ferrero's explanation. He has observed with masterly skill that the dramatic action

17. L. FERRERO, *Interpretazione di Catullo*, cit., 297.
18. Cf. Cic. *De orat.* 2,277; Plin. *Nat. Hist.* 8,74; Plut. *Quaest. Rom.* 31.
19. Cf. Varr. *L.L.* 5,61; Non. 516,19 M.; *Dig.* 24,1,66; Plut. *Quaest. Rom.* 1.

is present only as it is changed into poetry, only as the poet himself participates in it as the bard and master of ceremonies[20]; for this reason Catullus leaves out those elements of the ritual that he would have been compelled to describe from the outside. By doing so, Catullus avoids the conflict between the descriptive and dramatic components and immediately gets to the heart of the ceremony, of which he chooses and emphasizes the colour and folk aspects more than anything else.

What has been said with respect to Catullus' freedom in treating the details of the ceremony is sufficient to reject the hypothesis of those (Lafaye, Pighi) who regard c. 61 as being meant to accompany the stages of the ceremony step by step. Apart from the obvious considerations on the little regard for conventional elements of the ceremony, the mild tone of the *fescennina iocatio* and of the epithalamium proper should have diverted the critics from looking for a perfect correspondence between the poem and the reality of facts.[21]

The mistake of those who interpret the poem as the exact reproduction of the phases of the wedding ceremony, or consider it as being meant to accompany it, has been facilitated by the fact that Catullus has striven to enliven the subject matter of his poem by introducing actual particulars in abundance and describing the scene as real; but at the basis of this technique, more than Catullus' intention to reproduce what was taking place in front of him, lies his search for the "dramatic" motif and especially his love for pictorial elements and popular customs; this is actually what sets his imagination afire more than anything else; therefore the procession of the *deductio*, with its realistic and picturesque details, constitutes the core of the poem.[22] The preference for colour elements is most evident, besides the description of Hymen, in the *deductio*: suffice it to mention the

20. L. FERRERO, *Interpretazione di Catullo*, cit., 295 f.

21. On dealing with my work in too laudatory tones, E. PARATORE, *Gli epitalami catulliani*, in "Mélanges de Philologie, de Littérature et d'Histoire ancienne offerts à P. Boyancé", Roma 1974, 529-555 has formulated the suggestive hypothesis that refrains, repetitions, anadiplosis, allitterations and the various figures of speech connected with them, in which c. 61 is rich, prove the primary musical structure of the poem, which regulated their introduction and frequency.

22. Cf. E. FRAENKEL, *Kl. Beitr.*, II 98.

bright torches, the bride's *flammeum*, the purple *lectus genialis.*

Catullus' love for folk elements too is a well-known motif of his art, and Eduard Fraenkel has put it in the right light apropos of c. 17 and c. 72[23]; in c. 61 it is present in the group of characters, sketched with rapid but incisive traits, who make up the wedding procession: the παῖδες προπέμποντες who shake the torches and sing the fescennine, the *concubinus* who throws the nuts and is going to offer his hair to the *cinerarius*, the *praetextatus* who accompanies the bride to the thalamus, the *pronubae* who see to the *collocatio.*

Therefore, c. 61 is firmly rooted in the reality of the celebration, but it is definitely detached from it and it develops in a special sphere, that is, art: it is a poem that could neither be defined Greek nor Roman, since this would grasp only one of its aspects. The definition coined by Eduard Fraenkel with regard to c. 62 is indeed perfectly suitable for it[24]; "It could never have come into being without the Greek seed, and at the same time it owes its strength, its freshness, and its particular flavour to the soil of Italy out of which it grew". This is, after all, the principal characteristic of Catullus' great art.

---

23. E. FRAENKEL, *Kl. Beitr.*, II 124 ff.
24. E. FRAENKEL, *Kl. Beitr.*, II 101.

BIBLIOGRAPHY

In the present edition the text of c. 61 is based on R. Mynors' reading (Oxford 1958). When I disagree with it, I always explain the reasons for my dissent.

ABEL, W., *Die Anredeformen bei den römischen Elegikern*, Berlin 1930.

APPEL, G., *De Romanorum precationibus*, in "Religionsgeschichtliche Versuche und Vorarbeiten" VII (1909) 2. Heft.

AUSFELD, C., *De Graecorum precationibus quaestiones*, in "Jahrb. class. Phil." Suppl. XXVIII (1903) 505-547.

AXELSON, B., *Unpoetische Wörter*, Lund 1945.

BARDON, H., *Propositions sur Catulle*, Bruxelles 1970.

−−, *Catullus. Carmina*, iterum edidit H. BARDON, Stuttgart 1973.

BEDNARA, E., *Aus der Werkstatt der daktylischen Dichter*, in "Arch. Lat. Lexik. u. Gramm." 15 (1908) 223-232.

BERGK, T., *Kritische Analekten*, in "Philol." 16 (1860) 577-647.

BIONDI, G.G., *Semantica di 'cupidus'*, Bologna 1979.

CALAME, C., *Les choeurs de jeunes filles en Grèce archaïque*, I-II, Roma 1977.

CARCOPINO, J., *La vie quotidienne à Rome à l'apogée de l'Empire*, Paris 1939.

CASTORINA, E., *Questioni neoteriche*, Firenze 1968.

CICHORIUS, C., *Mancia*, in "Rhein. Mus." 73 (1920) 124-126.

CITRONI, M., *Funzione comunicativa occasionale e modalità di atteggiamenti espressivi nella poesia di Catullo*, in "Stud. Ital. Fil. Class." 50 (1978) 90-115; 51 (1979) 5-49.

DELLA CORTE, F., *Personaggi catulliani*, Firenze 1976.

−−, *Catullo. Le poesie*, Verona 1977.

ELLIS, R., *A Commentary on Catullus*, Oxford 1889.

ESTEVEZ, V.A., *The Choice of Urania in Catullus 61*, in "Maia" 29-30 (1977-78) 103-105.

ÉVRARD-GILLIS, J., *La récurrence lexicale dans l'oeuvre de Catulle. Étude stylistique*, Paris 1976.

FEDELI, P., *Il carme 30 di Catullo*, in "Studia Florentina Alex. Ronconi sexagenario oblata", Roma 1970, 97-113.

FERRERO, L., *Interpretazione di Catullo*, Torino 1955.

FORDYCE, C.J., *Catullus*, Oxford 1961.

FRAENKEL, E., *Vesper adest*, in "Journ. Rom. Stud." 45 (1955) 1-8 = Kl. Beitr. II 87-101.
−−, *Horace*, Oxford 1957.
−−, *Two Poems of Catullus*, in "Journ. Rom. Stud." 51 (1961) 46-53 = Kl. Beitr. II 115-129.
−−, *Review of the Commentary by C.J. Fordyce*, in "Gnomon" 32 (1962) 253-263.
FRIEDRICH, G., *Catulli Veronensis liber*, Leipzig/Berlin 1908.
GRANAROLO, J., *L'oeuvre de Catulle. Aspects religieux, éthiques et stylistiques*, Paris 1967.
GRILLI, A., *Nota a un frammento adespoto e Catullo, carme 61*, in "Studi classici in onore di Q. Cataudella", vol. III, Catania 1972, 95-97.
HAFFTER, H., *Untersuchungen zur altlateinischen Dichtersprache*, Berlin 1934.
HAUPT, M., *Quaestiones Catullianae*, Leipzig 1837 = *Opusc.* I 1-72.
−−, *Observationes criticae*, Leipzig 1841 = *Opusc.* I 73-142.
HECKENBACH, J., *Hochzeit*, in "R.E.P.W." VIII 2 (1913) 2129-2133.
HEUSCH, H., *Das Archaische in der Sprache Catulls*, Bonn 1954.
HOFMANN, J.B., *Lateinische Umgangssprache*, Heidelberg 1951[3].
−−, SZANTYR, A., *Lateinische Syntax und Stilistik*, München 1965.
JACHMANN, G., *Review of the Commentary by W. Kroll*, in "Gnomon" 1 (1925) 200-214.
KAIBEL, G., *Theokrits Ἑλένης Ἐπιθαλάμιον*, in "Hermes" 27 (1892) 249-259.
KÖRBER, V., *De Graecorum hymenaeis et epithalamiis*, Breslau 1877.
KROLL, W., *C. Valerius Catullus*, Stuttgart 1960[4].
LAFAYE, G., *Catulle et ses modèles*, Paris 1894.
LA PENNA, A., *Problemi di stile catulliano*, in "Maia" 8 (1956) 141-160.
LEJEUNE DIRICHLET, G., *De ueterum macarismis*, in "Religionsgeschichtliche Versuche und Vorarbeiten" XIV (1914) 4. Heft.
LENCHANTIN DE GUBERNATIS, P., *Il libro di Catullo*, Torino 1965.
LIEBERG, G., *Observationes in Catulli carmen sexagesimum primum*, in "Latinitas" 22 (1974) 216-221.
LÖFSTEDT, E., *Syntactica*, I[2] Lund 1942; II Lund 1933.
MAAS, P., *Ὑμὴν ὑμήν*, in "Philol." 66 (1907) 590-596.
−−, *Hymenaios*, in "R.E.P.W." IX 1 (1914) 130-134.
MANGELSDORFF, E.A., *Das lyrische Hochzeitsgedicht bei den Griechen und Römern*, Hamburg 1913.
MANSON, M., *Puer bimulus (Catulle, 17,12-13) et l'image du petit enfant chez Catulle et ses prédécesseurs*, in "Mél. Ec. Fr. Rome" 90 (1978) 247-291.
MANTERO, T., *Crocina candidus in tunica (Catull. 68,134)*, in "Studi di poesia latina in onore di A. Traglia", I, Roma 1976, 161-192.

MEISTER, K., *Die Hausschwelle in Sprache und Religion der Römer*, Sitzungsber. Heidelb. Akad. Wiss., Philol.-Hist. Klasse, 1924/5; 3. Abh.

MERKELBACH, R., *Sappho und ihr Kreis*, in "Philol." 101 (1957) 1-29.

MEYER-LÜBKE, W., *Lat. 'manciola', 'manciolum', 'peciolus'*, in "Rhein. Mus." 72 (1917/18) 153-154.

MÜLLER, L., *De re metrica poetarum Latinorum praeter Plautum et Terentium*, Leipzig 1894[2].

MUNRO, H.A.J., *Criticism and Elucidations of Catullus*, Cambridge 1878.

MUTH, R., *"Hymenaios" und "Epithalamios"*, in "Wien. Stud." 67 (1954) 5-45.

NISBET, R.G.M. - HUBBARD, M., *A Commentary on Horace: Odes. Book 1*, Oxford 1970.

NORDEN, E., *Aus altrömischen Priesterbüchern*, Lund/Leipzig 1939.

——, *Agnostos Theos*, Stuttgart 1956[4].

——, *P. Vergilius Maro. Aeneis. Buch VI*, Stuttgart 1957[4].

OTTO, A., *Die Sprichwörter und sprichwörtlichen Redensarten der Römer*, Leipzig 1890.

PAGE, D., *Sappho and Alcaeus*, Oxford 1955.

PARATORE, E., *Catullo e gli epigrammisti dell'Antologia*, in "Miscell. di Studi Alessandrini in memoria di A. Rostagni", Torino 1963.

——, *Gli epitalami catulliani*, in "Mélanges de Philosophie, de Littérature et d'Histoire ancienne offerts à P. Boyancé", Roma 1974, 513-555.

PASQUALI, G., *Il carme 64 di Catullo*, in "Stud. Ital. Fil. Class." N.S. 1 (1920) 1-23.

PERNICE, E., *Griechisches und römisches Privatleben*, in Gercke-Norden, *Einleitung i.d. Altertumswiss.*, II[3], Leipzig 1922, 1-82.

PERROTTA, G., *Cesare, Catullo, Orazio e altri saggi*, Roma 1972.

PICHON, R., *Index uerborum amatoriorum*, Paris 1902.

PIGHI, G.B., *La struttura del carme LXI di Catullo*, in "Humanitas" 2 (1948/49) 41-53.

REITZENSTEIN, R., *Die Hochzeit des Peleus und der Thetis*, in "Hermes" 35 (1900) 73-105.

RIESE, A., *Die Gedichte des Catullus*, Leipzig 1884.

RHODE, E., *Der griechische Roman und seine Vorläufer*, Leipzig 1900[2].

RONCONI, A., *Studi catulliani*, Brescia 1971[2].

ROSS, D.O., *Style and Tradition in Catullus*, Cambridge/Mass. 1969.

SALVATORE, A., *Studi catulliani*, Napoli 1965.

SAMTER, E., *Geburt, Hochzeit und Tod*, Leipzig 1912.

SCHMIDT, R., *De Hymenaeo et Talassio*, Kiel 1886.

SKUTSCH, O., *Metrical Variations and Some Textual Problems in Catullus*, in "Bull. Inst. Class. Stud. London" 16 (1969) 38-43.

SNELL, B., *Sapphos Gedicht Φαίνεταί μοι κῆνος*, in "Hermes" 66 (1931) 71-90 = Ges. Phil. Schr. 82 ff.

SOMMER, F., *Handbuch der lateinischen Laut- und Formenlehre*, Heidelberg 1948³.

SVENNUNG, J., *Catulls Bildersprache*, Uppsala 1945.

VAHLEN, J., *De deliciis orationis Catullianae*, Ind. lect. hibern. Berol., 1896/7, 3-18 = *Opusc.* II 214-234.

VOLLMER, F., *P. Papinii Statii Siluarum libri*, Leipzig 1898.

WACKERNAGEL, J., *Vorlesungen über Syntax*, I² Basel 1950; II² Basel 1957.

WEST, M.L., *Textual Criticism and Editorial Technique*, Stuttgart 1973.

WHEELER, A.L., *Tradition in the Epithalamium*, in "Amer. Journ. Phil." 51 (1930) 205-223.

——, *Catullus and the Tradition of Ancient Poetry*, Berkeley 1934.

WILAMOWITZ-MOELLENDORFF, U. v., *Sappho und Simonides*, Berlin 1913.

——, *Hellenistische Dichtung in der Zeit des Kallimachos*, Berlin 1924.

WILLIAMS, F., *Callimachus Hymn to Apollo. A Commentary*, Oxford 1978.

WILLIAMS, G., *Some Aspects of Roman Marriage Ceremonies and Ideals*, in "Journ. Rom. Stud." 48 (1958) 16-29.

——, *Tradition and Originality in Roman Poetry*, Oxford 1968.

WILLS, G., *Sappho 31 and Catullus 51*, in "Gr. Rom. Byz. Stud." 8 (1967) 167-197.

ZICARI, M., *Scritti catulliani*, Urbino 1978.

ZIEGLER, K., *De precationum apud Graecos formis quaestiones selectae*, Breslau 1905.

ACC. *Trag.* 234 b R³.: *33*.

ACHILL. TAT. 1,4,3: *122*.

ACR. (PS.) *ad* Hor. *Sat.* 1,2,98: *94*.

AESCH. *Agam.* 306: *64*; 1448: *60*; 1485 ff.: *58*.

– *Prom. uinct.* 555 ff.: *8*; 1044: *65*.

– *Suppl.* 823 f.: *58*.

AESCHIN. 3,111: *139*.

AGROEC. *Gramm.* VII 125,5 K.: *75*.

ALCM. 35 D. = *PMG* 55 Page: *38*.

ANACR. 17 Gentili: *29*; 71 Gentili: *97*.

Anth. Lat. 711,2 R.: *40*.

Anth. Pal. 5,4,5 f. (Philodem.): *81*; 5,5,1 f. (Statil. Flacc.): *81*; 5,158,2 (Asclep.): *52*; 5,171 (Meleag.): *80*; 6,76,5 (Agathias): *59*; 7,1 (Asclep.): *81*; 7,19,1 f. (Leon.): *10*; 7,324 (adesp.): *50*; 7,466 (Leon.): *100*; 8,1 (Meleag.): *81*; 9,58,7 f. (Antipat.): *67*; 9,258,1 f. (Antiphan.): *41*; 9,331 (Meleag.): *41*; 12,145,3 f. (adesp.): *130*; 12,208,1-4 (Strat.): *80*.

APOLL. RHOD. 3,1178: *40*; 3,1185: *40*.

APRISS. *ap.* Varr. *L.L.* 6,68: *92*.

APUL. *Met.* 1,6: *81*; 4,19: *38*; 6,12: *38*; 8,16: *38*.

ARCHIL. 94 D. = 174,1 Tarditi: *20*; 104 D. = 203 Tarditi: *113*.

ARIPHR. *PMG* 813,10 Page: *58*.

ARISTAENET. *Ep.* 1,1: *122*.

ARISTOPH. *Ach.* 237: *23*; 241: *23*; 665: *23*.

– *Aues* 1720 ff.: *13*; 1721 ff.: *78*; 1740 f.: *78*; 1759 f.: *78*.

– *Equit.* 559: *23*.

– *Lys.* 72: *52*.

– *Pax* 434: *23*; 1316 ff.: *13. 27*; 1333 f.: *13. 78. 86*; 1337 ff.: *13*; 1344 ff.: *144*; 1346: *13*.

– *Ran.* 330 f.: *21*; 403-410: *30*; 875 ff.: *30*.

– *Thesm.* 319: *23*.

ARISTOT. *Mir.* 832 b 23: *52*.

ARNOB. *Nat.* 3,25: *114*.

AUGUSTIN. *Ciu.Dei* 14,18: *116*.

AUSON. 384,6 Peiper: *33*.

AVIEN. *Ora marit.* 127: *40*.

BALB. *ap.* Cic. *Att.* 9,7b,2: *74.*
BED. *Gramm.* VII 276,17 K.: *75.*
Bell. Alex. 14,5: *98*; 60,5: *108.*
Bell. Hisp. 33,4: *94.*
BION. 12(9),1: *80.*
BION. (PS.) *Epithal. Achill. et Deidam.* 17 ff.: *122.*

CAEL. *ap.* Cic. *Fam.* 8,2,1: *82.*
CAEL. AURELIAN. *Acut.* 1,15,142: *39*; 2,37,192: *39*; 2,37,197: *39*; 3,21,
    208: *39.*
– *Chron.* 4,1,9: *39*; 5,7,84: *39.*
CAES. AREL. *Epist. ad uirg.* 3,2: *21.*
CAES. BASS. *Gramm.* VI 263,13 K.: *48.*
CALLIM. *Frg.* 2a,42 ff. Pf.: *26. 143*; 392: *13*; 572: *40.*
– *Hym.* 1,32 f.: *130*; 1,92 ff.: *49*; 2: *86*; 2,4: *64*; 2,4-8: *63*; 2,29: *59*; 2,80
    ff.: *36*; 3,113 ff.: *49*; 3,249: *67*; 3,252 f.: *130*; 4,75: *40*; 4,109: *22*;
    4,175 f.: *130*; 4,226 f.: *59*; 4,323 f.: *36*; 5: *6*; 5,18: *32*; 5,27 ff.: *122*;
    5,33: *23. 70*; 5,43: *70*; 5,55: *70*; 5,137-139: *86.*
CALP. SIC. 1,12: *40.*
CALV. 4 Morel: *15*; 5: *15*; 6: *15.*
Carm. Lat. Epigr. 950,1 f. B.: *119.*
CASS. DIO 48,44,3: *111.*
CAT. *Agr.* 22,2: *108*; 32,2: *73. 75.*
CATULL. 2,5: *125*; 4,14-15: *101*; 7,3 ff.: *131*; 8,11-12: *101*; 11,13-14: *50*;
    11,21-24: *68*; 17: *157*; 21,1-3: *101*; 34,2: *44*; 34,13-17: *52*; 35,15: *114*;
    36,11-14: *19*; 36,12 ff.: *31*; 37,7-9: *101*; 40,3: *47*; 45,15-16: *110*; 45,20:
    48.101; 46,6: *34*; 48,2 f.: *128*; 50,15: *142*; 51,5: *142*; 51,9: *75*; 54,2:
    142; 58,1-2: *100*; 58,4: *24*; 59,5: *142*; 62: *18. 157*; 62,1-4: *63*; 62,4: *92*;
    62,8: *64*; 62,34 ff.: *15*; 62,39 ff.: *68*; 62,43: *15*; 62,49-58: *72*; 62,54: *73*;
    62,59: *126*; 62,59 ff.: *126*; 62,60-61: *100*; 63,8: *24*; 63,47: *38*; 63,61:
    100; 63,79: *38*; 64: *16*; 64,20: *92*; 64,22 f.; *22*; 64,26-27: *100*; 64,69-70:
    45; 64,89 f.: *30*; 64,92 f.: *114*; 64,95-96: *19*; 64,143-4: *100*; 64,195: *23*;
    64,240: *24*; 64,269: *30*; 64,303: *24*; 64,309: *24*; 64,334: *145*; 64,364:
    24; 64,374: *114*; 64,403-4: *108*; 65,12 ff.: *31*; 66,11: *92*; 66,18: *125*;
    66,31: *47*; 66,35: *38*; 66,36: *34*; 67,1: *100*; 67,18: *126*; 68,34-35: *45*;
    68,57 f.: *31*; 68,68: *39*; 68,89: *34*; 68,125: *24*; 68,141: *44*; 68,156: *39*;
    72: *157*; 87,1 f.: *128*; 91,2: *100*; 98,1 f.: *129*; 107,4-5: *100.*
CELS. 3,7,2: *98.*
CHARIS. *Gramm.* I 32,17 K.: *50.*
CHARIT. *Erot. Gr.* I 1, p. 416,69 Hirschig: *79.*
CHOEROB. *Schol. in Theodos. Canon.* p. 252,21 Hilgard: *15.*
CHORIC. *Or.* 1 p. 15 Förster: *10*; 1 p. 16: *123*; 2 p. 24: *138*; 6 p. 40: *145.*
CIC. *Acad.* 2,22: 141.

– *Att.* 2,8,1: *93*; 2,24,1: *48*; 5,20,5: *25. 100.*
– *Brut.* 324: *98.*
– *Cael.* 48: *101*; 79: *58.*
– *Carm. frg.* 11,75 Morel: *146.*
– *Catil.* 3,22: *100.*
– *Cluent.* 14: *112*; 202: *98.*
– *De orat.* 1,251: *44*; 2,277: *155*; 2,290: *98.*
– *Diuin.* 1,28: *28*; 2,84: *107.*
– *Fam.* 9,16,7: *93*; 15,4,10: *100.*
– *Fin.* 1,58: *39.*
– *Marc.* 25: *98*; 27: *98.*
– *Off.* 1,54: *57*; 1,58: *45*; 2,24: *82.*
– *Phil.* 13,10: *98.*
– *Rep.* 1,64: *82.*
– *Rosc. Amer.* 74: *141.*
– *Top.* 11: *45*; 12: *45*; 71: *45.*
– *Tusc.* 4,70: *48.*
– *Verr.* 2,3,277: *100*; 2,4,5: *39.*
CIL VIII 24787,3: *58.*
CLAUDIAN. *In Eutr.* 1,32 f.: *130.*
CLEANTH. *Collect. Alex.* 1,15 f., p. 227 Powell: *58.*
COLUM. 2,2,28: *75*; 3,2,30: *58*; 6,37,9: *119*; 10,230: *38*; 10,294: *38.*
CORN. BALB. *ap.* Seru. *ad* Verg. *Aen.* 4,127: *27.*
CORN. NEP. *Epam.* 5,9: *141.*
Culex 70 f.: *33*; 402: *44.*
CURT. RUF. 3,11,10: *141*; 8,13,24: *141*; 10,2,23: *99*; 10,8: *99.*

DEMETR. *De eloc.* 167, p. 37 Radermacher: *135.*
Dig. 24,1,66: *155.*
DION. HAL. *Comp.* 201-202: *66.*
DION. HAL. (PS.) VI 1, p. 263,9 ff. Usener-Radermacher: *96-97*; VI 1, p.
   264: *137-138*; VI 1, p. 270: *10. 123*; VI 1, p. 271: *137. 138. 145.*

ENN. *Ann.* 1 V². : *25*; 5: *39*; 352: *122.*
– *Scaen.* 112 f. V². : *83*; 202: *38*; 229: *22*; 284: *22*; 316: *50.*
Epist. Sapph. 155: *94.*
Epithal. Laurent. (*PLM* III 42) 33-35 Baehrens: *123*; 69 ff.: *118.*
Etymol. gen. s.v. Αὐροσχάς: *73.*
Euang. Matt. 1,25: *120.*
EUR. *Alc.* 151: *67*; 177 f.: *50*; 395: *67.*
– *Androm.* 1218: *79.*
– *Bacch.* 83: *23*; 152: *23*; 370 ff.: *20.*
– *Cycl.* 104: *22*; 495 ff.: *78.*

– *Hec.* 635: *67.*
– *Hel.* 637 ff.: *79.*
– *Hipp.* 525 f.: *21.*
– *Ion* 125 f.: *21.*
– *Iph. Aul.* 1299: *70.*
– *Tro.* 308-340: *12*; 311 ff.: *78*; 840 f.: *21.*
– *Frg.* 781, 14-31 N²: *13*; 781,27: *78.*
EVEN. 2,3 D.: *41.*

FEST. 83,11 L.: *112*; 282: *116*; 282,22 ff.: *28. 90*; 364: *53.*
FRONT. *Epist.* 84,6 van den Hout: *74.*

GAI. 1,64: *57.*
GREG. NAZ. *Carm. mor.* 1,249 ff. (= Migne III 522 ff.): *56.*

HEPHAEST. *Ench.* 15,26 p. 55 Consbruch: *123.*
HERACL. *Pol.* 64: *120.*
HEROD. 1,47,3: *130*; 2,53: *99.*
HES. *Erga* 235: *199.*
– *Theog.* 420: *59.*
– *Frg.* 211,6 ff. Merkelbach–West: *78*; 221,7 ff.: *9*; 240,11: *31*; 310,2: *39.*
HES. (PS.) *Scut.* 273-280: *9*; 274: *9*; 277: *27*; 281: *86.*
HESYCH. s.v. θυρωρός: *135*; s.v. κτυπία: *133*; s.v. κτυπιῶν: *133*; s.v. νυμφαγωγός: *88.*
HIMER. *Or.* 9,4 Colonna: *10*; 9,8: *56*; 9,16: *34*; 9,19: *10. 35*; 9,21: *138.*
HOM. *Hymn.* 3,165: *50*; 4,1 f.: *19*; 7,1: *19*; 15,1: *19.*
– *Il.* 1,37 ff.: *18. 19*; 2,461: *34*; 2,800 f.: *129*; 3,277: *20. 66*; 4,422 ff.: *30*; 5,31: *20*; 5,544: *22*; 7,448: *64*; 8,554 ff.; *130*; 9,385 f.: *129*; 10,394: *83*; 11,68: *67*; 11,441: *100*; 11,452: *100*; 16,514 f.: *59*; 18,61: *67*; 18,493: *9*; 24,62-63: *9.*
– *Od.* 6,158 f.: *78*; 6,163: *35*; 6,231: *67. 70*; 7,183: *145*; 11,245: *50*; 11, 618: *100*; 17,545: *64*; 18,389: *100*; 24,192 f.: *78.*
HOR. *Carm.* 1,2,25 ff.: *49*; 1,2,30 ff.: *20*; 1,3,27: *22*; 1,10,9 ff.: *52*; 1,12,1 ff.: *49*; 1,12,13 ff.: *20*; 1,15,5: *31*; 1,21,1: *130*; 1,26,9 f.: *59*; 1,36,18 ff.: *40*; 2,1,39: *42*; 2,8,21-24: *51*; 3,3,18 ff.: *31*; 3,4,40: *42*; 3,6,47 f.: *58*; 3,11,13 f.: *60*; 3,13,15: *41*; 3,18,1 f.: *21*; 3,18,3-4: *18*; 3,18,15: *25*; 3,21,13 ff.: *52*; 3,26,6 f.: *23*; 3,30,16: *60*; 4,5,23: *139*; 4,5,30: *73*; 4,12, 18: *114*; 4,14,5-13: *30.*
– *Carm. saec.* 23: *69.*
– *Ep.* 2,9 f.: *73*; 4,9: *40*; 10,1: *31*; 10,16: *24*; 15,3-6: *73*; 15,5 f.: *40*; 16,13-14: *31*; 17,45: *60.*
– *Epist.* 1,1,87: *112*; 1,11,4: *99*; 1,18,18: *99*; 1,20,15: *101*; 2,2,170: *75.*
– *Sat.* 1,3,7: *44*; 1,5,43: *82*; 1,5,56: *72*; 2,3,171: *90*; 2,6,87: *101.*

Hymn. Orph. 6,10: *18. 21*; 16,5: *58*; 60,9: *59*; 68,8: *59*.
HYPER. 1,5 Kenyon: *88*.

ISID. *Orig.* 9,17,12: *107*; 11,2,28: *108*.
IUST. 16,5,4: *65*.
IUVEN. 2,120: *111*; 11,154: *65*.

LAEV. 9 Morel: *119*.
Laus. Ps. 81: *38*.
LIBAN. VI 516,11 Förster: *49*.
LIV. 1,9,12: *96*; 1,16,3: *60*; 2,20,8: *141*; 2,23,4: *141*; 3,38,9: *141*; 4,25,11:
    99; 6,25,1: *141*; 8,32,2: *141*; 9,36,10: *98*; 22,6,3: *141*; 26,41,24: *141*.
LONG. *Erot. Gr.* IV 33, p. 177,47 Hirschig: *79*.
LUCAN. 7,787: *70*; 9,839: *61*.
LUCIAN. *Com.* 41: *124. 140*.
LUCIL. 117 M.: *72*; 249 f.: *94. 99*; 781: *101*.
LUCR. 1,6-8: *51*; 1,21 ff.: *59*; 1,47: *69*; 1,932: *38*; 3,9 f.: *51*; 3,286: *104*;
    3,647: *74*; 3,734: *104*; 4,815: *74*; 4,1278 ff.: *103*; 5,785: *33*; 5,1402: *25*;
    6,1178: *41*.
LYGD. 4,31-34: *122*.

MACROB. *Sat.* 1,15,21: *53*.
MARTIAL. 6,22,1: *94*; 6,27,3 f.: *139*; 6,43,2: *41*; 6,47,1: *41*; 9,67,8: *146*;
    9,70,9: *99*; 10,38,7: *80*; 11,2,5: *91*; 12,49,4: *94*; 14,185,2: *90*.
MENAND. 382,5 Körte: *119*.
MENAND. (rhet.) *Rhet. Gr.* III 400,31 ff. Spengel: *49*; III 401,22 ff.: *56*; III
    402,10 ff.: *34*; III 404,5 ff.: *35. 67. 123*; III 404,11 f.: *66*; III 404,27 f.:
    139; III 404,29 ff.: *27*; III 405: *135*; III 405,19 ff.: *124*; III 405,28 ff.:
    66; III 406,4 ff.: *136*; III 407,8: *139*; III 407,16: *145*; III 407,20: *136*;
    III 407,20 ff.: *138*; III 407,23 f.: *139*; III 409,8 ff.: *27*.
MUS. *Her. et Leand.* 58: *122*.

NAEV. *Com.* 90-91 R³.: *103*.
NIC. *Alex.* 618 ff.: *32*.
NON. 516,19 M.: *155*.
NONN. 24,88: *25*; 33,67 f.: *25*.

Octauia 4: *70*.
OPPIAN. *Hal.* 1,644 f.: *139*.
OVID. *Am.* 1,8,53: *146*; 1,14,54: *146*; 2,16,41: *73*; 3,3,5 ff.: *122*.
– *Ars* 1,59: *130*; 1,253 f.: *130*; 2,575: *146*.
– *Fast.* 2,155: *34*; 5,683 f.: *44*.
– *Her.* 4,137: *146*; 5,47 f.: *73*; 6,122: *58*; 6,133: *119*; 11,116: *100*; 18,15

ff.: *80*; 18,34: *69*; 21,162: *26*; 21,165 f.: *26*.
– *Met.* 1,147: *100*; 2,525 f.: *120*; 3,423: *122*; 4,393: *26*; 8,151: *100*; 10,1: *26*; 11,614 f.: *130*; 12,215 ff.: *79*; 13,790: *54*; 14,621: *34*.
– *Trist.* 1,5,47: *130*; 4,5,31 f.: *139*.

PALLAD. *Hist. Mon.* 1,2: *120*.
PAPIR. *Dig.* 48,16,18: *98*.
Paroem. Gr. II 4 Leutsch: *131*.
PARTHEN. 32 Martini: *15*.
PAUL. *ap.* Fest. 3 L.: *113*; 55: *50*; 56,1: *26*; 76,6: *80*; 172: *88*. *89*; 331: *75*.
PERS. 1,10: *90*.
Peruig. Ven. 13: *33*.
PETR. 43,1: *128*; 87,8: *146*; 120,94: *38*.
PHAEDR. *App.* 10,4: *146*.
PHOC. (PS.) 178 D.: *139*.
PIND. *Nem.* 7,1 ff.: *58*. *60*; 7,96 ff.: *59*.
– *Olymp.* 2,2: *49*; 2,98: *130*; 4,1 ff.: *30*; 14,1 ff.: *60*; 14,10 ff.: *58*.
– *Pyth.* 3,30 ff.: *143*; 6,49: *42*; 9,46 ff.: *130*.
– *Frg.* 139 Snell: *25*.
PLAT. *Euthyd.* 294 b: *131*.
– *Leg.* 4,712 b: *18*. *21*.
PLAUT. *Amph.* 139: *60*; 177 f.: *99*; 839: *103*; 1065: *22*.
– *Asin.* 41: *115*; 328: *108*; 812: *146*.
– *Aul.* 808: *82*.
– *Bacch.* 938: *114*.
– *Capt.* 218: *74*; 792: *98*.
– *Cas.* 798: *70*; 798 ff.: *14*; 804: *70*; 806: *71*; 815: *70*; 815 f.: *106*; 815-821: *103*; 832: *44*; 839: *14*; 881 ff.: *120*.
– *Cist.* 63: *115*; 112: *65*; 173 ff.: *103*; 211: *128*; 682: *141*.
– *Curc.* 169: *100*.
– *Epid.* 72: *65*; 537: *141*; 607: *100*.
– *Men.* 787 f.: *103*; 961: *141*; 1064: *141*.
– *Mil.* 369: *55*; 501: *125*; 521: *141*; 1003: *125*; 1339: *65*; 1351: *60*.
– *Most.* 188 f.: *103*; 224-226: *103*; 329: *128*; 855: *114*; 953: *99*.
– *Pers.* 541: *115*.
– *Poen.* 315: *99*; 431 ff.: *130*; 1179: *99*; 1187 ff.: *20*; 1258: *125*.
– *Pseud.* 208: *100*; 702 f.: *92*.
– *Rud.* 2: *50*; 128: *99*; 222: *99*.
– *Stich.* 152: *99*.
– *Trin.* 853: *128*; 863: *141*; 1048: *100*.
– *Truc.* 379: *99*; 381: *99*.
PLIN. (sen.) *Nat. hist.* 5,130: *32*; 8,74: *155*; 9,38: *33*; 15,86: *89*; 16,75: *28*.
PLIN. (iun.) *Epist.* 6,20,14: *141*; 9,6,2: *141*; 9,23,5: *141*.

– *Pan.* 17,1: *141.*
PLUT. *Galb.* 9: *120.*
– *Lyc.* 15: *53.*
– *Quaest. Gr.* 36,299 b: *21.*
– *Quaest. Rom.* 1: *155*; 29: *107*; 30: *120*; 31: *155.*
PMG 7,5: *64.*
POLL. 3,40: *88*; 3,41: *88*; 3,42: *135.*
POMER. 3,6,4 (= LIX 482 B Migne): *93.*
POMP. *ap.* Cic. *Att.* 8,6,2: *74.*
POMPON. *Com.* 57 ff. R³.: *25. 26.*
PORPH. *ad* Hor. *Epist.* 2,1,145: *86.*
Priap. 86,10: *33.*
PRISCIAN. *Gramm.* II 170,10 K.: *15*; II 189,2 K.: *80.*
PROCL. *ap.* Phot. 321 a 17 Bekker (= V 162,17 Henry): *143-144.*
– *Hymn.* 1,46: *59.*
PROP. 1,2,28: *41*; 1,20,12 ff.: *34*; 2,3,10-12: *122*; 2,6,23: *140*; 2,7,3: *104*;
    2,7,13: *57*; 2,9,3: *140*; 2,15,1 f.: *80. 81*; 2,30,26: *42*; 2,30,40: *59*; 2,32,
    37: *34*; 2,34,76: *34*; 3,1,5: *42*; 3,3,14: *42*; 3,7,5-8: *60*; 3,12,38: *140*;
    3,13,24: *140*; 3,16,4: *41*; 3,17,1 ff.: *60*; 4,1,1: *69*; 4,5,7: *140*; 4,11,69:
    58.

QUINTIL. *Decl. min.* 298 p. 178,10 Ritter: *65*; 306 p. 203,28: *98.*
– *Inst.* 4,2,124: *141.*

Rhet. Herenn. 3,23: *93*; 3,25: *93*; 4,44: *24*; 4,63: *82.*
RUFINIAN. *Rhet. Lat. Min.* p. 56,7 Halm: *104.*

SALL. *Cat.* 26,5: *93.*
– *Iug.* 14,11: *60.*
SAPPH. 1,5 L.-P.: *23*; 2,5 f.: *36*; 2,9-10: *36*; 27: *10*; 30: *10*; 31,1 ff.: *35*;
    44,31 ff.: *35*; 105: *11*; 105 a: *35*; 105 c : *35. 67. 68*; 110: *135*; 111: *12.*
    87; 111,5-6: *35*; 112: *11*; 112,1-2: *79*; 112,5: *124*; 113: *66*; 115: *11. 72.*
    124; 116: *11. 144*; 117: *11. 144.*
SCHOL. *ad* Eur. *Phoen.* 344: *88.*
– *ad* Eur. *Tro.* 315: *88.*
SCHOL. *ad* Theocr. 18: *133.*
SCRIPT. HIST. AUG. *Alex. Seu.* 52: *52.*
SEM. *Frg.* 7,81-82 D.: *55.*
SEN. (pat.) *Contr.* 2,1,7: *58.*
SEN. (fil.) *Const. sap.* 15,1: *65.*
– *Epist.* 51,13: *98*; 121,1: *98.*
– *Herc. fur.* 586: *70*; 821: *70*; 953: *40.*
– *Marc.* 24,1: *98.*

– *Med.* 5: *70*; 67-70: *27*; 113: *93*; 385: *40*.
– *Oed.* 343: *40*.
– *Tro.* 970: *40*; 1092: *40*.
SEPTUAG. *Ge.* 4,1: *120*.
SER. SAMMON. (= *PLM* III 157) 1073 Baehrens: *75*.
SEREN. *ap.* Non. 539,13 M.: *52*.
SERV. *ad* Verg. *Aen.* 3,686: *104*; 6,353: *104*; 7,695: *86*.
– *ad* Verg. *Buc.* 8,30: *89*.
– *ad* Verg. *Georg.* 1,383: *34*; 3,31: *10*.
SIDON. APOLL. *Carm.* 24,62: *70*.
SIL. IT. 6,452: *70*; 9,360: *40*; 9,614: *40*; 12,482: *54*; 16,208: *38*.
SOPH. *Aiax* 695: *20*.
– *Ant.* 781 f.: *20*; 1117: *22*.
–*Oed. tyr.* 167: *23*.
STAT. *Sil.* 1,2,11 ff.: *117*; 1,2,31 ff.: *51*; 1,2,166: *146*; 1,2,236 f.: *79*; 1,2, 242 ff.: *66. 69*; 1,2,266 f.: *137*; 1,2,271 ff.: *139-140*; 1,3,37: *41*; 1,3,46: *41*; 1,3,98: *99*; 1,4,31: *38*; 4,3,101: *25*.
– *Theb.* 7,224: *70*.
STEPH. BYZ. 131,7: *34*.
STRAB. 14,1,45: *34*.
SUET. *Aug.* 83: *90*.

TAC. *Ann.* 6,31: *22*; 11,27: *111*.
– *Hist.* 4,44: *119*; 12,18: *141*.
TER. *Andr.* 282 ff.: *103*; 964: *82*.
– *Eun.* 593: *65. 117. 120*; 1085: *98*.
– *Heaut.* 1018: *139*.
– *Hec.* 150: *44*.
– *Phorm.* 724: *58*.
TERENT. MAUR. *Gramm.* VI 341 K.: *91*.
THEOCR. 2: *7*; 2,103 ff.: *107*; 3: *7*; 11,77: *129*; 12,34: *80*; 15: *7*; 15,100: *19. 32*; 17,38-40: *110*; 17,43 f.: *139*; 18: *8. 12. 13. 14. 16*; 18,1 ff.: *43*; 18,2 f.: *27. 144*; 18,9-15: *87*; 18,16 f.: *79*; 18,20 f.: *66*; 18,21: *139*; 18,29-30: *36*; 18,32 ff.: *66*; 18,38: *106*; 18,49: *145*; 18,51 f.: *137. 145*; 18,54: *136*; 18,54 ff.: *87*; 18,55: *69*; 18,58: *18*; 20,21 ff.: *40*; 22,37 ff.: *41*; 30,25 ff.: *131*.
TIB. 1,3,19 f.: *107*; 2,1,25: *64*; 2,5,9: *58*; 3,11,17: *110*.
TICID. 1 Morel: *15. 80. 81*.
TITIN. *Com.* 106 R³.: *66*.
Trag. Inc. Frg. 184 R³.: *39*.
TURPIL. *Com.* 42 R³.: *119*.
TZETZ. *Schol. ad* Lycophr. 4,13 Scheer: *9. 78*.

ULPIAN. *Dig.* VII 1,7,3: *75.*

VAL. AEDIT. *Epigr.* 2,2 Baehrens: *65.*
VAL. FL. 4,266: *40*; 5,538: *38.*
VAL. MAX. 9,10 *ext.* 2: *65.*
VARR. *ap.* Non. 112 M.: *28*; 112,23-25: *90*; 531,8: *117.*
– *ap.* Seru. *ad* Verg. *Aen.* 4,166: *116.*
– *ap.* Seru. *ad* Verg. *Buc.* 8,29: *107.*
– *L.L.* 5,61: *155*; 5,129: *94*; 10,12: *82.*
– *R.R.* 1,16,6: *75*; 1,26,1: *75*; 2,8,1: *65.*
– *Sat.* 10 B.: *102.*
VERG. *Aen.* 1,274: *58*; 1,693: *24*; 3,561: *114*; 4,1179: *24*; 5,43: *69*; 5,721:
   83; 6,117: *60*; 6,258: *23*; 6,500: *22*; 6,605 f.: *114*; 6,644: *25*; 6,779:
   64; 6,792: *22*; 6,839: *22*; 6,973: *24*; 7,213: *22*; 7,363: *32*; 7,429: *38*;
   7,556: *22*; 7,701 f.: *34*; 8,293 ff.: *52*; 8,407: *83*; 9,56: *40*; 10,720: *92*;
   11,601: *40*; 11,785 ff.: *20*; 12,67 ff.: *122*; 12,558: *40.*
– *Buc.* 2,44: *99*; 3,38: *75*; 4,18-20: *40*; 4,61: *138*; 8,30: *89*; 10,62: *34.*
– *Georg.* 1,16 f.: *38*; 1,187: *44*; 1,360: *101*; 1,383: *34*; 1,448: *101*; 2,7 f.:
   21; 2,105 f.: *130*; 2,248: *44*; 3,11: *41*; 3,40 ff.: *59*; 3,333: *114.*

XEN. *Conu.* 9,2: *129.*

GENERAL INDEX

Alexandrinism in Catullus *25; 32; 34; 41; 70; 81; 107; 122; 149 ff.*
alliteration *22; 70 108; 141.*
allocutio sponsalis 134 f.
ἀναδίπλωσις in the prayer *20; 23.*
anaphora *81.*
assimilation *55.*
auspices for the wedding *28.*

Callimachus *13.*
– his influence on Catullus *6; 36; 63; 70; 86.*
cena nuptialis 111.
changes made by Catullus in the ceremony *50; 115-118; 143; 152; 154.*
chorus of maidens in the wedding song *42.*
cinerarius 94.
collocatio 120.
colour elements *28; 74; 156.*
comparison (between the bride and natural elements) *35; 40; 67; 68; 124.*
 – between the groom and natural elements *71.*
compromise between Greek and Roman customs *97 f.*
conuentio in manum 47; 53.

dance in the hymenaeus *27.*
dare nuces 89.
deductio 88.
diminutives *33; 54; 67; 119.*
"Du-Stil" *51 f.*

εἰκάζειν *11; 34; 72.*
(Roman) elements *73; 86; 87-89; 96; 98; 103; 106.*
elements (fusion of Greek and Roman ones) *3.*
end of lines (Greek technique) *92.*
epithalamium (meaning of the term) *8.*
(Roman) ethics *96.*

gemination *100.*

Hymenaeus (meaning of the term) *8.*
hymn (technique) *19.*
hyperbole *109.*

idea of marriage in Rome *57.*
invocation to the god *19.*

lectus genialis 112.
litotes *126.*

μακαρισμός *78 f.*
metaphor *64.*
myrtle (symbolism of) *32.*
mythology (in Catullus) *25.*
morigera (uxor) 104.

neoterics (their wedding songs) *15.*
neoterism *33.*

obscenity (in the *fescennina iocatio*) *87.*
offensio pedis 107.
originality of Catullus *152.*

paronomasia *76.*
pherecratic *29.*
Plautus (Roman elements) *15.*
— wedding ceremony of the *Casina 14.*
ποικιλία *5; 23; 34; 150; 153.*
polyptoton *31.*
postposition of particles *75.*
pronuba 103; 116-118.
proverbs *129-131.*
pueri praetextati 106; 115.

raptio 47; 53.
reality or poetic fiction *4 f.; 97; 157.*
refinement of style *70; 73; 81.*

Sappho (creator of the *genus*?) *9 f.*
— licentious elements in her epithalamia *12.*
— arrangement of the book of the epithalamia *10.*
— her influence on Catullus *6; 36; 66 f.; 72; 150.*
— a model for the authors of wedding songs *10.*

– main themes of her epithalamia *10.*
– reconstruction of her fragments through Catullus *7.*
series of interrogatives *48 f.*
– of relatives (in the prayer) *19 f.*
sermo communis 4; 64; 74; 93; 98; 153.
similes *30.*
style of the prayer *5; 17 ff.; 51 f.; 58-60; 74; 125; 152.*
style of the prophecies *31.*

Theocritus *13 f.*
– his influence on Catullus *7; 13 f.; 16; 41; 66; 106; 145.*
τόποι *35; 51; 56; 66; 77; 80; 96 f.; 113; 122; 123 f.; 138; 139; 144; 151.*

wedding torch *28.*

INDEX VERBORUM

ac 39; 114.
accubo 111; 114.
aditum ferre 38.
adsero 73.
amaracinus 24.
amaracus 24; 27.
anilitas 108.
Aonius 40.
Asius 34.
aspice ut 114.
at potest 59.
audio i.e. intellego 93.
– i.e. oboedio 65.
– in sacral language 74.
ausit 60.

beatus 78.
bona Fama 58.
bonus 44.
brachiolum 119.

caelites 50.
cinerarius 99.
cito 44.
cognosco 119.
colloco 120.
colo 19; 31.
concubinus 94.
coniugator 45.
cultor 22.
cupidus 52.

deditus + in and abl. 74.
dicax 93.
dies i.e. sol 69.
domus ... domina 39.

eniteo 33.
eo i.e. abeo 65.
erro 40.
erus 82.
excitus 25.

felix 78.
femina 69.
floridulus 125.
floridus 33; 54.
flos hyacinthinus 67.
foris 108.
frigero 39.

gaudium gaudere 82.
genus 19; 22.
glaber 101.

Hamadryades (nymphae) 34.
hilaris 25.
hodie atque heri 99.
hortulus 70.
huc et huc 40.
huc huc 23.

Idalium 32.
–ier 44; 60.
immineo 114.
implico 75.
indidem 141.
ingenero 141.
inscius 141.
integer 44.
inuoco 52.
io 91.
iocatio 93.

ita 125.
item 44.
iuuenta 146.
iuuo 128.

laetus 21.
lentus 75.
liberos dare 58.
licet 85.
linquo 37.
ludo 129.
ludus 129.
luteus 24.

male i.e. *uix 100.*
manciola 119.
multa milia 129.
munus 44; 146.

nam 30.
ne + imperat. *126.*
ni 104.
nitens 125.
niueus 24.
noscito 141.
noua nupta 70.
nox uaga 83.
nympha 41.

o 21.
otium 3.

pellere pedibus 25.
penite 115.
pergo + inf. *38.*
Phrygius 32.
plaudere pedibus 25.
probrum 74.
procax 93.
prodeas 71.

pronuba 43.
pudor ingenuus 65.
puellula 54.
pulsare pedibus 25.

quare age 38.
queo 60.
quis deus 47.

rapio 27.
raptio 27.
reuincio 39.

satis diu 98.
secubo 74.
semihians 142.
si uidetur (uidebitur) 74.
sine te 58.
sino 108.
soccus 24.
sordeo + dat. *98.*
stirpe niti 58.

te uolente 60.
tenax 40.
Thespius 39.
tinnulus 25.
– tio 93.
tondeo 99.
transfero 108.
tremulus 108.

ueni 23.
uenio + dat. *83.*
uiden ut 64.
unguentatus 101.
usque dum 108.

zonula 52.

ἄκουε 74.
ἄκουσον 74.
ἄνευ σέθεν 58.
'Αόνιος 40.

βαῖνε 23.

γάρ 30.
γένος 22.
γιγνώσκω 119.

δᾳδες νυμφικαί 88.
δύναμις θεοῦ 56.
δύναται γάρ 59.

ἐλθέ 23.
εὐδαίμων 78.

ζώνη 52.
ζώνιον 52.

θεσπικός 39.
θυρωρός 135.

ἱκοῦ 23.

κλύε 74.
κλῦθι 74.

λείπω 78.

μάκαρ 78.
μακάριος 78.
μόλε 23.

νυμφαγωγός 88.
νυμφευτής 88.
νυμφεύτρια 88.
νὺξ θοή 83.

ὄλβιος 78.
ὁμόνοια 145.
οὐρανίωνες 50.

παῖδες προπέμποντες 42; 88; 91.
παίζω 129.
παράνυμφος 41; 88.
πάροχος 88.
προηγητής 88.

συμπαίζω 129.

INDEX OF NAMES

Abel W. *81.*
André J. *89.*
Andrieu J. *103.*
Appel G. *44; 52; 59; 74; 126.*
Ardizzoni A. *41.*
Ausfeld C. *18; 19 23; 74.*
Axelson B. *43; 69; 126.*

Bailey C. *41.*
Bardon H. *28; 110; 147.*
Bednara E. *24.*
Bentley R. *121.*
Benveniste E. *57.*
Bergk T. *48.*
Biondi G.G. *37.*
Bömer F. *22; 31.*
Bowra C.M. *10.*

Calame C. *14.*
Cantarella R. *144.*
Carcopino J. *121; 154.*
Castorina E. *15; 138; 150; 153.*
Cichorius C. *119.*
Citroni M. *15; 109; 110; 130; 148; 153.*

D'Arbela E. *37.*
Dawes R. *134; 135; 144.*
Della Corte F. *18; 29; 37; 63; 73; 102; 110; 148.*
Deubner L. *7.*
Diehl E. *34.*
Dutoit E. *130-131.*

Ehlers W. *99; 114.*
Ellis R. *25; 61; 62; 81; 91; 111.*

Enk P.J. *80.*
Ensor E. *51.*
Estevez V.A. *25.*
Évrard-Gillis J. *23; 31; 44; 48; 56; 73; 81; 100; 101; 105; 127; 129.*

Fedeli P. *45; 142.*
Fehrle E. *32.*
Ferrero L. *28; 29; 65; 67; 69; 93; 95; 98; 100; 105; 109; 113; 123; 128; 137; 138; 140; 143; 146; 147; 155; 156.*
Fordyce C.J. *29; 31; 32; 34; 35; 45; 53; 55; 57; 58; 62; 63; 67; 81; 83; 91; 96; 101; 104; 108; 112; 115; 116; 134; 141.*
Fraenkel E. *21; 37; 49; 62; 68; 69; 72; 73; 86; 91; 97; 142; 156; 157.*
Friedländer L. *111.*
Friedrich G. *75; 77; 111; 112; 142; 143.*

Gentili B. *97.*
Gerber D.E. *12.*
Giangrande G. *54.*
Gow A.S.F. *33; 86; 100; 114; 139.*
Granarolo J. *37; 64; 74; 110.*
Griffiths A. *64; 125.*
Grilli A. *28.*
Guglielmino F. *37.*

Haffter H. *40; 82.*
Hahn E.A. *64.*
Haupt M. *41; 48; 51; 75; 121; 134.*
Heckenbach J. *28; 87; 117.*

Hehn V. *32.*
Heine R. *120; 148.*
Heinze R. *30; 93.*
Helbig W. *26.*
Heraeus W. *91.*
Herzog-Hauser G. *116.*
Heusch H. *45; 60; 83; 104; 114; 126.*
Hofmann J.B. *31; 38; 39; 49; 55; 74; 98; 100; 104; 108; 114; 115; 126; 128; 142.*
Hoppe P. *99.*
Hosius K. *119.*
Housman A.E. *142.*
Hubbard M. *22; 31; 39; 42; 51; 52; 58; 59; 60; 64; 73; 114; 119; 130.*

Jachmann G. *15; 28; 35.*
Jakobson R. *82.*

Kaibel G. *13; 67.*
Kannicht R. *79.*
Kiessling A. *30; 93.*
Kirk G.S. *12.*
Koechling J. *26.*
Körber V. *7.*
Krenkel W. *101.*
Kroll W. *25; 31; 36; 42; 45; 55; 63; 64; 68; 74; 75; 77; 81; 91; 94; 99; 114; 116; 121; 129.*

Lachmann K. *92.*
Lafaye G. *5; 6; 112; 115; 156.*
Landgraf G. *141.*
La Penna A. *5; 23; 149; 151; 153.*
Latte K. *108.*
Lejeune Dirichlet G. *77; 79; 80; 81.*
Lenchantin De Gubernatis M. *56; 96; 112.*
Leo F. *86.*
Lieberg G. *12; 26; 31; 37; 41; 56;*

67; 134; 144; 147.
Lier B. *81.*
Lloyd-Jones H. *12.*
Lobel E. *123.*
Löfstedt E. *47; 48; 83; 142.*

Maas P. *8; 11; 14; 18; 20; 91; 150.*
Maass E. *42; 125.*
Maehly J.A. *29.*
Mangelsdorff E.A. *7; 10; 13; 14; 34; 67; 106; 117; 121; 136; 138; 143.*
Manson M. *57; 75; 90; 138.*
Mantero T. *26; 28; 74.*
Marx F. *94; 99.*
McKay K.J. *67.*
Martin J. *41.*
Meister K. *107.*
Merkelbach R. *36.*
Meyer-Lübke W. *119.*
Morelli C. *7.*
Müller L. *92; 142.*
Munro H.A.J. *91.*
Muth R. *8; 20; 136; 144.*
Mynors R.A.B. *18; 121; 134.*

Neudling Ch.L. *29.*
Neue F. *108.*
Nisbet R.G.M. *22; 31; 39; 42; 51; 52; 58; 59; 60; 64; 73; 114; 119; 130.*
Nock A.D. *51.*
Norden E. *3; 19; 20; 21; 22; 23; 24; 25; 29; 51; 58; 59; 60; 64; 75; 77; 92; 104; 108; 138; 147.*

Oberhummer E. *32.*
Ogilvie R.M. *96; 99.*
Otto A. *99; 130.*

Page D. *10; 12; 68; 123.*
Paratore E. *153; 154; 156.*
Parroni P. *18; 41; 62; 68; 102.*

Pascucci G. *64.*
Pasquali G. *7; 112; 113.*
Pernice E. *26; 28; 117.*
Perret J. *99.*
Perrotta G. *51.*
Pfeiffer R. *13; 26.*
Pflugbeil K. *69.*
Pichon R. *129.*
Pighi G.B. *5; 37; 77; 91; 156.*
Pleitner C. *134.*
Puelma M. *53.*
Putnam M.C. *26; 54.*

Rehm B. *25.*
Reitzenstein R. *7; 8; 9; 56; 73.*
Riese A. *4; 18; 50; 57; 90; 92; 98;*
    111; 125; 134.
Robert L. *131.*
Rohde E. *36.*
Ronconi A. *22; 24; 33; 39; 50; 52;*
    54; 70; 76; 82; 100; 101; 119;
    124; 125; 128; 129; 142.
Roscher W. *34.*
Ross D.O. *24; 39; 75; 93; 126;*
    142.
Rossi L.E. *78; 135.*
Rostagni A. *3; 6; 8.*
Rothstein M. *140.*
Russo C.F. *9.*
Rzach A. *139.*

Salvatore A. *147.*
Samter E. *88; 107; 113.*
Schanz M. *119.*
Schmidt R. *26; 96.*
Schneider O. *32.*
Scholfield A.F. *33.*
Schrader J. *62.*
Schuster M. *62.*
Skutsch O. *95; 109.*

Snell B. *34; 35; 78.*
Sommer F. *45; 60; 64.*
Stanford W.B. *30.*
Süss W. *34.*
Svennung J. *25; 30; 34; 35; 58; 64;*
    73; 81; 99; 122; 131; 141; 142.
Szantyr A. *31; 38; 49; 55; 100;*
    104; 108; 114; 115; 126; 128;
    142.

Tartari Chersoni M. *32.*
Testorelli E. *82.*
Thomas K.B. *45.*
Thomson D.F.S. *134.*
Traina A. *23; 56.*

Vahlen J. *60; 99.*
Vollmer F. *51.*

Wackernagel J. *41; 55; 64; 125;*
    126; 139.
Wagener C. *108.*
Wagenvoort H. *144.*
West M.L. *135.*
Wheeler A.L. *6; 7; 11; 72; 96; 102;*
    115; 137; 140; 145; 147.
Wilamowitz-Moellendorff U.v. *5; 6;*
    9; 10; 17. 25; 26; 29; 35; 37; 39;
    42; 59; 63; 77; 91.
Williams F. *59; 86.*
Williams G. *4; 14; 15; 53; 87; 90;*
    103; 104; 106; 116; 117.
Wills G. *3; 12; 35.*
Wissowa G. *86.*
Wölfflin E. *45.*

Zicàri M. *62.*
Ziegler K. *125.*
Zuntz G. *79.*